# Hampton Court

# *Hampton Court*

## The Palace and the People

## ROY NASH

Macdonald & Co
London & Sydney

Again, for Joyce

First published in 1983 in Great Britain by
Macdonald & Co (Publishers) Ltd
London & Sydney

Maxwell House
74 Worship Street
London EC2A 2EN

ISBN 0 356 09155 4

Filmset in Monophoto Apollo by
SX Composing Ltd, Rayleigh, Essex
Printed and Bound in Great Britain
by Purnell and Sons (Book Production) Ltd.,
Paulton, Bristol

# Contents

Acknowledgements  vi

Illustrations  vi

Foreword  vii

1  The Earliest Years: Wolsey and Henry VIII  9

2  The Earliest Years: Edward VI, The Boy-King  33

3  The Earliest Years: Lady Jane Grey and Mary Tudor  43

4  The Earliest Years: Elizabeth I  51

5  The Embattled Years: James I  65

6  The Embattled Years: Charles I  77

7  The Embattled Years: Cromwellian Interlude  95

8  The Embattled Years: Charles II  103

9  The Embattled Years: James II  121

10  The Middle Years: William III and Mary II  125

11  The Middle Years: Queen Anne  143

12  The Hanoverians: George I  151

13  The Hanoverians: George II  161

14  The Hanoverians: George III  173

15  The Hanoverians: George IV and William IV  183

16  The Later Years: Victoria  191

17  Legends and Ghosts  199

18  The Palace Today  203

Selected Bibliography  206

Index  209

# *Acknowledgements*

The author and publishers wish to express their grateful thanks to the many people who offered generous advice and guidance on the preparation of this book and, in particular, the following: M. V. Bishop, MVO, the Lord Chamberlain's Office; Ian Gray, Resident Superintendent, Hampton Court; P. E. Butler, the Department of the Environment; Robert Gibbins (for assistance with research); Mrs Karen Finch, OBE, Textile Conservation Centre; John Griffiths, RIBA, Director, Building Conservation Trust; Jenny de Gex (picture research); the Librarian and Staff, Guildhall Library, London; the Librarian and Staff, London Library; the Librarian, the Reform Club, London.

# *Illustrations*

The following colour photographs are reproduced by gracious permission of Her Majesty the Queen, photographed by Julian Nieman: 1, 3, 4, 5, 9, 13, 16, 17, 18, 19, 23.
Colour photograph 12 is reproduced by kind permission of Viscount de l'Isle from his collection at Penshurst Place, Kent.
All other colour photographs are by Julian Nieman.

The author and publishers wish to acknowledge the following for permission to reproduce the black-and-white illustrations:
Reproduced by gracious permission of Her Majesty the Queen: pp. 20, 21, 26, 32, 60 (top), 64, 67, 71 (bottom), 78, 79, 84, 85, 87, 96, 102, 105, 112, 116, 122 (top), 124, 129, 131, 150, 155 (left), 160, 162, 167, 173, 174, 182, 186, 188.
Ackermann Publishing: p. 10. Ashmolean Museum, Oxford: p. 13 (top). Bodleian Library, Oxford: p. 52. British Museum: p. 60 (bottom). Building Conservation Trust: p. 204 (bottom). College of Arms: p. 27. Cresswell Photographic Studios: p. 205. Guildhall Library: p. 171 (top). Mary Evans Picture Library: pp. 31, 46. Fotomas Index: pp. 48–9, 71 (top), 72, 88, 104 (left), 141, 154, 176, 177, 184 (bottom), 189. Leger Galleries, London: p. 119. London Transport: pp. 198, 202. Macdonald: pp. 13 (bottom), 17, 24, 28, 53 (centre), 83, 106–7, 127, 137, 148, 171 (bottom), 179, 180, 190, 192, 200. Macdonald/Julian Nieman: pp. 11, 204 (top). Mansell Collection: pp. 22, 89, 104 (right), 117, 123, 193, 196. National Gallery, London: pp. 42, 76. National Monuments Record/Wren Society: p. 128 (bottom). National Portrait Gallery: pp. 8, 34, 37, 39, 50, 53 (top right), 94, 98, 100, 105 (bottom right), 120, 122 (bottom), 128 (top), 142, 144, 153, 155 (centre and right), 184 (top). Thames and Hudson: pp. 135, 139. Victoria and Albert Museum: pp. 85, 118.

# Foreword

To its millions of visitors over the years Hampton Court Palace has been the romantic and somewhat awe-inspiring backdrop to an enjoyable summer afternoon's outing. Yet it is far more than that and has much more to offer than a brief tour of its state apartments and a leisurely stroll around its gardens can provide.

For, in so many ways, Hampton Court is a vital part of all our lives. Here, down the centuries, there lived, for varying periods, the sovereigns, the power-seekers and the policy-makers whose energies, intrigues and sometimes corrupting influences marked out the path along which the nation struggled towards its destiny.

In an age of rapid and bewildering change and in which we are deluged, as never before, with simplistic solutions to social and political problems, we would do well to remind ourselves that the achievements we tend to take for granted — the checks and controls on power, the right to be governed only by those to whom we give our consent by secret ballot — were won by hard struggle and sacrifice.

The purpose of this book, therefore, is not merely to document the building's physical development but to tell something of the story of the many extraordinary and colourful people who inhabited the palace and whose lives and actions are part of the mainstream of British history.

In quoting from contemporary documents I have modernised both spelling and punctuation except where the original forms more precisely convey the 'flavour' of the period.

Roy Nash, London, 1983

*Cardinal Wolsey. God may have called him to be a prelate but his tastes were worldly and he wanted his palace to be the envy of Europe's monarchs.*

# 1
# *The Earliest Years*

## WOLSEY & HENRY VIII

IN THE DISTANCE A JINGLE of bridles and accoutrements, a thin haze of dust rising from the churned-up dry ground and, slowly coming into view, a breath-taking shimmer of sunlit scarlet. The little group of country folk, caught unawares, hastens to the edge of the beaten track. The men uncover their heads, the women curtsey low.

The fast trotting procession of some three dozen riders, every one blood-red dressed, is past in seconds and soon lost to the westwards. But through their respectfully half-lowered eyes the onlookers have registered a sight they will remember always – the face of the man in the midst of the riders, a face whose expression bore an awesome fusion of arrogance and spirituality. They have looked upon the second most powerful man in the realm, the great Cardinal Thomas Wolsey himself. And no need to wonder where he is bound. In that direction in which he rides, in his crimson velvet cloak and his feet in gilt stirrups, he goes to his wonderful, new, fairy-tale palace at Hampton Court.

THE ROYALL PALACE OF HAMPTON COURT

*The palace beloved of Kings. Hampton Court as it was seen in the reign of George I by the painter Leonard Knyff. This engraving, from the original, was presented to the Earl of Sunderland.*

The palace, its elegant Tudor bricks crimson like the regulation dress of the Cardinal and his retainers, stands majestically on the north bank of the Thames in Middlesex – one mile from the villages of Hampton and Hampton Wick, thirteen miles from Charing Cross.

Across the drawbridge and over the moat, the Cardinal and his men entered the palace by way of the Great Gatehouse in the west front. As they passed, the two ranks of exceptionally tall yeomen, hand-picked as the guardians of the Gate, came smartly to the salute. Beyond the gatehouse the clatter of horses' hooves echoed around the first spacious courtyard known as the Base Court.

Waiting there to greet Thomas Wolsey, their master, were three principal officers of his household, each bearing his white stave of office: a priest who served as a steward; a knight who served as a treasurer; and the Cardinal's comptroller.

Wolsey dismounted somewhat heavily for he was a shortish, stoutish man in his forties, no longer young in terms of a sixteenth-century lifespan. His brown eyes under their drooping lids searched around the courtyard with that glint of hostile suspicion appropriate to a man of power in a time of dangerously high-powered politics. At a glance they took in the surrounding perfection of Tudor architecture – the picturesque turrets, the gables with their gargoyles and pinnacles, the mullioned windows, the bewitching craziness of the carved and

*Everywhere small details catch the eye, the creative work of designers, masons and joiners.*

twisted brickwork of the chimneys. Then, in a trice, he swept away to the seclusion of his private apartments. Thomas Wolsey was home again.

And to Wolsey Hampton Court was his favourite home. He had his palace in London, called York Place and later to become part of the Palace of Whitehall. But his health was far from robust – he suffered from dropsy and colic – and he found it impossible to settle comfortably in London where he was troubled by the smog and the chill, damp air drifting from the river.

It was said that he consulted a group of wise doctors from Padua as to where he might live with less hardship so long as the place was not more than twenty miles from the capital. But, whoever advised him, Wolsey finally settled on the ancient manor of Hampton Court for, although it stood beside the Thames and was only ten feet above the average river level, the site was remarkably free from damp. (The dryness was thought to be due partly to the gravelly nature of the soil and partly to the fact that the river itself acted as a storm drain to carry away surface waters.)

When Wolsey leased Hampton Court, the manor consisted of two thousand acres and its name had nothing whatever to do with a royal Court – 'court', in this case, simply meant the part of the property retained by the lord of the manor for his own use.

The peak year for Wolsey, son of a prosperous butcher from the Suffolk town of Ipswich, was 1515. In that year he received his Cardinal's hat from Rome, his King, Henry VIII, appointed him Lord Chancellor of England, and work began on his new palace at Hampton Court which he had determined should be one of the world's most brilliant and luxurious mansions.

Money was no object. From a variety of sources, including the bishoprics of Bath, Worcester, Lincoln, Hereford, Durham ( and later Winchester), there flowed into his coffers an annual income that in modern values we should need to count in millions. In his new post as chief counsellor and adviser to the monarch he had acquired immense command over men and affairs. A prelate he might be by God's choosing, but he thirsted after the ostentatious display of wordly wealth and power and saw no contradiction between the two interests. His worldliness extended, indeed, to the keeping of a mistress. It was widely believed that her family name was Lark and that the Cardinal had children by her. Wolsey's personal confessor, Thomas Lark, chaplain to Henry VIII, may have been her brother.

Wolsey's architect for the palace was the master mason, Henry Redman, although there is little doubt that the Cardinal himself provided the basic outline plan. The new building was designed to cover some eight acres and the main structures, mostly two storeys high, were built around a series of courtyards, two large – Base and Inner (later called Clock) Courts – and several smaller. There was, of course, a chapel and, most notably, a Great Hall, the social centre where guests were to be wined and dined while entertained by minstrels in the gallery.

Wolsey converted the adjoining land into two parks, and gardens were laid out. Building materials included chalk brought from Taplow and Windsor, timber from Cobham Park and stone from Reigate in Surrey.

In many ways the facilities were far in advance of the times. For example, an elaborate sewage system, employing pipes three feet wide and five feet high, was connected to the garderobes – early forms of indoor lavatories – and continued to operate right up until 1871.

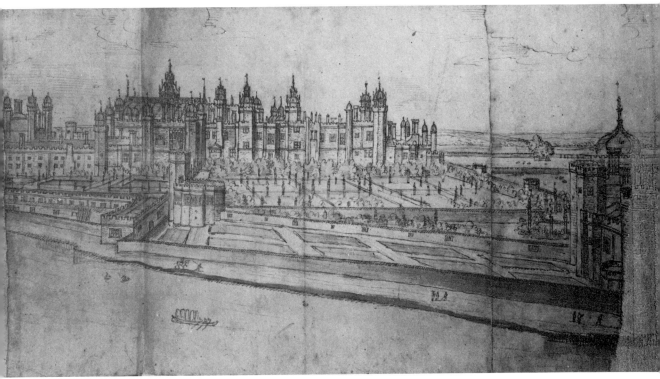

*Hampton Court from the river. The palace and the Thames were made for each other and this is a sixteenth-century view by the artist Wyngaerde.*

Through lead pipes a supply of fresh water was brought in from Coombe Hill, three-and-a-half miles away. The complex system ran through the nearby village of Surbiton, under the Thames above the point where it is now spanned by Kingston Bridge, and so to the palace. Each pipe was around two-and-a-half inches in diameter and half an inch thick – some two hundred and fifty tons of lead were used and the laying down of the system cost an astonishing £50,000. While most Londoners drank contaminated Thames water – and paid the price in often-fatal sickness – Wolsey's household enjoyed the healthful benefits of sparkling spring water.

Altogether, if one counted every small closet and walk-in cupboard, there were one thousand rooms in Wolsey's completed palace – two hundred and eighty of them always to be kept ready for guests.

Only the best carvers, painters and gilders were employed, many of them Italian immigrants. For instance, eight high-relief terracotta medallion busts of the Roman Emperors, set into the turrets on each side of the Great Gateway, were modelled by the Italian, Giovanni da Maiano, at a cost of £2.30 each. On the west side of the Inner (or Clock) Court was placed a similarly-designed medallion displaying the arms of Wolsey fixed to an archiepiscopal cross, supported by two cherubims and surmounted by a Cardinal's hat. Below Wolsey's monogram, 'T.W.', appeared his motto: *Dominus michi adjutor* (The Lord My Helper).

*Coats-of-arms, like these shown here on the palace exterior, form a delightful Hampton Court 'trade mark'.*

Material, if not Heavenly, help had certainly ensured that Wolsey's own apartments were sumptuous. Light shining through deep-bayed oriel windows illuminated carved and painted ceilings. The walls were emblazoned with cloth of gold and dazzling tapestries from a collection so vast that in each room they were changed weekly. Most of these tapestries were from Flanders and some consisted of a hundred or more pieces, usually scriptural in subject – the stories, among others, of Christ, John the Baptist, David and Samson. Others illustrated the Triumphs of the Italian poet, Petrarch: the Triumphs of Death, Fame, Chastity, Divinity and Love.

Apart from cloth of gold and tapestries, Wolsey's other most favoured hangings in his own and his guest-rooms were of crimson, blue, green, tawny, violet and yellow velvet. The Cardinal imported magnificent carpets in batches of fifty to a hundred, the choicest brought from the East by way of Venetian merchants. Uncarpeted floors were strewn with rushes impregnated, for the delectation of visitors' nostrils, with saffron.

Furniture and fittings were equally splendid: tables and chairs carved from oak or cypress, richly ornamented cupboards, five Chairs of State, covered with cloth of gold, for Wolsey and his most distinguished guests. (Buying-agents were commissioned almost continuously to scour the Continent for the richest and rarest of decorations, furniture and *objets d'art*.)

Wolsey himself slept in a great four-poster bed with gilt posts and a canopy of which the underside – the first sight to catch the Cardinal's eyes on waking – was of red satin with a flamboyantly needleworked red rose encompassed by garters and portcullises and fringed in white, green, yellow and blue silk.

His mattress was of wool, covered with fine holland cloth, and his pillow-cases were the same but some of them had been seamed with black silk and fleur-de-lys of gold, others with white silk and fleur-de-lys of red silk. White lamb's wool lined the blankets and Wolsey had a choice of counterpanes in blue damask, red satin or blue and yellow silk. The needlework decorations depicted flowers, birds and roses. Lest any guest should for a moment be in danger of forgetting where he was, he could not escape the reproduction of Wolsey's arms and motto – even on the profusion of red leather or crimson or blue cushion covers, and embossed on the fire-tongs in the monster fire-places.

Throughout the palace was to be seen a formidable array of gold and silver plate and ornaments – crosses, candlesticks, bells, chalices, goblets, flagons, bowls, basins, saucers, dishes, dinner plates. There were gold spoons, including several sets of thirteen representing Christ and the Apostles, a bowl with a lid encrusted with rubies, diamonds, and pearls, and a gold salt cellar embellished with jewels.

In 1527 the visiting Venetian ambassador made a rapid calculation and estimated the total worth of that array at three hundred thousand golden ducats – not less than around £3,000,000 in today's money.

Such a vast 'home' as Hampton Court required an equally vast staff and, if one counted all the officials, retainers and servants, the number came to at least five hundred. For special occasions the resident household would be supplemented by a few score lords and other nobles and everyone had a place, high or low, in the elaborate, well-defined domestic and social structures.

In the upper sectors of the hierarchy Wolsey was served by a chamberlain, vice-chamberlain and ten lords, each of whom was allowed two servants, except for the Earl of Derby who rated five. There were twelve gentlemen-ushers, six gentlemen-waiters, eight grooms of the chamber and forty-six yeomen of the chamber. Ever at hand to assist the Cardinal in his primary role as Chancellor were two principal secretaries, two clerks of the signet and four resident constitutional lawyers. And so the list of retainers went on and interminably on. Along a gallery, crossing a courtyard, you could any day see heralds and minstrels, doctors and apothecaries, surveyors and auditors, a keeper of the chamber, a keeper of tents.

Wolsey's chapel, agleam with gorgeous silver crosses, candlesticks and other richly-jewelled ornaments, was ruled over by a Dean and a sub-Dean. A Gospeller read the gospel and a Pisteller the Epistle. In the choir were twenty-eight men, twelve of them priests, and twelve boys; and that number was augmented by other choristers on festive occasions. (On weekdays Wolsey said Mass in his private apartments, attended by sixteen priests and chaplains.)

Of his immediate top-executive staff, the household comptroller had a deputy, the cofferer, who was in direct daily control of the staff, three marshals, two yeomen-ushers, two grooms and an almoner.

Two principal chefs presided over the main kitchen, where the food for banquets was prepared, assisted by five clerks and supervisors – who kept the accounts and attended to the ordering of produce – twelve kitchen hands and scullions and a yeoman of the pastry. In the Cardinal's private kitchen an especially grandiloquent figure ruled the roast – the Master Cook, who went about his daily chores with a gold chain hung around his neck. His watchful eyes surveyed the work of six kitchen hands, a yeoman and groom of the Larder, two grooms and two pages of the Cellar. Lesser mortals attended to the duties of the Scullery, the Scalding-House (where the dishes and cooking pans were washed), the Ewery (where casks of water, table linen and towels were stored), the Laundry, the Bake-House and the Wafery (where cakes and pastries were prepared).

The palace's 'outside' staff and servants included a Master of Horse, yeomen and sixteen grooms of the stables, a sumpter-man, who drove the pack horses, a saddler and a farrier, a yeoman of the Cardinal's coach and a yeoman of his barge. And since Wolsey often rode a mule, rather than a horse, there was also a muleteer.

When the Cardinal ventured forth on a long journey his coach was attended by four footmen in scarlet coats trimmed with black velvet four inches wide. If he should be bound for London, Wolsey would carry in his right hand an orange from which the fruit had been removed and replaced by a sponge soaked in vinegar mixed with spices. Held to his nose this protected him from the stinking throng of common people inevitably waiting to greet him.

Whenever he entered Westminster Hall, then the meeting place of the law courts, his gentlemen-ushers cleared the way for him with the cry: 'On, my lords and masters, on before! Make way for my Lord's Grace!' Ahead of his progress were borne two great crosses of silver and a magnificent silver-gilt mace. A retainer carried the Great Seal of England and a bareheaded nobleman the Cardinal's hat.

'All this number of persons,' proudly wrote George Cavendish, Wolsey's principal gentleman-usher, surveying the entourage, 'were daily attendant upon him in his house, down-lying and uprising.'

Except on special occasions, and when the law courts were not in session, Wolsey led a quiet, routine life at Hampton Court. He rose early and, having said Mass in private and breakfasted, he emerged at around eight o'clock dressed in his cardinal's robes. Altogether his collection of robes, copied exactly as to colour and cut from those worn by cardinals in Rome, was said to have cost around £3,000 in contemporary values.

He passed the morning in giving audiences to distinguished visitors, in writing and signing state documents and corresponding with the King. In the afternoon he walked in the gardens, if the weather permitted, but in the palace galleries and cloisters if it was cold and rainy. Occasionally he hunted the stag. At dusk he would again promenade through the palace, intoning divine service with one or other of his chaplains, and afterwards dine in private with a few close friends.

Wolsey jealously guarded such privacy as he could obtain and nothing angered him more than to learn that someone had turned up at the palace without an appointment and on the off-chance of being granted an audience. No matter how important they were – or thought themselves to be – they would be sent packing. Occasionally some innocent, who had not previously felt the cutting edge of the Cardinal's temper, would track him down as he strolled through the parkland. That was fatal indeed, and one messenger slunk away, red-cheeked, when the infuriated Wolsey snapped, 'If ye be not content to tarry (interfere with) my leisure, depart when ye will!'

Palace servants were only too well aware of the rule that Wolsey had laid down for the times when he walked out alone: none was to approach him closer than a man might fire an arrow. And, since good archers could make arrows fly long distances, a servant was best advised not to come even within sight of his master. Good servants served him well when they were needed – otherwise they went to ground when he was 'at leisure'.

It was when there were important State visitors to be received that the household and staff at Hampton Court really excelled themselves. As when the Constable of France arrived with one hundred of his nobles, their guards and servants: in all, six hundred people.

The whole place was set flurrying and scurrying weeks in advance of the guests' arrival, for Wolsey was resolved that the jealous French should be left in no doubt as to Tudor England's capacity to impress and overawe. Carpenters, joiners, masons and others were set energetically to work, renovating, scouring, redecorating and refurbishing every room, nook and cranny. Extra costly ornaments, rich drapes and tapestries were set in place.

Wolsey summoned the senior officials of the household and commanded them, as Cavendish reported, 'neither to spare for any costs, expenses or travail to make them [the French] such a triumphant banquet as they may not only wonder at here but also make a glorious report thereof in their country to the great honour of the King and his realm'.

Emissaries were sent to the richest town and country houses to borrow the services of their best cooks to assist the palace chefs. Every carcase of meat, every barrel of fish was minutely examined for quality. Fruit and produce of even slightly less than perfect condition were rejected.

On the evening of their arrival, the Constable of France and his chief nobles found huge welcoming fires burning in the spacious hearths of their rooms. On their bedside tables stood decanters of the Cardinal's most select wines and outside their doors hovered yeomen ready to attend to any and every request – a kind of instant and reliable medieval room-service.

In the Chamber of Presence the light from scores of candles, some fat as rolling pins, was reflected and magnified by the fabulous display of gold and silver plate covering the banqueting tables, hanging on the walls and displayed on stately sideboards. The silver of a pair of great candlesticks had alone cost £200.

'Now,' reported Cavendish, 'was all things in a readiness, and supper time at hand. My lord's officers caused the trumpets to blow to warn to supper, and the said officers went right discreetly in due order and conducted these noble personages from their chambers unto the chamber of presence where they should sup. And they, being there, caused them to sit down; their service was brought up in such order and abundance, both costly and full of subtleties, with such a pleasant noise of divers instruments of music, that the Frenchmen, as it seemed, were rapt into a heavenly paradise.'

Wolsey's chefs and pastry cooks had surpassed themselves with their culinary art and prepared many of their dishes in the form of miraculous food-sculptures. There were offerings that came shaped as castles and old St Paul's Cathedral, complete with steeple, as well as beasts, birds and fowls of diverse kinds. There were fish and pastry concoctions designed to represent scenes depicting duelling, jousting and dancing. And, something that particularly astonished Cavendish, a cake made in the form of a chessboard with confectionery chessmen.

Cunning Wolsey, who had an unerring instinct for the value of personal

*Supper in the Presence Chamber. Wolsey himself was probably the host for this 'minor' occasion; it was not unusual for him to entertain hundreds to a single meal.*

publicity in international affairs, made a dramatic late entry to the banquet at the end of the first course. He was dressed in riding clothes, booted and spurred in a deliberate pose intended to convey to the visitors that, at the hub of English power, lavish banquets were such routine affairs that nobles would think little of coming into them straight from the hunting field. Embarrassed and awkward, caught in the middle of their energetic efforts to dive into the food, the Frenchmen began hastily to scramble to their feet. But, with lofty generosity, Wolsey bade them remain seated, took his place at the top table and, beaming, called to them to enjoy themselves.

Minstrels continued to play while the endless courses flowed across the tables and Cavendish, seated near to his master, was able to observe the Cardinal 'laughing and being as merry as ever I saw in my life'.

Wolsey had every reason to be merry. He believed implicitly in the political theory that 'foreigners' took notice not of words but of demonstrations of affluence and power. And what Frenchman present could doubt that any chief minister capable of putting on such a show of inordinate luxury must speak for a powerful, self-confident monarch?

Half way through the meal Wolsey lifted a golden bowl of hippocras – wine flavoured with spices – and toasted the Constable of France with the words: 'I drink to the King, my sovereign lord and master, and to the King, your master.'

This toast was the signal for the general circulation of wine, of which there was an unlimited supply. And the guests took such advantage of the hospitality, and exchanged so many toasts and pledges of goodwill that, said Cavendish, many of them 'were fain to be led to their beds'.

The banquet was, as Wolsey had planned it should be, a solid investment. When they had emerged from their hangovers, the Frenchmen went home brimming over with gossip about the wonderous sights they had seen at the court of the English Henry's chief minister. As Cavendish put it, they made 'a glorious report in their country, to the King's honour and that of his realm'.

From time to time Henry VIII himself would go with a party of friends to Hampton Court for a night of carousing and festivity. And, thanks to the records left by George Cavendish, it is possible to reconstruct a typical, royal festive occasion:

It is dusk of a spring evening and the sky above the Thames at Hampton is crimson-streaked from the setting sun. Silently upstream glides the great ornamental barge of the King, followed by a clutch of smaller barges filled with men of the royal court.

As the barges come alongside the landing stage, a pair of decorative cannons in front of the palace break the silence with a welcoming bark. Wild-fowl lift up suddenly from the river in a turbulence of fluttering wings.

The King's friends, nobles and gentlemen, step ashore first and form themselves into two inward facing ranks. All are masked and dressed as shepherds, except that their smocks are made of fine cloth of gold, set with panels of red satin, and their visored caps are also of satin.

Then, from his own barge, comes the King, similarly masked and dressed. He is plump, but not yet as gross as he will popularly be remembered, light upon his feet, and he walks with an easy, swinging grace.

Henry passes through the ranks of his friends, lighted in the thickening gloom by sixteen torch-bearers who precede him at a steady pace marked by a drummer boy's tap-tap. Caps are doffed with a flourish, eyes behind the masks are smiling. In the King's wake the courtiers fall in, two by two, and the procession moves on towards the palace.

Inside, Wolsey and his entourage, noblemen, ladies and gentlemen, are seated at supper in the Presence Chamber, the tables covered with perfumed damask cloths, the gallant scene illuminated, as always, by fat wax candles. Wolsey and his guests know the King is approaching for they, too, have heard the cannons' salute, but they profess cheerful ignorance. It is all a game, a charade, this supposedly surprise visit by the King. It has been played many times before; childish, perhaps, but Henry enjoys a touch of frivolity and who is Wolsey to deny this simple indulgence to the man who has raised him to fame and fortune?

Meanwhile, and all in the game, Wolsey has commanded Lord Sands, his Lord Chamberlain, and his chief guest, Sir Henry Guilford, the King's comptroller, to go off to enquire into the reason for the cannon fire. Solemnly they do the Cardinal's bidding and return, half-smiling, to say that they have spied strangers, possibly 'ambassadors from some foreign prince'.

Then says Wolsey (word-perfect in the dialogue of make-believe): 'I shall desire you, because ye can speak French, to take the pains to go down into the Hall to encounter and receive them, according to their estates, and to conduct them into this chamber, where they shall see us, and all these noble personages, sitting merrily at our banquet, desiring them to sit down with us, and to partake of our fare and pastime.'

Lord and knight depart and within minutes the clamour of drums and fifes is heard beyond the chamber. Then the doors are flung wide and the 'strangers' enter in pairs, bowing low in salute to the Cardinal. By no sign does the King identify himself.

Still persuing the charade's 'scenario', the Lord Chamberlain announces that the visitors, 'who can speak no English', have informed him in French that, hearing of the Cardinal's 'triumphant banquet, where was assembled a number of excellent fair dames', could do no other than hurry to the palace to view 'their incomparable beauty'.

Now the masked arrivals circulate among the tables, greeting the ladies with special gallantry, until the company is silenced by Wolsey declaring that he believes there must be among them 'some noble man, whom I suppose to be much more worthy of honour to sit and occupy this room and place than I, to whom I would most gladly, if I knew him, surrender my place according to my duty.'

The Lord Chamberlain pretends to inquire of the visitors, again in French, if there is indeed present such a nobleman who would be prepared to accept the Cardinal's place if his Grace should point him out. The answer is 'yes'. Gravely, Wolsey points to the masked figure of Sir Edward Neville, gentleman of the King's Privy Chamber, who is of the same build and stature as Henry. Immediately, there is an outburst of glee since everyone, including the playacting Cardinal, knows very well that this is not the King.

But the game has reached its climax. King Henry steps forward, unmasks Sir Edward and then lifts the mask from his own face. The whole company rises to its feet and applauds wildly; the King grins as happily as a prankster schoolboy, turning from side to side to acknowledge the ovation.

The charade most rewardingly concluded, the King and his friends retire to change into fresh and even more splendid apparel, tables are cleared and the real banquet for which everyone has been waiting is ready to begin. Humbly, Wolsey vacates his place under the canopy of state and Henry, on his return, is cheered into it.

So now the main festivities of the evening are launched with a choice (as Cavendish reports) of 'two hundred dishes or above, of wonderous costly meats and devices, subtley devised. Thus passed they forth the whole night with banqueting, dancing and other triumphant devices, to the great comfort of the King, and pleasant regard of nobility there assembled.'

Such were the golden days at Hampton Court when King Henry and Wolsey were still close friends and allies and all seemed set fair for the two men who, between them, ruled a kingdom of splendid potential.

Henry would often drop in at the palace in the course of a day to discuss affairs of state with Wolsey and, in fine weather, they could be observed walking through the gardens together, deep in animated conversation. On other days letters regularly arrived from London addressed to 'Mine own good Cardinal' and ending 'Written with the hand of your loving master, Henry R.'

But, as surely as he had risen, the unfortunate Thomas Wolsey was destined to fall. At first the differences between monarch and confidant were personal and mainly trivial, although one was to have far-reaching consequences for Hampton Court.

In Henry's mind there had slowly festered a certain jealousy about his chief minister's high living and, during one of those garden strolls, the King suddenly asked why the Cardinal had felt moved to build so majestic a home for himself.

Wolsey, perhaps caught off guard, perhaps instinctively resorting to idle flattery, made a fatal reply. 'To show,' he purred, 'how noble a palace a subject may offer to his sovereign.'

As though snapping open a trapdoor King Henry instantly accepted the Cardinal's generous 'offer'. By the summer of 1525 Hampton Court and all its treasures had formally been conveyed to the King, although Wolsey was allowed to remain in residence but only, in effect, as a royal 'tenant'.

In 1528 Wolsey spent the months of July and August shut away in Hampton Court as a refugee from yet another of the many plagues – this time 'the sweating sickness' – which regularly afflicted London. There he received a letter from Henry begging him have a care for his health and to 'keep out of the air, have only a small and clean company, not to eat too much supper, or drink too much wine'.

*Catherine of Aragon (1485–1536), Henry VIII's first Queen. Henry's tortuous campaign to divorce her led to England's break with the Church of Rome.*

But the mainspring of the King's affection was rapidly running down. Soon Henry was plunged into the long and complex adventure of trying to persuade the Pope to annul his marriage to Catherine of Aragon, his first wife who had failed to provide him with a son. In that business he looked to Wolsey for aid.

At first it had seemed that Wolsey might triumph once more in his role as a wily negotiator. In collusion with Henry he sought to argue the case that, under Church law, the King had contracted a non-marriage since Catherine was the widow of his brother, Arthur. The manoeuvre failed and suddenly Wolsey found himself relegated from King's friend to King's enemy, his downfall speeded by the personal antagonism of Anne Boleyn whom Henry had by then taken openly as his mistress.

In disgrace and fearful of his fate, Wolsey set off for his diocese of York. He fell sick, was unable to complete his journey and on his way back to London was arrested for high treason. His death at Leicester, on 29 November 1530, spared him from the Tower of London and the executioner's block; and towards the end he uttered his famous words. 'If I had served God as diligently as I have done the King, He would not have given me over in my grey hairs.'* He was fifty-five.

There is a curious footnote to Wolsey's last days. For most of his adult life he had been burdened with the belief that the name 'Kingston' boded ill for him; and never, in any of his journeys between London and Hampton Court, would he pass through Kingston-upon-Thames, even though that was the most convenient route.

As he lay in his final sickness he was told that the Constable of the Tower had arrived with orders to take him into custody. He asked one of his attendants to

*Ill-fated Anne Boleyn (1507–1536). The morning after her execution on his own orders, King Henry appeared at the palace with a feather in his cap. Nine days later he married his third wife, Jane Seymour.*

---

* Translated more poetically by Shakespeare as: Had I but served my God with half the zeal
I served my King, he would not in mine age
Have left me naked to mine enemies.

*There is a fictional basis to this domestic scene of Henry VIII with Jane Seymour and the future boy-king, Edward. For Jane did not live to see her son grow to the age represented here.*

remind him of the Constable's name and he was told – Mr. Kingston. Whereupon a look of fear and anguish came into his dying eyes. 'Ah, Mr Kingston,' he repeated and slapped his thigh and breathed a deep sigh of despair.

By the time of Wolsey's death Henry VIII had already moved into Hampton Court with Anne Boleyn although he was still officially married to Catherine.

He at once set about enlarging the palace, adding a number of new structures including an extra gallery, library, study and a set of kitchens. On the north-east side he built himself a bowling alley and an indoor court for tennis, the game originated by fourteen-century English and French nobles and now known as 'real tennis'. The court was lighted by twelve windows, six on each side, covered with wire-netting to safeguard the glass of which there was altogether one hundred and twelve square feet. Henry was a keen and skilful player and wore a type of tennis slippers and specially made shorts.

He was thirty-nine and no longer a particularly pretty sight on the tennis court. His body was now more bulging than comfortably plump, his once-abundant red hair thinning, his fine skin turning blotchy and there was a hint of rheuminess in his eyes.

He did not greatly resemble the jolly 'bluff King Hal' created by legend and, in more modern times, by Charles Laughton's classic movie portrayal. He was scholarly, in a rather ponderous vein, not notably witty, and generous if he took to you, dangerous if he did not.

Surprisingly, for all his final total of wives and mistresses, he was prudish and abhorred smutty jokes or public references to sex. (It is said that, on being jocularly advised that France's many beautiful girls could best be judged by sampling each in bed, Henry blushed and changed the subject. Some thought that the root of his curious shyness lay in a nagging suspicion that women responded

*Typical court for 'real' tennis and similar to that built by Henry VIII at Hampton Court. 'Real' tennis, as distinct from modern lawn tennis was played indoors and was originally developed by the French and English aristocracy in the fourteenth century.*

to him not for himself but for his crown and majesty.)

Like Wolsey before him, Henry brought to Hampton Court his own great retinue – again, around five hundred in number. At the top of the household tree were a Lord Steward, Lord Treasurer, the Astronomer-Royal, priests, secretaries and physicians; at the bottom, cup-bearers, yeomen, ushers, pages, cooks, scullions and grooms.

Each night a bevy of grooms, pages and yeomen prepared Henry's bed, laying each of the sheets in one sweeping movement at the military-style command of a gentleman-usher. Always a yeoman searched with a dagger through the straw on which the King's mattress was laid to ensure that no infernal devices or foreign bodies were concealed. For, despite the well-guarded gatehouses, Henry complained that the palace was far too accessible to 'unmeet persons, rascals and vagabonds'.

The final responsibility for running the whole place rested with the Board of Green Cloth, under the command of the Great Master of the Household – the royal equivalent of modern Top Management. The Board's two senior executives, treasurer and controller, issued the daily orders, saw to it that the food was ordered, fires were lit, candles replaced, charcoal delivered and the palace cleaned. Each day they totalled up the wild life that had sacrificed itself in the previous twenty-four hours to keep the Court and household nourished – often six oxen, forty sheep and a thousand or more pullets, larks, pheasants, partridges and pigeons.

Although the senior officials were vigilant accountants, 'custom and practice' decreed that they turn a blind-eye to the widespread petty theft which provided 'perks' for the palace menials. Each group had its place in the pecking order of recognised 'fiddling'. Thus, there were those entitled to tap the wine-kegs, others to make off with the 'surplus' blankets, 'liberate' the generous portions of left-over meat that could have been turned into royal pies, or sell off the tallow candle-ends that could have been melted down to make fresh candles.

Oddly, the one thing that defeated the palace managers was who should clean up the mess left regularly by the royal mastiffs on the royal rugs. There were no volunteers and no one, apparently, with sergeant-major powers to draw up a 'volunteer' list. Consequently, the proud palace, outwardly so glorious, inwardly stank of a mixture of less than hygienic humans and the ripe offerings of their canine friends. Henry himself did issue some ordinances for 'doggs to be kept in kennels and other meete places', but they seem not to have been very effective.

In addition to his enlargements to the palace, Henry undertook some other major works. He partly rebuilt Wolsey's chapel, added a new quadrangle, Cloister Green Court (south of the chapel) but, most important of all, replaced the Great Hall by a much larger structure.

Each of his three great new kitchens included a fireplace with ample room for the roasting of an ox. And one of those kitchens, thirty-seven feet long by twenty-seven feet wide, still survives.

Henry also built what was described in the building accounts of his surveyor, a 'Mr Williams, priest', as the King's 'Newe Wyne Sellar'.

This famous cellar, sixty feet by thirty feet, had a brick-groined roof supported by pillars nearly eleven feet tall. It was entered by steps leading down from Cloister Green Court and lighted by windows set into the outer, south-east wall. Wide brick benchings, on which the wine casks could stand, were built up eight inches above floor level, leaving gangways of around six feet in width traversing the whole cellar. The records show that the master-masons, bricklayers and carpenters employed in the construction received one shilling a day (5p) for an eight-hours-a-day, six-day working week, and the lesser-skilled men from about eightpence down to sixpence ($2\frac{1}{2}$p). By the general standards of the time in those trades the wages were good.

Much of the wine would have been Rhenish, or the white varieties imported from the Canary Islands and known generally as 'Sack'. It was measured as a hogshead (sixty-three gallons), a pipe (two hogsheads) and a tonne (two pipes).

The Court and household were great imbibers and, although modern money equivalents can be estimated only roughly, Henry's Hampton Court bill for all types of drink would today run at not less than £1,000,000 a year. At dinner (then the universally accepted term for the midday meal) and supper the routine provision at the private table for the King and his special, personal guests was six gallons of beer and ale and four quarts of wine. At each of the two main daily meals the Great Master of the Household's table was supplied with ten gallons of ale and four quarts and two pitchers of wine.

On important festive occasions Henry entertained in his new Great Hall on which work started in 1531 and was completed five years later. Workmen laboured by night, by candlelight, as well as by day for the King was impatient to see the work finished.

The Hall, still one of the palace's masterly showpieces, is one hundred and six feet long, forty feet wide and sixty feet high. Within the carved foliage of the lovely hammer-beam roof are the royal arms, in some places intertwined with those of Anne Boleyn. There, too, is carved Anne's badge, the representation of a falcon. At the lower end of the Hall an oak screen supports the minstrel's gallery.

On a dais, one step up above floor level and lighted by the great bay window, Henry sat at High Table for his banquets and, below him, his guests were at tables ranged along the main walls. In winter a large fire was set in a stone hearth in the middle of the floor, its smoke drifting upwards to gratings in the roof which are now closed off.

Adjoining the Hall, Henry built his Great Watching (or Guard) chamber immediately above the wine cellar where some of Wolsey's tapestries representing Petrarch's 'Triumphs' are now to be seen.

*The Great Hall in Tudor times. Then, as it is now, this magnificent structure was one of the showpieces of the palace and the focal point for festive occasions.*

As soon as she was installed, Anne, daughter of one of Henry's diplomats, the Earl of Wiltshire, made it clear that she was as much in charge of Hampton Court as Henry. She was attractive, with dark eyes and raven hair, but quick tempered and bossy. She was not without creative gifts and produced some exquisite embroidery; but she also liked to gamble at cards and shovel-board, the more aristocratic ancestor of what was to develop into shove-ha'penny. Unhappily for her, and more particularly for the King's privy purse, she was an unlucky gambler and on one occasion her bets amounted to the then sizeable sum of £200.

Her presence in the King's life contributed to a change of course in British history and was a crucial factor in the gradual development of the Reformation which was to end the link with Rome and the papacy. For Henry was now absolutely determined to end his twenty-four year marriage to Catherine and make Anne his Queen despite a likely rupture with the Vatican. In the end, and with the aid of English and European universities acting as adjudicators, he proved to himself (at least) that the marriage had been 'unlawful' and he banished Catherine and her daughter, Mary, from the Court.

On 23 May 1533, with Parliament's reluctant acquiescence, the marriage was at last formally annulled. And Henry, incidentally, may be regarded as the father of the 'division' system of Parliamentary voting for he thought up the notion of requiring those Members who were for his divorce (the Ayes) to move to one side of the chamber and those against (the Noes) to the other side. In those days of supreme royal power such a division was akin to an unrefusable offer since it gave Henry visible evidence of his opponents; and many of the 'Ayes' voted more for the preservation of their necks than positively for the divorce. They were no doubt wise in their discretion for the Reformation, as it proceeded, was ruthless and bloody.

Among the earliest victims was Wolsey's successor, that remarkable and tragic figure of history, Sir Thomas More. As he lay in the Tower, awaiting the axe for having disputed Henry's right to challenge the Pope, he heard tell of how Anne Boleyn was dancing the night away at Hampton Court. Prophetically, he declared: 'These dances of hers will prove such dances that she will spurn our heads off like footballs, but it will not be long ere her head will dance the like dance.'

Anne could not, in any case, go on dancing much longer for she was already pregnant – a condition that, four months before the annulment of his marriage to Catherine, had encouraged Henry secretly and bigamously to take her as his wife.

Desperately and irrationally, Henry had convinced himself that Anne would present him with his badly-needed son and heir. But to his acute frustration and anger she was delivered of a daughter, the Princess Elizabeth. A year later she miscarried and in January 1536 another child was still-born. According to rumour that last tragedy was a direct result of Anne's entering a room at Hampton Court and discovering the King in a fumbling embrace with a lady-in-waiting, Jane Seymour. If there was truth in the gossip then Henry was indeed his own worst enemy. For the dead baby was a boy.

Henry had begun to build a set of rooms for Anne at the palace, the Queen's New Lodgings, but he now no longer wished to see her there nor anywhere. His spitefulness boiled over against both Anne and Catherine. He pressured

*King Henry and his third Queen, Jane Seymour (c1509–1537). She died a few days after giving birth, at the palace, to the boy who was to become, if briefly, Edward VI.*

Parliament into accepting an Act denying the succession to Catherine's daughter, Mary, whom he had fathered, and vesting it in Princess Elizabeth, although he still hoped that Elizabeth would not have to ascend the throne. He had not abandoned hope of begetting a son who would be the next King.

Anne was finally disposed of by a series of charges, some probably valid, others trumped-up, of adultery and incest. Awaiting execution in the Tower she asked one final favour of her husband: could she please be beheaded in the civilised French manner by a sword instead of the more humiliating axe? Not wishing to appear unreasonable, Henry granted her wish and on the Tower Green, on 19 May 1536, Anne Boleyn was dispatched by a swordsman especially imported for the occasion from France.

That same night Henry dined merrily with the vivacious Jane Seymour at Hampton Court and the next morning appeared with a feather in his cap. Even to modern society, accustomed to bloody violence, Henry Tudor's mind must appear dark and forbidding. He had once called Anne his 'own darling', had suffered excommunication by Rome in order to marry her, and then ordered her brutal murder. And all the time he had worried, as he always did, over the literal meaning of the scriptures. But the truth was that the mystical significance of religion played little or no part in Tudor lives and neither did the majority of people concern themselves with the inner Christian message. Ends justified means. And Henry, doting upon his new-found love at Hampton Court, was morally no worse than Stalin, four centuries later, idly reflecting in the Kremlin that it was good to plot the destruction of an enemy and then retire to a quiet, refreshing sleep.

Certainly the King felt no pangs of conscience or remorse in proceeding at once to complete the apartments he had begun for Anne and furnishing them for Jane.

Ten days after Anne's head was severed, Henry married Jane at York Place. Some people thought her a 'lady fair and graceful', but she was shortish, deathly-pale in complexion and by no means a beauty. All the same, Henry believed himself once again to be deeply in love and he set about, as far as possible, to eliminate the reminders of Anne Boleyn at Hampton Court.

The records show, for instance, that money was spent on 'twenty vanes paynted and new alteryd from Queen Annes arms unto Queen Janes with theyr badges'. Master carvers were set to work on roof and other timbers, dexterously changing the initials A and H, joined in true-lovers' knots, to J and H.

Henry resumed his accustomed Hampton Court life. Despite his girth he sat well on a horse and he jousted in the nine-acre Tilt Yard he had built on the north side of the palace. There the lists and the pavilion were richly adorned with arms, banners and gold-and-silver embroidered tapestries. On a fine summer's day the competing knights were an unforgettable sight in their brilliantly colourful array, astride their sumptuously caparisoned horses and surrounded by glittering groups of esquires and pages, heralds and minstrels.

The King was preceded into the arena by the marshal of the jousts, dressed in cloth of gold, the royal approach signalled by the beating of drums and a fanfare of trumpets. Behind the marshal came the pages, squires and footmen, walking in line with great dignity. And then, Henry entered, in a coat of silver, escorted by thirty gentlemen-at-arms walking beside his horse and resplendent in velvet and white satin.

In the jousts Henry gave a good account of himself and the spectators rose as

*Henry VIII revelled in jousting and took the same risks as his knights. One one occasion he lay unconscious for two hours after being toppled from his horse. Here, in this contemporary etching, he shows off in front of Catherine of Aragon — before he had tired of her.*

one body, with a cry of exultation, whenever his lance unhorsed an opponent. His jousting was no mere exhibitionism and he fully shared his knights' dangers. He once came close to serious injury when a lance struck his helmet and, on another occasion, he lay unconscious for two hours after being toppled from his horse.

The bouts were conducted with highly formalised courtesy and ceremony. Honour and chivalry were two much-repeated Tudor watchwords; and if you were the King you might wield your unlimited power pitilessly in political and religious matters but you were expected to display gentlemanly grace and gallantry on such public occasions as the tournaments.

Apart from jousting, hunting and tennis, one of Henry's other great passions was music. He enjoyed singing and had a full-blooded baritone voice. He also composed attractive songs, although a line from one of them – 'Whoso loveth, should love but one' – can hardly be said to have come from the heart.

He had good reason to sing and rejoice on 12 October 1537 when, at Hampton Court, Queen Jane gave birth to a son, the future Edward VI. From church steeples throughout the kingdom the bells pealed and in the towns and villages bonfires were lit. Henry was so overcome by the reward of his endless prayers that he dashed off a note to his chief adviser, Thomas Cromwell, declaring that, in bringing about the happy event, God 'hath shown himself the God of England – or rather an English God, if we will consider and ponder His proceedings with us'.

Three days later the infant Prince was baptised in the palace chapel in the presence of a huge assembly of the great and noble, including the three-year-old Princess Elizabeth. The Prince was carried into the chapel by the Marchioness of Exeter, accompanied by her husband and the Duke of Suffolk, the little group processing under a canopy borne aloft by four gentlemen of the King's Privy Chamber. Behind them walked the baby's godmother, the twenty-one-year old Princess Mary, to whom the King had refused the royal succession.

Two peers carried basins covered with towels and a third held a taper of virgin wax. The ceremony was performed by the Archbishop of Canterbury at a silver font placed on a dais in the centre of the chapel choir. At its conclusion, Garter

*The baby prince Edward, later to be Edward VI, is carried towards the font of the Chapel Royal for his christening. The Marchioness of Exeter supports the infant in her arms and the gentlemen of the King's Privy Chamber bear the canopy.*

King-of-Arms intoned: 'God of his Almighty and infinite grace, give and grant good life and long to the right high, right excellent and noble Prince, Prince Edward, Duke of Cornwall, and Earl of Chester, most dear and entirely beloved son to our most dread and gracious lord, King Henry the Eighth.'

But Henry himself was not there to hear those words or witness the christening. He stayed at Jane's bedside, anxiously watching over the Queen, for soon after the birth a bad cold and inadequate diet had suddenly sapped her strength. She wrote a letter to Thomas Cromwell announcing the arrival of her son and signed it 'Jane the Queene', but that was her last action. Nine days later, at midnight on 24 October, Jane Seymour died and Henry's rejoicing turned to deep melancholy and despair. He could not bear to linger in the surroundings of the tragedy and fled to Windsor.

Jane's body was embalmed and then moved into the Presence Chamber for its lying-in-state. The whole darkened room was draped in black, and the windows were shuttered. The only light came from twenty-four tall tapers burning beside the catafalque. For a week, day and night, masses were said and dirges sung by the side of the dead Queen. On 31 October the body was removed to the chapel and further rites continued until 12 November when the coffin was taken out to Clock Court and placed on a funeral carriage drawn by four horses draped in black velvet. On top of the coffin, in accordance with royal tradition, lay a waxen effigy of Jane wearing a gold crown and with a golden sceptre in the right hand. Headed by Princess Mary, as chief mourner, the funeral procession wound its slow way to Windsor Castle where Henry awaited it and where the Queen was buried in St. George's Chapel.

For a year after Jane's death, Henry stayed away from Hampton Court but the work of completing the new additions to the palace continued. A suite of apartments for the King was built facing on to Green Cloister Court (but eventually demolished in William III's time). A water gallery was erected to connect with the royal landing stage at the river's edge and the gardens were further developed, studded with sun-dials and stone pedestals surmounted by heraldic beasts and engraved with the King's arms.

Many varieties of flowers, still familiar today, were to be seen in the flower-beds: pinks, primroses, marigolds, stocks, carnations, sweet-williams, holly-hocks, daffodils, paeonies and, of course, roses. Gardens were, in general, a great feature of Tudor England; and Elizabeth Burton, the historian of English domestic life, has estimated that between 1548 and 1597 no fewer than one hundred and twenty-one different varieties of trees, shrubs, vegetables and flowers were introduced into the realm.

The two parks, Bushy, and what was then called House (now Hampton Court) Park, were divided by brick walls and Henry extended the manor by buying up surrounding land on both sides of the river. He also built a 'mount' – a popular outdoor feature which consisted of a man-made hillock topped by a summer-house.

The newly-acquired land, stretching as far as the Surrey villages of Byfleet, Esher and Weybridge, was enclosed and intended by Henry as a hunting ground. The locals, who were not pleased by the creation of this 'chase', but dared not incur the King's wrath by openly protesting, had the land freed and the enclosing fences removed in the subsequent reign of Edward VI.

By 1539 Henry was beginning to think about the acquisition of a new wife. But this time his intentions were basically political rather than romantic. He had come to the conclusion that it would be expedient to secure an alliance through marriage with the Protestant German princes, and was 'advised' to choose twenty-four-year-old Anne of Cleves. Henry had never met her but Thomas Cromwell, somewhat stretching the matchmaking prospects, reported that her charms were highly spoken of. He glossed over the fact that she spoke nothing but German and knew little of music.

On New Year's Day 1540, Henry sailed down the Thames to Rochester to meet Anne's ship, took one look at his bride-to-be and immediately fled back to the royal barge. 'I like her not! I like her not!' he howled to Cromwell. 'Say what they will, she is nothing fair.'

However, a marriage contract had been concluded and Henry was trapped. 'Is there no remedy then, but that I must needs put my neck in the yoke?' he asked, and was told there was none. He refused to share his bed with his new bride, spent the 'honeymoon' period working over plans for divorce, and eventually succeeded in having the marriage annulled on the grounds of non-consummation. Anne, who made only one brief visit to Hampton Court, alone, consented to the divorce, was given lands with an income valued at £3,000 a year and disappeared into obscure retirement in England.

The farcical disaster did nothing to dissuade Henry from pursuit of a wife and immediately Anne was safely off his hands he returned once more to Hampton Court, this time in the company of yet another bride, Catherine Howard, the Duke of Norfolk's niece. The record of their marriage is missing but the ceremony is believed to have been held at the palace on 8 August 1540, the day Henry presented Catherine in the chapel as the new Queen.

In appearance they were an ill-matched pair: Henry now fifty and bloated, Catherine still in her twenties – her actual birthdate is uncertain – small, hazel-eyed, auburn-haired and quite the prettiest of the King's wives.

At first the marriage went well. Henry was proud of his lovely young wife and for five months, in 1541, they lived continuously at Hampton Court in almost total privacy, interrupted only by the King's meetings with his Privy Council. But tranquility was short-lived. To his dismay Henry quickly began to realise that beyond a pretty face and figure Catherine had not much to offer him. She was feather-brained and flighty and an insatiable spender. His health was deteriorating, he was cursed with intractable leg ulcers and he craved a bit of domestic peace and quiet instead of incessant silly chatter.

Catherine, too, had her enemies, including the sinister Archbishop Thomas Cranmer, and very soon rumours of her infidelities were being breathed into Henry's ears. The ultimate offence, it was said, was Catherine's illicit sexual relations with her cousin, Thomas Culpepper. As soon as he was told, the King wept bitterly, left Hampton Court and never again set eyes on Catherine. She was beheaded at the Tower on 10 February 1542, having uttered her famous last words: 'I die a Queen, but I would rather have died the wife of Culpepper.'

In the background, during the two-year failed marriage, some construction work continued at Hampton Court and the latest new addition was the remarkable and famous astronomical clock. It was made by Nicholas Oursian to the design of the Bavarian astronomer, Nicholas Cratzer. The clock shows the hour, month, day of the month, number of days since the start of the year, phases of the moon and the time of high water at London Bridge. But since it was designed before the astronomical discoveries of Galileo and Copernicus it inaccurately depicts the sun revolving around the earth. The dial, seven feet and ten inches in diameter, consists of three separate copper discs superimposed upon each other and all turning at different speeds.

Henry had grieved sorely over his 'betrayal' by the late Queen but very soon he was back at Hampton Court once more with another Catherine, Catherine Parr, aged thirty-one and twice a widow. She was no raving beauty but she had the great merits of being affectionate and domesticated. They were married in the Holyday Closet, next to the chapel, on 12 July 1543.

Only around twenty people, including the Princesses Mary and Elizabeth, attended the ceremony and it may well have been that Henry, now a little sensitive about the uncertainties of matrimony, thought it wise to keep the proceedings private. The new Queen made a present of £20 to Princess Mary and probably gave a similar sum to Elizabeth, although the historical record is not precise.

Catherine lavished greater attention on Henry than he had enjoyed from any of his other wives. She bathed his ulcerated legs and some of the soothing talk she employed during her private nursing encouraged the King towards a degree of reconciliation between himself and his daughters, Mary and Elizabeth. And she was kind and considerate, too, to the motherless Prince Edward, who was developing into a frail and sickly youth.

The general view of Henry's friends was that, at last, he had found himself a quiet, gentle wife who would be a faithful and loving support to him in his declining years. But illness and the past disappointments of married life had turned the King into an obsessively suspicious oaf.

At first he was irked and then more darkly doubtful about Catherine's form of piety which seemed to him to place rather too much emphasis on mysticism and not enough on the outward trappings of religion. After she had ventured to disagree with him on a point of theology he complained: 'A good hearing it is when women become such clerks [scholars]; and a thing much to my comfort to come in mine old days to be taught by my wife!'

The shape of that dreaded medieval word 'heresy' began to form in his mind and he went so far as to order the Queen's rooms to be searched and for preparations to be made for her arrest. He summoned Catherine to him and put her

through his own kind of religious catechism. But the Queen's mind was a good deal sharper than her ailing husband's and, rather than risk being trapped in elusive doctrinal argument, she disarmed him completely by declaring: 'I refer my judgment in this, as in all other cases, to Your Majesty's wisdom, as my only anchor, supreme head and governor.'

*Hampton Court as Henry VIII left it. Here it is Tudor-perfect but later sovereigns were unable to leave well alone and the original perfection was marred.*

At once poor, muddle-headed Henry cried: 'Then perfect friends we are now again, as ever at any time heretofore!'

Unfortunately, he had forgotten to rescind the orders for Catherine's arrest and no sooner had the touching reconciliation been accomplished than the Lord Chancellor, Wriothesley, arrived with forty yeomen to take the Queen to the Tower. Wriothesley, who was simply obeying instructions, was obliged to stand white-faced and humiliated while Henry subjected him to a venomous tongue-lashing for supposed stupidity and incompetence.

In the summer of 1546 Henry entertained the French ambassador, Claude d'Annebaut, who had come to ratify the peace treaty concluded between England and France. Little Prince Edward, accompanied by a velvet-and-gold coated retinue of eight hundred, met the ambassador a short distance from Hampton Court, and the Frenchman was duly impressed.

In Tilt Yard and House Park great tents, pavilions and temporary wooden houses had been erected and for six days there was feasting, hunting, dancing and the staging of masques and mummeries. At the end of it all Henry presented the ambassador with £1,200 worth of silver plate as a parting gift.

Henry had participated in his last great State occasion. After his guests had departed he slowly sank into sickness and misery. His gross body was a nauseating sight for his attendants to look upon. His suppurating legs caused him agony, his temper was foul, his distrust of everyone around him (except for Catherine) tedious to bear.

Towards the close of the year he was taken to Westminster Palace and it was clear that his time had run out. On 28 January 1547 he announced to the watchers at his bedside that he would 'take a little sleep'. The sleep developed into a coma and a few hours later he died, having briefly recovered consciousness just before the very end and uttered (according to one account) the despairing cry: 'All is lost!'

*Edward VI (1537–1553).
The young King was studi-
ous and highly articulate
but, despite frail health, he
also enjoyed the outdoor life
and was often to be seen
hawking and hunting in the
palace parks. Portrait attri-
buted to William Stretes.*

# 2
# *The*
# *Earliest Years*

## EDWARD VI, THE BOY KING

THE NEW KING WAS THE NINE-YEAR-OLD BOY, Edward VI, son of Henry VIII and Jane Seymour, and born, as we have seen, at Hampton Court on 12 October 1537.

Edward's most notable characteristics were his auburn hair and delicate, extremely pale skin – something then thought very attractive – and his intelligence which, compared with other boys from the top social strata, was well above average. He kept a kind of diary (or his *Chronicle* as it has come to be known) written in rather archly adult style which has led to Edward usually being described as 'precocious'.

He spent most of his earliest years at Hampton Court, brought up until the age of six, as he himself wrote, 'by women'. (His mother, of course, had died a few days after his birth.) Henry VIII, always desperately worried that he might lose the son and heir for whom he had prayed, took the most stringent precautions against disease or murder. The royal nursery was at all times the most hygienic, best guarded apartment in the palace.

Every piece of cutlery, every plate, dish, bowl, every drinking vessel handled by the young Prince was thoroughly scoured before use. Food tasters sampled every morsel of food. Edward's rooms were cleaned and scrubbed twice a day and no dogs were allowed near them. No member of the Prince's suite was permitted to have contact with any stranger who came to the palace.

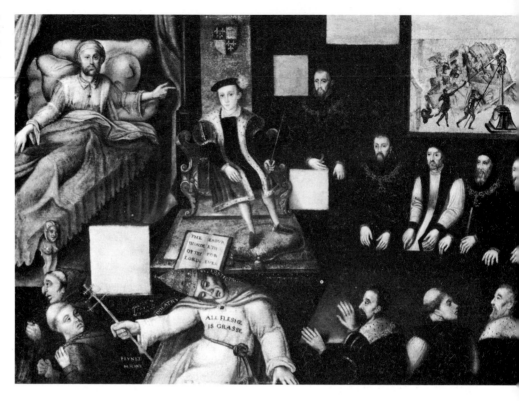

The cosseting of the Prince extended to allowing him to eat as much as his childish heart desired with the result that he developed into an unhealthy fat toddler. And this nearly cost him his life when he was just four. Despite the Hampton Court hygiene, he contracted malaria and it looked for some time as though the combination of overweight and infection would be too much for his heart.

King Henry was almost hysterical with worry, and the agony was heightened by his discovery, which coincided with the boy's illness, of the adultery of his current wife, Catherine Howard. The Prince's recovery was so slow that by the time it was complete Catherine Howard was dead (by Henry's hand) and buried.

A popular roundelay of the child's infant years ran:

> God save King Henry with all his power,
> And Prince Edward, that goodly flower,
> With all his lords of great honour –
> Sing on, troll away, sing, troll on away,
> Heave and how, rumbelow, troll on away.

In 1543, Edward was introduced (at Hampton Court) to yet another step-mother, Catherine Parr. But, again as we have seen, she treated the boy with great kindness and he responded with affection and trust.

By then Edward had moved out of the world of women governesses into the hands of two tutors, Dr Richard Cox and Sir John Cheke. Cox, a former Provost (headmaster) of Eton, was a militant Protestant who had great influence on

Edward's religious attitude. Cheke, Oxford University's first Regius Professor of Greek, shaped the Prince's interest in expressing himself in writing and helped to develop his enthusiasm for the Greek and Latin classics. Three of his schoolboy exercise books, filled with quotations from Cicero and Aristotle, have been preserved.

Both Cox and Cheke had commendably advanced views on the system of royal education. Rather than isolate the Prince as a solitary student, they arranged for him to be taught as one of a group. Consequently, he was usually surrounded at Hampton Court by at least fourteen schoolfellows, most of them sons of peers.

Nor was there any neglect by his tutors of non-academic activities. They gave the Prince instruction in outdoor sports and games, in dancing and also in music for which Edward had inherited his father's love. Edward was a competent lute-player.

The Prince enjoyed hawking, hunting and tennis, often in the company of two of his closest friends, Barnaby Fitzpatrick, son of the Baron of Upper Ossory, and Henry Sidney, son of his Chamberlain, Sir William Sidney. Barnaby has often been described as Edward's whipping-boy – that is to say he literally bore the beatings intended as a punishment for the Prince. (The employment of whipping-boys as stand-ins for princes was a long-established practice but it seems to have ended with the end of Edward's childhood.)

By the time his father died, Edward was a well-educated, articulate little boy able to understand many of the important events taking place around him. It is all the more touching therefore, to note that, childlike, one of the things that most impressed him at Henry VIII's funeral was, as he recorded in his *Chronicle*, that the Court officers 'broke their staves, hurling them into the grave'.

On 19 February 1547, young Edward, in a silver gown embroidered with gold and wearing a white velvet cap covered with shimmering diamonds and pearls, rode in a great State procession from the Tower to the Palace of Westminster.

As the boy passed through the crowded streets, upright and confident on his crimson caparisoned horse, riding beneath a huge canopy held aloft by six mounted knights, Londoners gazed with awe upon their new King. In Cornhill a group of children, not much younger than himself, greeted him with their specially-composed poem which began: 'Hail, noble Edward, our King and Sovereign.' In Cheapside the Lord Mayor presented him with a purse that held a thousand crowns, equivalent to the then magnificent sum of £250. But those around him saw then that he was still very much a child, for all his learning. He could not understand why he, a King, should be thought in need of money. He half-turned in his saddle and asked: 'Why do they give me this?' He was told it was the custom of the City.

Next day, in a ceremony reduced from its usual twelve hours to seven, Edward was crowned in Westminster Hall – three times. Archbishop Cranmer placed upon his head, in turn, Edward the Confessor's crown, the Imperial Crown and a third crown, custom-made to fit comfortably.

Young as he was, Edward knew himself to be a Protestant. The lesson had, in any case been driven home by his tutor, Richard Cox. But Cranmer could not forbear to remind him of it during the Coronation ceremony, and in an exaggeratedly fussy admonition he told the boy: 'You are Supreme Head of the Church, elected of God, and commanded *only* by him.'

Edward was King, but in name only. His uncle, Edward Seymour, Duke of

Somerset (Jane Seymour's brother), was his guardian and adviser but, by means that had no legal basis, Somerset was appointed Lord Protector. It was an office that offered great power; and power appealed to the Duke.

In June 1547 King Edward returned to the place of his birth and boyhood – to Hampton Court. There he continued his lessons with Sir John Cheke. He was happy to be back with his tutor, whom he both respected and loved, and happy to be back at games and sports with his friends. His young friends treated him as an equal and on many an afternoon the palace servants could hear the half-giggling, half-protesting shrieks of the King of England as some companion bested him in a schoolboy scuffling, knock-about game. But, despite his exuberant spirits, strong for a boy whose health was far from robust and who looked always sickly, Edward could be touchy and dominant. One of the famous stories told of him is that when he was struggling one day to grasp something or other out of his reach, a young friend pushed forward a large Bible for him to stand on. Edward turned on his friend and refused the offer in a sudden, chilling cry of anger.

On another occasion one of Edward's boyish pranks shocked the courtiers by its total lack of royal discretion. The young King, having undertaken the tedious chore of conferring knighthoods on men in whom he had no personal interest, decided that he would like to create a knight of his own choice. He picked on another of his friends, Nicholas Throckmorton, and with whooping, giggling cries of 'Kneel!' chased him through the palace galleries brandishing a sword. Throckmorton, half amused and half alarmed, for he, at least, was sensible enough to appreciate the embarrassment the King was certain to cause, hid in a cupboard. But there Edward found him, commanded him to come forth and instantly tapped him upon the shoulder and dubbed him knight. The Court was appalled but the King's prerogative could not be denied, even when exercised as part of a silly, thoughtless game. Throckmorton was now Sir Nicholas and would remain so. (His lasting memorial, involving a slight modification in spelling, is Throgmorton Street, in the City of London.)

But life was far from being all fun and games for Edward. His restless Protector, Somerset, was ever busy organising his future. As a means of securing union between England and Scotland, he was intent on marrying the King to Mary of Scotland. He raised an army and marched against the Scots who were defeated and massacred at Musselborough, in the last battle to be fought between the two kingdoms as separate states. Leith was burned but the English were forced to withdraw from Scotland for lack of supplies.

At Hampton Court, Edward found himself caught in the centre of rivalry that had developed between Somerset and his brother, Thomas Seymour, who had been given command of the navy. Thomas, a handsome, sad-eyed man, with a full beard and a voluminous moustache, was bitterly jealous of Somerset, mainly on the grounds that he was taking more than his fair share of State 'perks'.

Ironically, the brothers' hostility was fattened by the apparently trivial matter of the King's pocket money. Somerset, in an effort to control England's rapidly rising inflation, was cutting back on public spending including Edward's personal allowance. (Edward and some of Somerset's political rivals, with the Earl of Warwick in the forefront, did not fail to notice that while the Protector preached the need for belt-tightening he was sparing no expense on building a great monument to himself in London's Strand: Somerset House.)

*St Nicholas Throcmorton*

*Sir Nicholas Throckmorton. In the course of a silly, boyish prank Edward VI knighted him. The courtiers were appalled at the breach of protocol but the King's prerogative could not be denied.*

Admiral Thomas Seymour saw the reduction in Edward's pocket money as a heaven-sent chance to drive a wedge between the Protector and the King, as one of Edward's letters shows:

My uncle of Somerset dealeth very hardly with me, and keepeth me so straight that I cannot have any money at my own will. But my Lord Admiral both sends me money and gives me money.

Unfortunately for him, Thomas Seymour's trouble was that he could not resist pushing his luck too far, too fast. Having won Edward's gratitude by his 'generosity' he tried to persuade the King that he, Thomas, would make an altogether more acceptable Protector than his brother, Somerset.

In January 1549, Thomas went personally to Hampton Court to press his case and there found the King walking and talking in one of the galleries with Somerset. Having come all the way from London, Thomas was not going to be put off by the presence of his brother and enemy. All the same, it was clearly not a good moment for an outright take-over bid and so he was obliged to unroll a classic nod-and-wink political statement. 'Within three or four years,' he pontificated, 'Your Grace shall be sixteen years old. I trust by that time Your Grace will help your men yourself, with such things as fall in Your Grace's gift.' Wisely, Edward and Somerset said nothing.

Admiral Seymour was not himself wise enough to see the danger inherent in that silent rebuff. On the night of 16 January, accompanied by two servants and armed with a pistol, he stole up to Edward's bedroom in the palace with the apparent intention of kidnapping the King. The door was locked and was guarded by Edward's dog which immediately began barking excitedly at the approach of the shadowy figures. In a panic, Seymour killed the animal with a single pistol shot.

In the stillness of the night and the silence of the sleeping palace, the shot rang out like a thunder-clap. Immediately, hoarsely-shouting yeomen came pouring into the corridor. And so swift was their arrival that in the light of their torches they could see the smoke still drifting from the pistol in Seymour's hand. Lamely he explained, 'I wished to know whether His Majesty was safely guarded.' Seymour was taken to the Tower, convicted of high treason and beheaded on 20 March.

Somerset was rid of both brother and rival but his own time was running out. He was a zealous reformer. During his 'reign' the Common Prayer Book was produced in English and the laws against witchcraft were repealed. Boiling in oil, the standard punishment for poisoners, was abolished and Somerset also tried (although unsuccessfully) to prevent the enclosure of land.

But, although many people in the countryside supported his opposition to enclosure, many were angered by the enforced Anglicising of church services and the forbidding of Mass. As a result of a combination of these factors, Somerset, and Edward by implication, found themselves faced with a revolution that was part political, part religious.

Led by a tanner, Robert Kett, the peasants of East Anglia rose against the land enclosures and tore down fences. Some were hanged by the enclosing landlords. On Whit Sunday 1549 the parishoners of Sampford Courtnay, in Devon, refused to hear the service in English and insisted on their priest conducting Mass in

*Edward Seymour, Duke of Somerset. He was guardian and adviser to the boy-king, Edward VI, and by means that had no legal·basis was appointed as the realm's Lord Protector. He lusted after power but in the end over-reached himself and ended with his neck beneath the executioner's axe. Young King Edward recorded that final event in his diary with the single, chillingly heartless sentence: 'The Duke of Somerset had his head cut off upon Tower Hill, between eight and nine o'clock in the morning.'*

Latin. The two concurrent revolts spread to the Midlands and Yorkshire, with much bloodshed. In East Anglia, cavalry led by the Earl of Warwick killed 3,500 peasants and in the West country some four thousand religious protestors perished. It was the French king, Henry II, who unwittingly prevented the uprisings from developing into civil war. Seeking to take advantage of the troubles he threatened to invade England and rebels and their persecutors united in defence of the realm.

When the danger from France had passed Somerset was confronted by strong opposition from a group of peers and other nobles who gathered under the banner of John Dudley, Earl of Warwick. In alarm Somerset whisked Edward away with him to Hampton Court where he set about turning the palace into a fortress protected by five hundred armed guards. From there he persuaded Edward to issue the following proclamation:

The King's Majesty straightly chargeth and commandeth all his living subjects with all haste to repair to his Highness at His Majesty's Manor of Hampton Court, in most defensible array, with harness and weapons to defend his most royal person and his entirely beloved uncle the Lord Protector, against whom certain persons have attempted a most dangerous conspiracy. And this to do in all possible haste. Given at Hampton Court the Fifth day of October in the Third year of his most noble reign.

The dried-out palace moat was filled with water, local villagers were exhorted to rally to the King's defence, and the Lord Mayor and Corporation of London were told to send reinforcements of one thousand men.

One evening after dark the King, shivering from a severe cold, was brought down to the western gatehouse (then a five-storey structure) to speak personally to the locals. He was hurried across the Base Court, his way lighted by the flare of torches, to the edge of the thirty foot moat. From there he shouted in his piping, feverish voice, across to the assembled group of gaping villagers, 'I pray you be good to us and our uncle.'

Then Somerset harangued the crowd, misguidedly warning them that if he, the Protector, died in defence of the palace, the King would also die. 'It is not I they shoot at – this is the mark they shoot at,' he shouted, grasping the King's hand. The tone was wrong, the content wheedling, the man himself unimpressive. The villagers listened in total silence and in silence they drifted away. With their feet they delivered their vote of no-confidence.

Somerset at least had enough sense to see the reaction as a likely reflection of the general popular will and he immediately abandoned the idea of relying on Hampton Court as a secure 'fortress'. With Edward and the whole palace guard he rode off to Windsor. Five days later he surrendered to the Earl of Warwick and was taken to the Tower.

Despite everything, Somerset for the moment survived. On 6 February 1550 he was freed on condition that he would not come within ten miles of the King. But by April he was restored to Court and in July 1551 was even received again at Hampton Court. Indeed, such was the apparent turn of events that on 18 July he actually joined with other members of the Privy Council in signing a royal proclamation urging the people 'to resort more diligently to common prayer than they had done, and especially to refrain their greedy appetites from that insatiable serpent, covetousness'.

Somerset himself may not have prayed quite hard enough for he soon found himself back in the Tower for the last time. In January 1552 he went, splendidly arrayed, to his execution. In his *Chronicle*, Edward recorded the event in a single, strangely callous sentence: 'The Duke of Somerset had his head cut off upon Tower Hill, between eight and nine o'clock in the morning.'

Before Somerset's death Hampton Court had seen its last great event of Edward's reign, a magnificent reception for the envoys of France with whose country the King had, after earlier confrontations, formed a new alliance. On

14 July 1551 the three diplomats, led by the Grand Marshal of France, Jacques d'Albon, were received in the Presence Chamber where Edward, seated beneath the canopy of State, addressed them in impeccable French:

My Lords, you are welcome for three reasons: one, thus is confirmed in perpetuity a good peace between my brother of France and myself; two, it enables me to meet the Grand Marshal, whom I have so long wanted to see; and three, that you all, being witnesses of the oath of loyalty I shall take towards your King, will remember how it will be kept . . .

Two days later, and again in the Presence Chamber, d'Albon invested Edward with the Order of St. Michael. One of the French envoy's secretaries afterwards said of the young English King that it was impossible to 'imagine a more beautiful face and figure, set off by the brilliance of jewels and robes, and a mass of diamonds, rubies and pearls, emeralds and sapphires – they made the whole room look as if lit up'.

The Order, on a chain of scallop shells, was placed around Edward's neck and the investiture was followed by the celebration of Communion in the palace chapel. At the end of the service, the Marshal and the other senior diplomat, François de Rohan, each kissed the boy-king's cheeks. That night there was a banquet in the Great Hall and Edward entertained his guests on the lute. The festivities, with tilting and tournaments, went on for a week, culminating in a great fireworks display.

Warwick now became the man of power, in Somerset's place, and during his 'reign' the final remnants of Catholicism were eliminated from the Church of England. Archbishop Cranmer's Forty-Two Articles – his formulation of the Christian faith – completed the creation of the Protestant church. The royal assent to those Articles, given on 12 June 1553, was Edward's last formal action.

Tuberculosis was far advanced in the young King's lungs and primitive and misguided medical treatment brought him to an agonising end. He was unable to eat, his hair fell out, and he developed gangrene in his toes and fingers. He remained conscious through it all and whispered prayers for his release through death as he lay in his bed at Greenwich. On 6 July 1553 this tragic and remarkable boy, not often remembered among England's Kings, died in the arms of an aide, Sir Henry Sidney, after reciting a final prayer of his own composition. He was not quite sixteen.

One of history's most tragic figures. Seventeen-year-old Lady Jane Grey (1537–1554), Queen for just nine days, is gently persuaded to present her neck to the executioner's block. She neither wanted nor sought the crown but was manipulated by unscrupulous power-seekers.

# 3
# *The*
# *Earliest Years*

## LADY JANE GREY & MARY TUDOR

THE UNCERTAINTY THAT HAUNTED THE REALM during Edward VI's brief reign was intensified by a power struggle over who was to be the dead King's successor. In his final days Edward had used his failing strength to argue a fiercely emotional case against the passing of the crown to his half-sister, Mary Tudor. He was certain that if she became Queen she would restore the authority of the Pope in England. In his will, signed just before his death and only hesitantly endorsed by the Privy Council, he denied the succession to both Mary and Elizabeth.

He was counselled and encouraged by Warwick (the Duke of Somerset's rival), who had now become Duke of Northumberland and was intent on securing the crown for his sixteen-year-old daughter-in-law, Lady Jane Grey.

Jane is another of history's tragic figures. She was wistfully beautiful, highly intelligent and well educated and might have lived a happy and rewarding life had she not been made a pawn in the political chess game. At the age of nine she was admitted to the household of Queen Catherine Parr and, after the Queen's death, became the ward of Catherine's fourth husband, Thomas Seymour, brother of Edward's protector, Somerset.

There had been unsuccessful attempts to arrange a marriage between Jane and King Edward but her eventual union with Northumberland's son, Guildford Dudley, was contrived solely for the purpose of trying to promote the Dudleys as successors to the Tudors. Jane protested desperately against the match and it is said that she gave way only after her father had beaten her. Her subsequent hatred for her husband and her in-laws was so vehement that it brought on a near-fatal illness.

Her despair deepened as the ruthless manipulators around her pushed her still further towards her ultimate and terrible fate. On 9 July 1553 she was taken by Northumberland to a meeting of the Privy Council and unceremoniously informed that she was to be the new Queen. She immediately fainted.

The next day she was required to announce her accession in a proclamation which she signed 'Jane the Queen'. But, despite the dangerous situation into which she had been pitchforked, Jane had not lost all sense of personal judgment. When her obnoxious husband announced that he would take the title of King she replied that he would do no such thing until Parliament approved.

Meanwhile, an extraordinary exchange of letters took place between Mary Tudor and Northumberland – she insisting that she was rightfully Queen and he retorting that because of the annulment of her parents' marriage she was illegitimate and should make her obeisance to Queen Jane.

But Northumberland had misjudged the public mood. In the southern half of the country, where news of the plotting had quickly spread and which, ironically, was predominantly Protestant, the people rose on behalf of Catholic Mary. With a force of ten thousand men she descended upon London and was at once acclaimed as the lawful Queen.

Unhappy Jane, her nine-day 'reign' at an end, was taken to the Tower along with her husband and father-in-law. She pleaded guilty to high treason but declared that she had neither sought nor wanted the crown. Even so, up to her very last minutes on earth she was subjected to humiliation and horror. At their executions on Tower Hill, on 12 February 1554, her husband was made to precede her to the block so that she witnessed the full bloody brutality of the axe which, a moment or two later, was visited upon her. Her odious father-in-law, Northumberland, behaved in character right up to his own execution. He begged Mary's mercy, nauseatingly denied his Protestant faith, and wrote to a friend: 'An old proverb there is, and that most true – a living dog is better than a dead lion. Oh, that it would please her good Grace to give me life – yea, the life of a dog!'

The original enthusiasm for Mary's accession did not long outlast Lady Jane Grey's death. Her Protestant subjects were especially outraged when, on 25 July 1554, the new Queen married Prince Philip of Spain in a move designed to unite England with the Catholic Habsburg Empire. On 23 August, plain and dowdy Mary, more masculine than feminine in appearance and voice, and her lantern-jawed husband, arrived at Hampton Court for their honeymoon.

It was a happy time for Mary, for she was genuinely in love with her husband, but not for Philip who did not return her affection. He had married solely for the prospect of enhanced power and, although he was outwardly courteous, he was unbearably bored. Worse still, he and his Spanish retainers despised the English as uncouth 'foreigners'. They were particularly offended by the drunkenness rife in the kingdom. They certainly had a point there, for excessive and oafish drinking long remained an English characteristic, a fact later noted in several of Shakespeare's plays, as in *Othello*, for example:

> . . . in England . . . they are most
> potent in potting; your Dane, your
> German, and your swag-bellied Hollander,
> – drink, ho! – are nothing to your English.

For the courtiers and servants, life at Hampton Court with Mary and Philip was oppressively dull. There was neither feasting nor festivities and the Queen and her consort usually dined alone, and frugally, on fish, eggs and oatmeal.

Mary withdrew into even greater seclusion at the palace in April 1555 when she believed herself to be pregnant. A nursery was prepared and official proclamations were drawn up ready with spaces into which the title of the expected infant, Prince or Princess, could be written. In London the church bells rang out and religious processions, led by torch-bearers after dark, wound their way through Cheapside and by Bishopsgate to the river.

On 23 April Mass was celebrated in the palace chapel after which the celebrants, led by Philip and including the Lord Chancellor, Privy Councillors, the Catholic Bishop of Winchester, knights, and priests in cloth of gold copes, paraded around the cloisters of Inner (now Fountain) Court. From her bedroom window Mary watched the procession over which hung a haze of smoke from burning tapers and censers.

But the Queen was depressed and worried by her condition. Her time came and went and there was still no sign of an early birth. Many people expected problems because Mary was thirty-eight, well into middle-age by the average life expectancy of the time, and perilously late for child-bearing. To cheer and encourage their royal patron, Mary's doctors brought 'three most beautiful infants' for her to see. And they emphasised that the babies had been 'born a few days previously at one birth, of a woman of low stature and great age like the Queen and who, after the delivery, found herself strong and out of all danger . . .' The sight, it was added, 'greatly rejoiced her Majesty'.

Mary delightedly reported that she could feel the movement of the unborn child in her womb and undoubtedly she appeared swollen enough. But her midwife was more outspoken and honest than the doctors for she said that, apart from the swelling, Mary exhibited none of the other usual signs of pregnancy. She was right. It was a false alarm and, as it later came to be realised, Mary was suffering from dropsy and other afflictions which together helped to produce the false outward appearances of pregnancy.

Mary desperately wanted a child, not merely for the personal satisfaction of motherhood but because a Catholic heir would ensure that the crown did not pass to her Protestant half-sister, Elizabeth.

Elizabeth's future and, indeed her life, were in jeopardy. Sir Thomas Wyatt, who led a rebellion against Mary, implicated Elizabeth in his conspiracy, although he withdrew the charge in his last moments on the scaffold. As a result Elizabeth was sent to the Tower and there was every likelihood that she would share Wyatt's fate.

It was during Mary's suspected pregnancy that Elizabeth was brought to Hampton Court and there held prisoner. Mary was hesitant about what to do

with her. Already the Queen had approved the burning of the first of her reign's Protestant martyrs but Elizabeth could not easily be disposed of. Mary had learned that when her own name was mentioned on public occasions in London the crowds were sullen and silent; when they heard Elizabeth's name they cheered.

At ten one night early in May, Elizabeth was unexpectedly summoned to the Queen's presence. It was a frightening moment for the twenty-two-year-old Princess, whose climb up the torch-lit privy stairs to the Queen's apartments might, for all she knew, mark the way towards the block.

Mary sat on a chair of state placed in the middle of her bed-chamber and, upon entering, Elizabeth curtseyed three times and fell on her knees before the Queen.

The encounter between the two royal half-sisters was one of high drama. In that room, with the flickering light of wax candles casting long and sinister shadows on bed posters and tapestry hangings, was to be decided not merely the fate of a young Princess but the future of a nation.

Both women were well armed for the verbal fencing that followed, but Elizabeth's wits were the sharper of the two. She seized the opening gambit by avowing that, whatever the Queen might believe to the contrary, she was a true and loyal subject.

'Then you will not confess yourself to be a delinquent, I see, but rather stand stoutly on your truth,' Mary answered curtly. 'I pray God your truth may become manifest.'

'If not, I will request for neither favour not pardon at your Majesty's hands,' Elizabeth countered.

Mary thought for a moment and then produced a trick question: 'Well, then, you stand so stiffly on your truth, belike you have been wrongfully punished and imprisoned?'

'I cannot and must not say so to your Majesty,' came the astute reply.

'Why, then, belike you will report it so to others?'

'Not so, as it please your Majesty. I have borne, and must bear, the burden myself; and if I may but enjoy your Majesty's good opinion of me, I shall be better enabled to bear it still, and I pray God when I shall cease to be one of your Majesty's truest and loyal subjects that then I may cease to be at all.'

It was a brilliant defence from a Princess who was both intellectually brilliant and cultivated and Mary found herself at a loss. She raised her eyes to the ceiling, muttered the Spanish words, *Sabe Dios* – God knows – and added: 'Whether innocent or guilty I forgive you.' Turning her head away she gestured, dispiritedly, that Elizabeth was to be led back to her room.

Legend says that Philip, who had been curious to see Elizabeth, eavesdropped on the historic interview from behind a concealing arras. Whether that was true or not, neither he nor Mary made any attempt from then on to threaten Elizabeth. Later, in fact, Philip advised Mary to re-admit Elizabeth to the Court and the sisters were reconciled. Philip treated the Princess with marked gallantry. Rumour inevitably suggested that he was in love with her but there is no precise evidence for that. (Later, after Mary's death, Philip was among Elizabeth's suitors – but his intentions were almost certainly politically based. Later still, when as King of Spain, he coveted the idea of returning to England as an invader, his hopes were shattered with the destruction of the Armada.)

Mary's reign was now nearing its end. After her disappointment over the non-existent child she was forced to move temporarily to Oatlands, near Weybridge in Surrey. Hampton Court had fallen into such neglect that it needed a full-scale spring-clean. Even for those none-too-fastidious times, the unhygienic state of the palace was plainly intolerable. Although they were tried, lavish doses of perfume could not alone make the place habitable. Nothing but an intense and thorough scouring would suffice.

Mary had further, and equally unfounded, expectations of childbirth and soon Philip tired of her constant sickness and disappeared to the Continent where he disported himself with a succession of mistresses.

He returned briefly and in 1557 he and Mary spent a few summer weeks at Hampton Court. She was back, alone, in August of the following year and once more she believed herself to be pregnant. That time, sensibly, her advisers persuaded her to keep her hopes secret and the advice was sound, for she was doomed to disappointment. It was the very last of her many unfulfilled hopes.

Mary Tudor's final days were passed at St James's Palace and she died there, on 17 November 1558, almost certainly from what we would now recognise as cancer. She was nearly forty-three.

The brutal murders of Protestants, carried out during her reign, earned Mary the title of 'Bloody Mary'. It was fully deserved. But, in the interests of truth, it

The Lady Jane, Proclaimed Queen

The Lady Jane and Fecknam a Preist

The Lady Jane Beheaded in y̆ Tower

needs to be said that intolerance and bigotry were then very much the hallmarks of institutionalised religion. In the far future the overwhelming majority of British people would be led towards a decent respect for the faiths and convictions of their neighbours. Few sovereigns who inhabited Hampton Court, during the centuries in which it remained a royal residence, had many lessons in enlightenment to offer.

*Contemporary Tudor history, strip-cartoon style. One set of frames tells of some of the main events in the life of Elizabeth I. The other set on the opposite page recounts the brief chronicles of Lady Jane Grey.*

*Gloriana. Elizabeth I (1533–1603) at the peak of her power. Fortunately her lips are tightly closed for the great defect of her appearance was a mouth full of decaying teeth. Dental caries may well have been the cause of much of her ill-health.*

# 4

# *The Earliest Years*

## ELIZABETH I

IT WOULD NOT HAVE BEEN SURPRISING if Queen Elizabeth had chosen to keep away from Hampton Court. After all, it was from there that her terrifying father ruled – the father who killed her mother, Anne Boleyn, when Elizabeth was only three – and it was there that she herself had come close to death at the hands of her half-sister, Mary. But from the time of her first visit as Queen in August 1559, nine months after her accession, she seemed to accept the palace without looking over her shoulder.

Her past, ominous experiences had affected her in other ways. They had toughened her and, in particular, had helped to develop her skill for cautious and sometimes tortuous diplomacy. She never revealed more of her inner thoughts than was absolutely necessary. Her tight lips were characteristic of her personality although what most impressed her courtiers and Hampton Court servants in those early days of the reign were her slender body, auburn hair, light blue eyes and her imperious bearing.

On that first visit to the palace marriage was uppermost in her mind. She had in fact gone there to meet James Hamilton, Earl of Arran, a Protestant and a member of the Scottish royal house, whom her advisers saw as the ideal husband whose marriage to the Queen would unite the English and Scottish crowns.

*William Cecil, 1st Baron Burghley, who served, in turn, the Duke of Somerset in Edward VI's reign, Mary Tudor and Elizabeth I. As a power behind the throne he did much to create the image of the great Elizabethan Age.*

Elizabeth walked and talked alone with Arran in the Queen's private garden, on the south side of the palace, but the meeting disappointed her. She was highly cultivated and well-educated. She spoke six languages, had read widely in Latin and Greek and, at the remarkably early age of eleven, had made an impeccable prose translation of the French poem, *The Mirror of the Sinful Soul*, by Margaret of Navarre. Arran, on the other hand, was neither very bright nor personable. William Cecil, later Lord Burghley, who was to remain the Queen's first minister for forty years, was equally disappointed by her rejection of Arran. But she insisted that she would take no husband who did not personally appeal to her, whatever the State considerations might be.

Elizabeth and Cecil had done their best to keep the meeting with Arran secret but da Guadra, the ambassador of England's suspicious ally, Mary's widower, Philip II of Spain, had planted his spies in the palace.

*Robert Dudley, Earl of Leicester, one of Elizabeth's 'favourites'. Rumour said that he and the Queen lived as man and wife at Hampton Court and, in 1586, a man turned up in Madrid claiming to be their illegitimate son.*

*Elizabeth and Leicester in the Knot Garden. This type of garden, with interlacing patterns of flowers and plants, was a great Tudor feature of mansions and country houses.*

Elizabeth, indeed, was soon plunged into a running battle of wits with ambassadors. The first to arrive at Hampton Court was de Noailles of France. He hurried down on 6 September to report that Arran, who had commanded the Scots Guards in the French wars against Spain, was now 'wanted' for the treachery of his pro-Protestantism. Could France be assured that if Arran appeared in England he would be arrested? Blandly, Elizabeth replied that the French authorities could rely on her co-operation *if* Arran appeared, but de Noailles was somewhat disconcerted by what he thought was the ghost of a smirk on the Queen's face. (Arran later made a second and more formal proposal to Elizabeth but in 1561 she delivered her final refusal. By that time the unfortunate Earl had made a similarly unsuccessful approach to his cousin, Mary Queen of Scots.)

Philip II himself had been a suitor for Elizabeth's hand but he, too, was refused. Unwilling to give up the pursuit of a potentially valuable political alliance he had suggested, as second choice, his cousin, the Archduke Charles of Austria. Elizabeth told the ever-scurrying Ambassador da Guadra that she would think about the matter. Meanwhile, however, da Guadra rushed off a dispatch to King Philip reporting on what he described as the 'very strange story' emanating from the Queen's lady-in-waiting, Lady Sidney, mother of the soldier-poet Sir Philip Sidney.

Lady Sidney, according to the ambassador, 'said there had been a plot to murder the Queen and Lord Robert Dudley [Lady Sidney's brother] at a banquet given at Lord Arundel's. The frightfulness of the danger . . . had so alarmed Elizabeth that she had positively determined to marry.'

In fact, for all the hustle and bustle that enveloped the subject, and the proposals from other foreign suitors that she purported to be considering, Elizabeth had no intention of marrying anyone. Her courtiers had made up their minds that she was in love with Lord Robert Dudley, later to be Earl of Leicester, and by 1561 her relations with Dudley had become a central topic of court gossip. Da Guadra, ever vigilant, reported that on a barge journey down the Thames, on which he was a guest, Elizabeth and Dudley behaved together with 'discreditable freedom'.

One rumour went so far as to suggest that the couple lived as man and wife at Hampton Court where Elizabeth had secretly given birth to a son, fathered, of course, by Dudley. Some support seemed to be given to that allegation when, in 1586, a man turned up in Madrid claiming to be that same illegitimate son and insisting that he had been brought up by Robert Sotheron, the son of the Queen's childhood governess.

According to the nineteenth-century Roman Catholic historian, John Lingard, the 'son', who called himself Arthur Dudley, provided the Spanish authorities with a detailed account of his life. The original document, written in English, has not been found but the Spanish summary described how the foster-father, Sotheron, was summoned to Hampton Court and told that 'a lady at court had been delivered of a child', and that the Queen wished to conceal the lady's 'dishonour'.

Sotheron was then led 'into the gallery near the royal closet' and handed the infant with orders to call him Arthur. At first Sotheron boarded the child with a miller's wife at Molesey, just across the river from the palace, but later took him into his own house and sent him to school in London.

Arthur Dudley, the Spanish summary went on, 'now concluded that there was some mystery respecting his birth, from the different manner in which he and his supposed brothers and sisters had been educated, but could not draw the secret from Sotheron till a few days before the old man's death when he learned from him that he was the son of Queen Elizabeth and the Earl of Leicester. He then consulted [two courtiers] who advised him to keep it secret, and return to the Continent. This he had done, but not before he had obtained an interview with the secretary of Leicester.'

Strangely (or perhaps significantly, if Arthur Dudley *was* an imposter), no details of that interview with the secretary were given.

The importance of the Arthur Dudley 'case' is that it strikingly illustrates just one of the many attempts that were made to discredit Elizabeth and especially to destroy the image of the 'Virgin Queen'. In a time of acute religious conflict it was natural for Catholics to wish to denigrate Elizabeth and for Protestants to defend her. Bigotry was an impediment to the truth on both sides. And there was ever fuel for rumour in the fact that all her life, even into extreme old age, the Queen liked to be surrounded by handsome young men; and she had her close favourites – the Earl of Essex and Sir Walter Raleigh, among others – after Leicester.

A Swedish diplomat, who observed Elizabeth at the palace, wrote to his king, Erick, who was among her suitors: 'I saw no signs of an immodest life, but I did see many signs of chastity, of virginity, and of true modesty; so that I would stake my life itself that she is most chaste. She is beautiful and eloquent and wholly worthy of your Majesty, in my judgment at least, if there is any in all Europe who is.'

That diplomat may well, of course, have adjusted the 'prospectus' to suit his master's wishful thinking but there is no doubt that a constantly fascinating subject of talk among the Hampton Court hangers-on was the Queen's sex life, or lack of it. The truth will probably never be known. Some, like the great Ben Jonson, believed that Elizabeth suffered from an unspecified handicap that made sexual intercourse physically impossible. But, in the light of modern medical science, there are grounds to support the theory of the essayist and biographer, Lytton Strachey, that Elizabeth's childhood psychological disturbances made ultimate sexual contact repugnant to her. And certainly she once confessed to Lord Sussex: 'I hate the idea of marriage for reasons that I would not divulge to a twin soul.'

But while the idle tongues at Hampton Court persisted in clacking, the Queen had other and more pressing matters on her mind. Inflation was rife and represented only one of the many economic problems that beset the realm. Antagonism between the supporters of Rome and the Protestants was much sharpened by European Catholic insistence that Mary Queen of Scots was the rightful sovereign of both Scotland and England. Elizabeth's throne looked far from safe.

Gradually the first signs of the Counter-Reformation were becoming evident – the movement spearheaded by the Jesuits, resourceful and resolute and dedicated to the restoration of the Catholic supremacy. In time, threats against Elizabeth's life were to become an ever-present anxiety. And, just as her half-sister, Mary Tudor, had burned hundreds of Protestant martyrs, so in due course would Elizabeth order the deaths of hundreds of Catholics.

Meanwhile, however, it appeared much more likely that disease, rather than assassination, might bring about the Queen's untimely removal from the throne. On 13 October 1562 she went for a walk in her Hampton Court gardens and by evening was overtaken by a high fever.

Her doctors feared for her life and some fifteen or sixteen members of her Council, who happened to be in London, were summoned to her bedside. While she lay oblivious to the world in a coma, her advisers adjourned to a next-door room to discuss the urgent question of her successor. It soon became clear that Elizabeth had smallpox and she, too, believed she was dying for, in one of her briefly conscious moments, she whispered to the courtiers around the sickbed that she wished Lord Robert Dudley to be appointed as the kingdom's Protector.

Then a few hours later, at midnight on 16/17 October, she rallied and regained full consciousness. The smallpox spots appeared and, like any woman of the time, she worried about how much disfigurement she might have to endure. In the event, she was relieved to discover that the blemishes were minimal.

Her skirmish with death, and especially the problem of her successor, had so shaken her advisers that on 5 November the Commons presented a petition begging her to marry. On behalf of the House, Mr Speaker declared that, without a known heir to the throne, the kingdom would face a multitude of crises, including the prospect of civil war and invasion by foreign armies. True to her accustomed form of avoiding either 'yea' or 'nay' when 'maybe' might serve, she returned an evasive answer.

Her Commons, however, lived in hope and two years later more proposals of marriage were still arriving. One, from the German Duke Casimir, was brought by young Sir James Melville, who was also envoy to Mary Queen of Scots. Elizabeth mulled over the offer, half-heartedly, and then rejected it.

A few months later Melville returned to Hampton Court but this time specifically on behalf of Mary whose potential threat to her throne was of greater moment to Elizabeth than the question of a husband. During his week's stay Melville met the Queen every day, and often three times a day, for negotiations. In his *Memoirs* he recalled:

She expressed a great desire to see her [Mary]; and because their so-much-to-be-desired meeting could not hastily be brought to pass, she appeared with great delight to look upon Her Majesty's picture. She took me to her bedchamber, and opened a little cabinet wherein were divers little pictures wrapped within paper and their names written with her own hand upon the papers. Upon the first that she took up was written *My Lord's Picture*. I held the candle and pressed to see the picture so named; she appeared loath to let me see it, yet my importunity prevailed for a sight thereof, and I found it to be the Earl of Leicester's picture.

Once again Elizabeth drew upon her capacity to prevaricate. She carefully shied away from the nub of the matter, the future relationship between the two crowns, and practised the art of feminine wiliness on Melville. For their walk-about discussions in the palace gardens she wore a different dress every day. And if her purpose was to divert Melville's attention from his diplomatic task by impressing him with her private personality, she certainly succeeded. Even if he had not been readily impressionable he could hardly have overlooked her constant change of costume since she openly begged for flattery by seeking his opinion: did he approve of her French attire, or perhaps the English, or the Italian?

Melville, as it happened, was as astute as she. Noting the just-perceptible extra emphasis she used in speaking of her Italian dress, he lavished special praise on that. And, like all those women who relish even invited compliments, she lapped up his response.

His 'opinion', he remembered, 'pleased her well, for she delighted to show her golden coloured hair, wearing a caul and bonnet as they do in Italy. Her hair was more reddish than yellow, curled in appearance naturally.'

We can well imagine them both, in that long-ago summer of 1564, strolling among the pinks and the roses, the honeysuckle and sweet briar, in and out of the palace bowers, across the soft English lawns; Melville's tongue treading as delicately through the conversation as his feet between the flower-beds, Elizabeth fishing almost as dexterously for compliments as for political information about her Scottish rival.

What colour of hair, she wondered aloud, did he think was reputed to be the best? Was her's the best, or that of his own Mary of Scotland? Which was the finest? Melville did his best, and a gallant best it was too, to answer the unanswerable. 'The fairest of both is not the worst fault,' he ventured, and then, with second-thought inspiration: 'You are the fairest Queen in England, and mine is the fairest Queen in Scotland.'

Later Elizabeth made cunningly certain that Melville should be witness to one of her accomplishments which she doubted Mary could equal. She arranged for her cousin, Lord Hunsdon, to take the envoy into one of the palace galleries adjoining a room in which she sat playing upon the virginals, an early form of the harpsichord.

As Melville wrote: 'After I had hearkened awhile, I took by [drew back] the tapestry that hung before the door of the chamber, and seeing her back was towards the door, I entered within the chamber, and stood a pretty space [a little time] hearing her play excellently well . . .'

Eventually Elizabeth turned and pretended to be surprised and angered by the intrusion. But the contrived annoyance swiftly subsided and the Queen commanded Melville to sit beside her and demanded to know who played best, she or Mary? 'In that,' Melville admitted, 'I found myself obliged to give her the praise.'

Elizabeth had inherited her love of music from her father, Henry VIII, and she delighted always in being surrounded by musicians. (Two of the famous composers of the age, Thomas Tallis and William Byrd, were successively Masters of the Music of the Chapel Royal.) She was as skilled upon the lute as the virginals and enjoyed singing, although opinions about the quality of her voice differed. One particularly reckless critic, Lord Oxford, was helped towards incarceration in the Tower by his comment that she had 'the worst of voices'.

Dancing was another of the Queen's favourite pastimes and she would rebuke her ladies 'if they do not dance to her liking, and without doubt she is mistress of the art, having learned in the Italian manner to dance high'.

She danced many a night away at Hampton Court, treading the measures of pavanes and galliards and country dances with such delightfully evocative titles as Flaunting Two, Leaves Green, Mopsy's Tune, Nobody's Jig and Shake-a-Trot.

For her diversion on quieter evenings the Queen often chose to play at cards, particularly primero, a type of early poker. She also tried her luck at a newly-devised game known as triumph (from which the term 'trump' is derived) and which survives, in an amended form, as whist. And she referred to a pack of cards with the word still used by North American players – 'deck'.

Dressing for the evening was inevitably a lengthy process for Elizabeth. She spent an interminable time merely applying her make-up. In the Tudor fashion she painted her nails red but she also whitened her neck and the exposed part of her bosom, in conformity with the popular belief that extreme whiteness was very feminine. The whitener was ceruse, made from a mixture of white lead and vinegar. For putting colour on her lips and cheeks she used a red dye known as fucus.

Her formal gowns (of which she had more than three thousand) were studded with jewels and covered layers of undergarments: a chemise-smock, a great hopped petticoat known as a farthingale, a laced bodice, skirt and kirtle. She wore the recently introduced knitted stockings, although one of her prize possessions was a black silk pair, and high-heeled shoes embroidered with gold and silver. As her brilliantly auburn hair gradually lost its lustre, she covered it with a red wig, intertwined with jewels and she had no fewer than eighty wigs to choose from.

But the most memorable feature of the dressed-up Queen was the enormous ruff with which she adorned her neck. Some of her ruffs were starched and pleated but others were stretched upon wires. The outer edges were needleworked with representations, as one contemporary put it, with 'the sunne, moone and starres, and many other antiques strange to behold'. Often when she entered the candle-lit Chamber of Presence she gave the impression of a goddess afloat on the ocean with her head set against a vast, billowing galleon foresail.

Like other noble ladies, Elizabeth often appeared in daytime clad in a man's style doublet and jerkin, buttoned up the front and with padded shoulders. Many people, however, frowned on this unisex garb and their criticism was summed up by the satirist, William Goddard:

> To see Morilla in her coach to ride,
> With her long locke of hair upon one side;
> With hat and feathers, worn in swaggering guise;
> With buttoned boddice, skirted doublet-wise;
> Unmaskt, and sit i' the booth without a fan:
> Speake, could you judge her less than be some man.

At night the Queen slept, as did most of her upper-class women subjects, in a simple night-smock and only in the morning changed into what was called a night-dress but which today would be regarded as a housecoat or dressing-gown.

Unfortunately, all the dressing-up, the make-up and the bejewelled elegance could not disguise her worst feature – a mouth full of blackened, decaying teeth. The English were notorious for their bad teeth and usually the only attention they gave them was to remove the most irritating particles of food with a toothpick: an iron instrument, like a small builder's nail, for men, and a wooden one for women. The Queen, not surprisingly, was a 'martyr' to incessant tooth-ache, and dental caries very likely contributed to some of her more general bouts of ill-health.

Elizabeth's personal vanity was such that nothing angered her more than any attempt by a lady at court to outdo the Queen in 'glamour'. And when, in February 1579, she noticed that ladies' ruffs were growing larger and some other aspects of their dress becoming increasingly extravagant she issued an extraordinary Hampton Court edict. It declared that:

No person shall use or weare such excessively long clokes, being in common sight monstrous, as now of late are beginning to be used, and before two yeares past hath not been used in this realme. Neither also shoulde any person use or weare such great and excessive ruffes, in or about the uppermost parts of their neckes, as had not been used before two yeares past; but that all persons shoulde, in modest and semely sort, leave off such fonde, disguised and monstrous manner of attyring themselves, as both was unsupportable for charges, and undecent to be worn.

Earlier, in 1568, Elizabeth had been engrossed in matters more pressing than unseemly court fashion. For then the crisis over Mary Queen of Scots reached a new peak. Mary's weak and corrupted husband, the Earl of Darnley, had been murdered, with her connivance, and she had married the murderer, the Earl of Bothwell. But she had been unable to safeguard her throne and was forced to flee into England and beg asylum from Elizabeth.

Mary's presence in the realm, however, was to make life even more hazardous for Elizabeth. Those determined to promote the Counter-Reformation and eliminate Protestantism rallied around Mary. The key to their success would clearly have been the removal of Elizabeth and so the kingdom simmered with plots and counter-plots and everywhere the shadowy figures of spies, secret agents and double-agents flitted energetically about their nefarious trade.

There was, indeed, no shortage of conspiring, would-be assassins, many of them communicating with one another by means of coded letters which were often intercepted and successfully 'broken' by skilful cypher experts. Sometimes, of course, the 'plots' were entirely imaginary, shrieked out by the unhappy victims of the rack who were prepared to 'disclose' anything to keep their limbs in their sockets.

Elizabeth appointed a commission of inquiry to look into all the implications of the crisis over Mary and summoned a progress-report meeting at Hampton Court on 30 October 1568. The facts so far available were alarming enough. In the north there was growing support for Mary and it was said that the Catholic Duke of Norfolk was planning to marry her. It seemed very possible that, with the aid of Norfolk's supporters and her Spanish allies, Mary could replace Elizabeth as Queen of England.

Precautionary measures were called for. Mary was put under close guard at Tutbury, in Staffordshire, and the Duke of Norfolk was sent to the Tower and subsequently executed for high treason.

On 14 December members of Elizabeth's Council again met at the palace and this time they were shown a casket purporting to contain evidence of Mary's conspiracy. One by one, in a kind of solemn conjuror style, the supposedly incriminating documents were plucked from the box. Among them were eight letters proving, so it was claimed, Mary's implication in Darnley's murder, and a sonnet to her composed by Bothwell. William Cecil vouched for the authenticity of the letters. The handwriting, he said, had been compared with that of Mary's letters to Elizabeth.

But some members of the Council came to the conclusion that the casket was much less of a valuable find than they had been led to believe. At best, the evidence appeared to be flimsy and consequently the Council meeting ended indecisively. Its only positive recommendation was that Elizabeth ought not to accede to Mary's plea for a personal confrontation between the two Queens.

Elizabeth herself seemed relieved that she would not be obliged to take drastic action against Mary. Indeed, when Mary's representatives, led by the Earl of Moray, came to see her at the palace at the end of January 1569, Elizabeth returned the letter casket to them, saying that there was not sufficient proof 'whereby the Queen of England should conceive or take any evil of the Queen, her good sister . . .' She even gave Moray a parting gift of £5,000.

Elizabeth was still hoping that somewhere, somehow, she and Mary could reach a final and peaceful settlement. But those hopes were not to be fulfilled. The issues were too large, the numbers of people involved far too many, and the international stakes far too high.

*Mary Queen of Scots (1542–1587). European Catholics insisted that she, and not Elizabeth, was the rightful claimant to the throne of England. Reluctantly, Elizabeth was finally obliged to order Mary's execution.*

*High drama as seen in a contemporary engraving. Mary Queen of Scots goes to the headsman's block at Fotheringay Castle, Northamptonshire, on the morning of 8 February 1587.*

Eventually the die was cast. In 1586 Sir Francis Walshingham, the head of Elizabeth's secret service, was able to convince the Queen that a conspiracy against her life had been undeniably proved by one of his undercover 'agents' and that Mary was clearly implicated.

On the morning of 8 February 1587 the great hall of Fotheringay Castle, Northamptonshire, was the setting for a powerfully tragic and poignant moment which has left its indelible mark on the pages of British history. Clad from head to foot in black satin, Mary mounted the improvised scaffold with great dignity and, before presenting her neck to the block, slipped off the outer garments and revealed herself in dazzling crimson underclothes. As the severed head rolled forward, the executioner snatched it up, held it aloft and showed it to be that of an elderly woman and covered by a wig.

Mary's death helped to hasten the war that had been brewing with Spain and the following year saw that great and memorable Elizabethan event, the destruction of the Armada. Suddenly it seemed as though all the louring clouds were lifting and that England was emerging into a new and more hopeful climate. The people rejoiced and the mood was one of celebration and festivity.

Festivities, too, remained great features of Elizabeth's Hampton Court. The palace and the Queen together shone on those occasions. Day and night there was music, singing and dancing. There were masques and there were plays, performed in the Great Hall where a stage of scaffolding, screens and canvas was put up. The minstrel gallery served as an upper storey for the 'set' and small oil lamps, ingeniously strung on wires below the Hall's roof, illuminated the stage. The pantry at the lower end of the Hall was reserved for use by the actors as their green room and they rehearsed in the Great Watching Chamber.

There was, of course, no stinting on food and drink for the celebratory occasions and contemporary accounts show that the annual bill ran to the then staggering sum of £80,000. The variety of dishes was as wide as the times could provide: venison, hare, rabbit, partridge, pheasant, teal, snipe, lark, capon and chicken. There was butter by the ton, eggs, milk, cheese and twenty varieties of seafood – oysters from Colchester and Whitstable, fresh-water eels from the Midlands, plaice, cod, turbot, skate, whiting and mackerel, grayling, mullet and herring, sturgeon and cuts of meat from stranded whales. For the guest's refreshment there were unlimited barrels of beer and hogsheads of wine.

On ordinary days the Queen and her Court followed the national pattern of meal times. The first main meal of the day was taken at mid-day, and always known as dinner (as it still is among many people in Britain) and the principal evening meal was supper, usually served between five and six in the evening. Like all her subjects, Elizabeth abided by the so-called 'fish day' laws which forbade people to eat meat on Fridays and during Lent and when fish was normally the substitute. The purpose of the laws was not, as might be thought, religious but to control the consumption of beef and mutton.

On non-festive occasions, Elizabeth ate little, picking at her food and preferring beer to wine. She breakfasted, soon after dawn, on manchet (a round loaf of white bread made of wheat flour) and a pottage of mutton or beef washed down with ale.

Dinner and supper each consisted of two courses. She and her ladies would have a first course choice at dinner of beef or mutton, veal, swan, goose, capon or rabbit, followed by fruit with custard and fritters with cheat (a form of wheatbread made with coarsely-sifted flour). For the second course there was usually a choice of lamb or kid, heron or pheasant, or chicken, pigeon or lark, all rounded off with tarts or mince-pies.

Supper began with boiled or roast mutton, capons or baked chicken with manchet. The second course was nearly always identical with the second dinner course for which the basic dishes had been re-heated.

Vegetables were mainly turnips, parsnips, carrots, cabbage, artichokes, asparagus, peas and beans. The Queen enjoyed green salads with her meat and many of the men courtiers were fond of sweet potatoes, or yams, principally in the belief that they were a powerful aphrodisiac.

Fruit played an important part in the menus and there was always plenty to choose from: raspberries, mulberries, strawberries, apples, pears, apricots and plums. And Elizabeth and her courtiers shared a taste for candied nutmeg, ginger and lemon, seed-cake and barley-sugar, honey and marmalade.

All the meat dishes at Hampton Court were heavily spiced, as much to overcome any lack of freshness as to add to tastiness. Venison pasty was a favourite Court dish and made from the meat of a young boar which had been specially raised on oats and peas. If the venison was 'off' – and it frequently was, in the absence of any refrigeration – the palace chefs would bury it three feet in the ground, wrapped in linen, for twenty-four hours. After that, they said, it was as good as fresh-killed but, just in case, they cooked it steeped in beer and served it smothered with rich sauces.

Sausages (then called 'sawsedges') were popular, too. And the Elizabethan agriculturalist, Sir Hugh Platt, produced a recipe for 'Polonion sawsedge':

Take the fillers of a hog; chop them very small with a handful of Red Sage: season it hot with ginger and pepper, and then put it in a great sheep's gut; then let it lie three nights in brine: then boil it and hang it up in a chimeny where fire is usually kept; and these sawsedges will last a whole yeere. They are good for sallads or to garnish boiled meats, or to make one rellish a cup of wine.

At private meal-times two gentlemen-attendants laid the table-cloth (first kneeling in salute) and two ladies scoured the royal gold plates by rubbing them with bread powdered with salt. Scarlet-liveried yeomen brought in the food from which one of the ladies cut slivers with a tasting-knife. Each of these small portions was then handed to a yeoman who chewed and swallowed it. If he showed no sign of dropping dead it was assumed that the dish was free of poison and ready for serving to the Queen.

Her Majesty drank her beer from gold or silver goblets but her courtiers used pewter, horn or glass drinking vessels. The choice of wines included muscadel, vernage (an Italian white), raspes (made from raspberries), clary (a wine mixed with honey, pepper and ginger), and white and red claret.

Table manners were not of the highest order and royal meals were generally accompanied by deep-bellied and thunderous belching. At first, foreigners found it a bit disconcerting but so much admired the palace cooking that they thought the meals worthy of good, stomach-rumbling tributes.

Everywhere palace guests could see the outward trappings of opulent royalty: magnificently wrought furniture, the richest tapestries of pure gold and fine silk and priceless Persian and Indian carpets. The royal throne, set beneath a velvet canopy in the Presence Chamber, was studded with diamonds, rubies and sapphires.

On Sundays and on Christmas Day there would be an interval in the festivities as Elizabeth and her guests paraded to chapel. First to march in solemnly went the Queen's personal guards, all young, straight and tall men, dressed in red coats faced with black velvet on which, back and front, was embroidered the Queen's arms in silver gilt. Each man carried a gilt halberd.

After the guards came the gentlemen of rank and members of the Council, two of them each bearing a royal sceptre and a third the royal sword in its red velvet scabbard embroidered with gold and set with precious stones and large pearls.

Then came the Queen, the yellowing skin of her face heavily painted with make-up – for we are close to the end of her reign and she is ageing now. The thinning hair, no longer lustrous, was curled and artificially thickened. Yet she still managed to look regal in her fine long gown with its train carried by a peeress who, in turn, was followed by twelve young ladies of noble birth. Impressive as she remained, Elizabeth would never again see herself in her glory for she had banished all mirrors from her sight. She could not bear to look upon the wrinkles and the vacant eyes that marked the rapidly fleeting years.

As she slowly processed out of the chapel at the end of the service the whole congregation fell upon its knees and the Queen bowed to each individual group, intoning the words: 'I thank you with all my heart.'

At night on her way to bed, the elderly Elizabeth would pass by pictures that inevitably reminded her of some of the great and tragic moments of her extraordinary life: pictures of Henry VIII, of Edward VI, her sad brother, of Philip of Spain, and of Mary Queen of Scots on the news of whose execution, on her orders, she had wept. She would pass rooms, too, that were filled with reminders of crucial times past: the bedroom in which Edward VI was born and where, soon after, his mother, Jane Seymour, died, and another bedroom in which the tester for the bed was worked by unhappy Anne Boleyn as a gift to Henry VIII, Anne's murderer.

Elizabeth paid her last brief visit to Hampton Court in September 1598. She was ill and tired but what she lacked in strength she made up for in spirit. On the day she left the palace to return to London the weather was foul and her cousin, Lord Hunsdon, discovering her ready to take her departure on horseback, chided her with the comment: 'It is not meet for one of Your Majesty's years to ride in such a storm.'

'*My years*!' she cried furiously, fixing Hunsdon with a devastating look, and then led the Court away with the shouted command to her ladies: 'Maids, to your horses quickly!'

She had one further memorably withering rebuke to deliver. In March 1603 she lay on cushions in her room at Richmond Palace trying gallantly to will sickness away. Anxiously, one of her aides, Robert Cecil, son of Lord Burghley, protested: 'Your Majesty, to content the people you must go to bed!' The Queen rested her pain-ridden eyes on Cecil for a brief moment. 'Little man,' she demanded, 'is "must" a word to use to princes?'

Early on the morning of 24 March, Elizabeth, the last of the remarkable Tudors, died. She was in her seventieth year, a great age for that time, and she had reigned for just over forty-four years.

*James I (1566–1625) who was also James VI of Scotland. On his first visit to Hampton Court he was preoccupied with an offer to his better-off subjects that few could afford to refuse – they could buy a knighthood for £30 or else pay a fine of £40.*

# 5
# *The*
# *Embattled Years*

## JAMES I

SURPRISING AS IT MAY SEEM in an age when there are still many nostalgic references to 'Gloriana' and 'the Elizabethan era', the people of England warmly welcomed James I to the throne mainly on the grounds that they had, in the end, grown weary of being ruled by a Queen and thought they would feel more 'comfortable' with a King again. They were to feel less comforted as time went by.

James was the son of Lord Darnley and Mary Queen of Scots and at the tender age of thirteen months had succeeded to the Scottish throne, as James VI, on the enforced abdication of his mother. He was brought up by the Earl and Countess of Mar and the Earl of Moray was appointed as Scotland's Regent.

At the time of his accession to the English throne he was thirty-seven, well-educated and cultivated (and rather arrogantly aware of being so), a spendthrift and, despite his marriage to Princess Anne of Denmark and the eventual fathering of seven children, a homo-sexual.

It is highly significant, and much in keeping with his life-style, that on his first visit to Hampton Court, in July 1603, his mind was preoccupied with a money-raising scheme. The idea, which originated from Lord Salisbury – that same Robert Cecil who had been Elizabeth's chief minister – was centred upon the sale of honours. The offer was one that few of the potential purchasers could afford to refuse: every-one with £40 a year or more in income from land was to be summoned to attend upon the King and receive a knighthood on payment of £30. Those declining the honour would be fined £40 so that, either way, the King was assured of a 'bonus'.

In fairness it must be said that James, who was normally not exactly over-sensitive when confronted by the prospect of money, hedged a little and wondered if the scheme might not be regarded as approaching the fringe of sharp practice.

Salisbury had no intention of seeing a bright idea go to waste. 'Tush, Sire!' he growled. 'You want the money and that will do you good. The honour will do them very little harm.'

The word rapidly spread that Hampton Court was offering the seventeenth-century equivalent of a rather special kind of 'summer bargain sale'. Within three days of the King's acceptance of the scheme, a Mr John Gammes of Radnor and a Mr William Cave of Oxfordshire turned up at the palace and became the first two fully paid-up knights of the realm.

Very soon hundreds of country gentlemen were converging on the palace and by 22 July the throng of customers was so vast that, for the sake of greater convenience, the King was obliged to transfer the investitures to the royal gardens at Whitehall.

There, on a single day, he conferred three hundred knighthoods, working rapidly through the long ranks of eager recipients. James suffered from a deep psychological aversion to looking upon the blade of a sword and therefore turned his head aside as he dubbed each knight, coming close at one moment to removing a gentleman's eye. (Legend had it that this curious trait in James arose from the shock sustained by his mother, while pregnant with him, on coming upon her favourite, David Rizzio, being hacked to death with daggers wielded by conspirators acting on Darnley's orders.)

Despite his initial hesitation, honours-for-money evidently came to be regarded by James as a solid business proposition for he later invented a new honour, the baronetcy, available for a fee of £1,000 a time with the money so raised being used to support English troops in Ulster. He was also lavish with the bestowing of peerages and created eleven peers in one day in the Great Hall at Hampton Court. Altogether he was to create one hundred and eleven peers, seven times as many as were recorded for Elizabeth's reign which was twice as long as his.

Addicted to lavish spending as he was, James was not a man to bother his head much about such trivial technicalities as accounting or budgeting and it was said of him: 'He was very liberal with what he had not in his own grip, and would rather part with a £100 he never had in his keeping then one twenty-shilling piece within his own custody.'

That 'liberality' was expressed on a sizeable scale. James regularly gave away around £100,000 a year to his courtiers and in only the second year of his reign spent £47,000 on jewellery. His fluffy-brained wife, Anne, was equally extra-vagant and within two years of the royal couple's arrival in England she had run up a debt for clothes and other personal luxuries of £40,500. And there is a neat touch of irony in the fact that one of the King's men friends, James Hay, had as his family motto: 'Spend and God will send.'

It cannot be said that the royal pair exuded any degree of glamour that might have gone some way towards compensating for their freedom with the nation's money. James, upon whom his new English courtiers gazed with curiosity at Hampton Court, was stocky, with bulbous eyes, unkempt reddish hair and an over-large mouth through which he dribbled when he spoke. His personal habits, too, left much to be desired and it was said that he never washed his hands but

*Anne of Denmark (1574–
1619), wife of James I. Like
her husband, she was a
reckless spender and within
two years of her arrival in
England she ran up a debt
for clothes and other personal luxuries of £40,500.*

simply wiped the finger-ends with a damp napkin.

Anne was fair-haired, long-nosed and had a small thin-lipped mouth. She looked shrewish and could be sharp-tongued but she was tolerant of her husband's peccadilloes and the couple had a curious arrangement under which he usually accepted as boy friends only those men whom she introduced.

Two of the overriding interests of her life were dancing and masques and it was largely due to her that festivities at Hampton Court were colourful affairs and that much encouragement was given to companies of actors.

The first of the masques to be 'supervised' by Anne was staged in the Great Hall at Christmas 1603 – the *Vision of the Twelve Goddesses* by the poet Samuel Daniel who had also been Elizabeth's Master of the Queen's Revels.

The stage was arranged as it had been in Elizabeth's time and Anne raided the late Queen's wardrobe, with its three thousand gowns, to find costumes for the twelve ladies of the court who were to 'star' in the amateur production. The scenery for the masque was designed by the great Inigo Jones.

Performances usually started around nine or ten in the evening and courtiers and guests would make their way to the Hall in groups, from their various lodgings in the palace, lighted by torch-bearers. Along each main wall were ranged rows of seats but everyone remained standing until the royal party arrived. At a few minutes before 'curtain time', the doors at the top end of the hall were thrown open, a herald bellowed the announcement, 'The King!' and the trumpeters sounded a brilliant fanfare. Then there entered James and the Queen who took their seats under the canopy of state set below the south oriel windows. At a sign from the King the masque began.

Much more important than the masques at that Christmas, however, were the plays presented by the King's Company of Comedians whose members had been accorded the status of officers of the royal households. Among those members was William Shakespeare.

Between 26 December and the night of 1 January, the Company presented no fewer than eight plays, although some of them were probably 'interludes' or one-act plays. No record of the titles has survived and they may possibly have included one or two by Shakespeare himself; almost certainly he appeared as one of the actors. The Company was paid £53, plus a £30 bonus to compensate for the fact that the players were deprived of going on to other profitable appearances in London where the plague had forced theatres to close.

On Twelfth Night the King and Queen entertained the French ambassador to a feast but, as soon as the meal was ended, James slipped away to his room to play at dice with some of his favourites and lost 500 crowns, or about £125 in modern currency.

James has sometimes been derisively described as 'the peacemaker' because of his antipathy to militarism, but he does seem to have had a genuinely optimistic belief in the precept, later coined by the twentieth-century's Winston Churchill, that 'jaw-jaw' is better than 'war-war'.

It was that trust in negotiations which encouraged him to try to heal the widening breach between the Anglicans and the Puritans by bringing representatives of the two sides together at a memorable conference which opened at Hampton Court on Friday, 14 January 1604.

The Puritans were a powerful and dedicated group of members of the Church of England who protested that insufficient steps had been taken to eliminate the rituals and trappings of Rome. They were also, and more crucially, a political force since, despite confusions about their doctrinal attitudes, they challenged the power of the Crown over Church and State. The nub of their demands was reform.

James was hopeful that these differences might be talked away. Therefore, in the King's Privy Chamber, part of which is now the Cumberland Suite on the east side of Clock Court, James, sitting on a chair a few feet forward of the canopy of state, presided over the gathering of bishops and deans headed by John Whitgift, Archbishop of Canterbury.

The four Puritan representatives stayed outside the room, sitting, we are told, 'on a form', and no doubt stony-eyed and tight-mouthed, stiff with conviction as only men of certainty in an uncertain world are self-confidently stiff.

James spoke for an hour and, all outward appearances to the contrary, he had a beguiling way with words. He had come to the conference, he said, 'like a good physician, to examine and try the complaints'.

On the following Monday, after a long week-end of waiting and brooding, the Puritans were admitted and given the opportunity of putting their case through their leader, Dr John Reynolds, President of Corpus Christi College, Oxford.

With marked dignity and calm, Reynolds outlined the Puritan objections to church doctrine and the King treated him, in turn, with the greatest civility, even rebuking the unpleasant Richard Bancroft, Bishop of London, for his ill-timed and boorish interruptions.

James also showed that he was not without a sense of humour. When Reynolds took exception to the marriage service dedication, 'With my body I thee worship,' the King quipped: 'Many a man speaks of Robin Hood who never shot in his bow! If you had a good wife yourself you would think that all the honours and worship you could do to her very well bestowed.'

In the end the Puritans' case cut no ice with the King and his humour gave way to irritation. But the conference remains to this day a most important event for English-speaking Christians throughout the world and all because of what amounted to something of an afterthought.

Reynolds, his principal argument completed, suddenly produced a suggestion that might, in modern parlance, be regarded as coming under the heading of 'any other business'. 'May Your Majesty,' he asked, 'be pleased that the Bible be new translated, such translations as are extant not answering the original?'

Bishop Bancroft could not resist breaking in with the sour comment: 'If every man's humour might be followed there would be no end of translating!' But James silenced him and, with remarkable quick-wittedness, made a pronouncement that was to have the most far-reaching consequences.

'I wish,' he said, 'some special pains were taken for a uniform translation, which should be done by the best learned in both universities [Oxford and Cambridge] then reviewed by the Bishops, presented to the Privy Council, and lastly ratified by royal authority to be read in the whole church, and no other.'

The wish was duly fulfilled and, in 1611, the James I Authorised Version of the Bible replaced the variety of versions designed by different religious sects, more to reinforce their individual prejudices than to record the original Christian message.

That, in itself, was a triumph for James and pleased him even more than what he afterwards saw as his forensic skill in handling the Puritans during the conference debates. If, he said, they had been students disputing with dons in college they would have been entitled not to considered answers but rather to have had 'the rod plied upon the poor boy's buttocks'.

Soon after the end of the conference the Court left the palace but James's heir, Henry, Prince of Wales, who was then eleven, moved in with his tutors for an eight-months' stay. He was, by all accounts, a lively, intelligent boy, fond both of learning and the outdoor life, and, as he grew older, openly critical of some of the seamier aspects of his father's behaviour. He was particularly angered by James's imprisonment in the Tower of Sir Walter Raleigh and asked: 'Why does my father keep such a bird in the cage?' (Sir Walter was held for conspiracy, later released but subsequently re-arrested on the original charge and beheaded.)

The might-have-beens of history are always fascinating, if not particularly rewarding, to consider, and it is possible to speculate that had Henry lived he might have been a successful King and England might have escaped yet another great political upheaval. As it was he died at the age of eighteen from a disease that was almost certainly typhoid; his death was assured by the crass medication of that time that included violent purgings which were in themselves enough to dispatch any chronically sick patient. So it was that the crown would pass not to Henry but to his younger brother who became Charles I.

Meanwhile, at Hampton Court young Henry indulged his taste for playing bowls and tennis, hunting and shooting, and was everywhere accompanied by his friend, the young Earl of Essex, dressed like himself in a green hunting suit.

The King and Queen rejoined their son in the autumn, bringing with them the lovely and tragic Lady Arabella Stuart, daughter of the Earl of Lennox. At the time of James's accession she was next in line to the succession and there were many who would have preferred to see her on the throne. James thought it expedient to act as her unofficial guardian, particularly to ensure that she did not enter into a marriage that might threaten the Crown.

In the event, Arabella secretly married William Seymour, grandson of Lady Jane Gray's sister, and the couple were promptly arrested for having broken their oath not to marry without the King's consent. She was confined at Lambeth and he in the Tower.

Arabella managed to escape, dressed as a man, and rode down to the Thames estuary where she boarded a ship for France. Sadly for her, the ship was intercepted by a British frigate and she herself was then sent to the Tower in June of 1610. By then, however, Seymour had escaped from that very same fortress by putting on a disguise smuggled in by his barber, Batten, and walking calmly out to freedom with a smile and a nod and a 'God-be-wi'-ye' to the unsuspecting guards. (For his part in the plot poor Batten ended up in the dungeons.)

Seymour succeeded in making his way to freedom and safety on the Continent but Arabella never saw her husband nor the outside world again. She lingered in dank confinement in the Tower until her death in 1615 at the age of forty.

Whether or not that tragedy, for which he was responsible, weighed on the King's mind we can only speculate. Certainly there were times when the courtiers at Hampton Court had good reason for wondering whether he cared much about what people might think of him. Apart from his habit of never washing, he changed his clothes only when special events made it imperative and he was not a fragrant figure. As he passed through the splendid rooms and galleries of the palace it was sometimes difficult for the servants to know whether his unsteady gait was due to his ill-formed legs or liquor or both. There was a much-repeated story that James went out riding one winter's night while befuddled with wine and fell head first into an icy stream so that only his boots were to be seen, waving frantically in the air.

Not unnaturally, many courtiers took their example from the King and the Court became noted for its unsavoury behaviour. One lady assigned to a leading role in a Hampton Court masque was reportedly so drunk that she had bodily to be removed from the stage.

However, kings are kings and will receive tributes from their subjects whether they deserve them or not; and it was in honour of James that Shakespeare wrote *Measure for Measure* and appeared in the cast at the performance staged at the palace by the King's players during Christmas 1604. Although probably no personal reference to the sovereign was intended, it is interesting that one of the principal characters, Vincento, the Duke, pardons the drunken prisoner Barnardine.

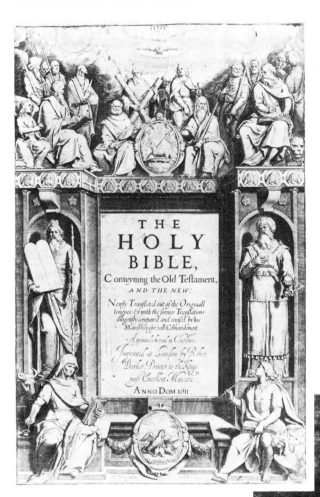

The version of the Bible authorised by James I. This arose directly out of a conference held at Hampton Court and, for that reason alone, the palace is of historical importance to all Christians.

Henry, Prince of Wales (1594–1612), eldest son of James I. Although he was only eighteen when he died he was openly critical of some of the seamier aspects of his father's behaviour. Of James's imprisonment of Sir Walter Raleigh he asked, 'Why does my father keep such a bird in the cage.'

Perhaps intentionally, however, the play does reflect another characteristic of James: his aversion to contact with the 'common people', something that was made crudely plain in a Hampton Court proclamation against the unauthorised hunting and killing of royal deer in which the King compared 'gentlemen and persons of better sort' with 'the corrupt natures and insolent dispositions of some of the baser sort'.

In *Measure for Measure*, therefore, Shakespeare makes the Duke declare:

> I do love the people,
> But do not like to stage me to their eyes;
> Though it do well, I do not relish well
> Their loud applause and aves [greetings] vehement.

*James I opens Parliament, 1604. The people of England had welcomed James on his accession but they soon became disillusioned and many were repelled by the dissolute life of the Court.*

James was particularly outraged by the way in which many of the 'baser sort' of people would persist in trotting after him on foot when he went out hunting from the palace. He may also not have relished being observed by prying eyes since, according to one foreign observer, James's hunting style was not particularly commendable.

In his account the visitor wrote: 'The hunt generally comes off in this way: the huntsmen remain on the spot where the game is to be found, with twenty or thirty hounds; if the King fancies any in particular among the herd, he causes his pleasure to be signified to the huntsmen, who forthwith proceed to mark the place where the animal stood; they then lead the hounds thither, which are taught to follow this one animal only, and accordingly away they run straight upon his track; and even should there by forty or fifty deers together, they do nothing to them, but chase only the one, and never give up till they have overtaken and brought it down. Meanwhile, the King hurries incessantly after the hounds until they have caught the game. There is, therefore, no particular enjoyment in this sport. Two animals only were caught on this occasion . . . His Majesty now and then uses longbows and arrows; and when he is disposed he shoots a deer.'

There were events other than masques, plays and hunting to relieve the boredom of the Court and not least of those was an extraordinary 'arranged' marriage at the palace in 1617. The facts have the ring of rather bad fiction.

Sir John Villiers, the mentally unstable Master of the Robes to Charles, Prince of Wales, had set his heart on marrying the attractive fifteen-year-old Frances Coke, daughter of Sir Edward Coke, the Lord Chief Justice, and his second wife, Lady Hatton. Frances was heiress to the vast personal wealth of Lady Hatton who heartily detested her husband and was bitterly against the proposed match. And Frances herself, who had not been consulted about the proposal, was in love with Sir Robert Howard.

King James approved of the marriage mainly because Villiers was the brother of his latest favourite, George Villiers, who was to become Duke of Buckingham. But Sir Edward Coke, who had offered only around £6,500 as his daughter's dowry, instead of the £10,000 demanded, and who had in other ways offended the King, swiftly became *ex*-Lord Chief Justice.

While the general hubbub and quarrelling over the marriage negotiations mounted towards a peak, indomitable Lady Hatton decided that action was preferable to argument and spirited Frances away into hiding at a relative's house near Oatlands, a few miles from Hampton Court.

Sir Edward Coke, growing increasingly concerned that the whole affair might permanently damage his public career, learned of the whereabouts of his wife and daughter and, having failed to flush them out by due legal process, formed the seventeenth-century equivalent of an American Western-style posse.

This strange group, composed of Coke's sons and other relatives and servants, set off to ride to Oatlands, led by Coke himself, resplendent in gleaming breast-plate and with sword in hand and pistols across his saddle.

They found the hide-away house barricaded but Coke – not so long ago one of the kingdom's principal upholders of law and order – cried out for his daughter to be produced and threatened: 'If death ensue, it will be justifiable homicide in me, but murder in those who oppose me!' Eventually, after much huffing and puffing around the house, one member of the posse broke in through a window and opened the main door to Sir Edward and the rest. Inside, they rampaged through the rooms, finding them all deserted, until at last Sir Edward discovered his wife and daughter cowering in a cupboard. Angrily he snatched the sobbing Frances from the protection of her mother's arms and rode off with her to his house at Stoke Poges, in Buckinghamshire, where he locked her in an attic.

On 29 September 1616, Frances Coke was taken, to her dismay, to Hampton Court and there, in the chapel, married to the oafish Villiers by the Bishop of Winchester. The King gave the bride away and the Queen and all the courtiers were in the congregation. The couple spent the 'honeymoon' night at the palace and, in true insult-to-injury fashion, half-tipsy James led the 'bundling' party of drunks which invaded the ill-matched couple's bedroom and bounced the bride and groom up and down on the mattress and rolled them about the bed.

Fortunately, however, the story had a happy ending. In 1620 Villiers sank into a period of complete insanity and the following year Frances left him and was reunited with her true love Robert Howard.

It must also be said, in the interests of fair reporting, that Edward Coke is remembered by history as an outstanding lawyer and Parliamentarian and his writings had a decisive influence on Anglo-American legal education. All the same, his wife never forgave him and on his death in 1628 said of him: 'We will never see his like again – thank God!'

The wine-and-roses days of Hampton Court were not to last so very long for James. By the latter part of 1618 it was clear that the Queen was slowly declining under a combination of gout, dropsy and tuberculosis. She died at the palace on 2 March 1619, at four in the morning, with the nineteen-year-old Prince of Wales (the future Charles I) at her bedside. James was in London and said to be ill; but some people thought his absence was due to his aversion to witnessing the deathbed scene.

Just before the end the Bishop of London leaned over the Queen's inert form and whispered: 'Madame, make a sign that Your Majesty is one with your God and longs to be with Him.' Shakily she raised both hands and they remained upright for a few seconds before falling back on the counterpane.

Despite the strange circumstances of their married life, James was genuinely grieved at the loss of Anne. As a tribute he wrote the following lines, the first of which makes a passing reference to a comet seen in the sky only a few days before and which, so the King believed, was a portent of the Queen's death:

> Thee to invite the Great God sent his star,
> Whose friend and nearest kin good princes are;
> Who, though they run the race of men and die,
> Death serves but to refine their majesty.
> So did my Queen her Court from thence remove,
> And left this earth to be enthroned above;
> She is changed, not dead, for sure no good prince dies,
> But, like the sun, sets only for to rise.

In the Queen's bedroom at the palace we may, to this day, see James in his morning dress in a portrait by Van Somer.

It has to be admitted that there were those who consoled themselves on the announcement of Anne's death with the thought that the State would at least be relieved of some of the pressure on its finances. Anne and her household had cost the treasury some £90,000 a year and, at the time of her departure, total royal debts amounted to close on £1,000,000. Indeed, the lying-in-state of her body was prolonged while money for the funeral was scraped together.

Anne had gone from a realm in which all was far from well. Despite those sneering cries of 'peacemaker', James had taken a pride in what he saw as his contribution to the avoidance of another Continental armed conflict. But hopes of a long-term peaceful settlement of the differences between European Protestants and Catholics ended in 1618 with the beginning of what was to be the Thirty Years' War and which would devastate Germany.

And James, who had thought he ruled in the kingdom, came to be ruled by the ambitious Duke of Buckingham who was already helping to sow the seeds of dissent between Crown and Parliament. Far off there could be detected the first stirrings of that political breeze which for James's son, Charles, would shape itself into a whirlwind.

Hampton Court was now supervised by the great architect Inigo Jones, as His Majesty's Surveyor of Works, and as we approach the reign of Charles I, we may note the special irony in the fact that Jones it was who designed the Banqueting Hall at Whitehall.

James, however, no longer much cared who supervised the palace or what might happen to it. Even although he was still only in his mid-fifties, he was growing rapidly senile. He paid his final visit to Hampton Court in September 1623 and died on 27 March 1625 from what was described as 'an ague'. He was fifty-nine and, at that moment, the nation was looking forward with anticipation to the reign of his son, Charles, happily already seen to be a man with a style and dignity very different from his father.

*Charles I (1600–1649) as he is popularly remembered, immortalised by Van Dyke. The degree of calm, dignified competence that he exhibited in the saddle was matched neither by political judgement nor imagination.*

# 6

# *The Embattled Years*

## CHARLES I

WHEN CHARLES I SUCCEEDED TO THE THRONE the population of England and Wales was around five million, with another million each for Scotland and Ireland. London, increasingly pushing out beyond the old City walls, was by far the largest city in the kingdom with more than 250,000 people. Of all the counties, Middlesex, which included Hampton Court, was the richest and, in general, prosperity was centred upon the southern half of the country and the Midlands, and poverty upon the northern counties.

Annual incomes ranged from around £3 a year for a Yorkshire husbandman, to £45 for a shopkeeper, £280 for a 'gentleman' – a middle-rank landowner – to £650 for a knight and, at the very top, £3,200 for a temporal lord. Slow changes were beginning to overtake a society that had not basically altered in structure since Elizabeth. The foundations for future large-scale overseas trade were laid and industry was developing: already primitive collieries in Yorkshire, Lancashire and the Midlands were producing some 65,000 tons of coal a year and those of South Wales 20,000.

The largest concentrations of labour were in fishing and in all the industries associated with wool. To Hampton Court, as to many noblemen's homes, came blankets from Witney, broadcloth from Leeds and plaids from Scotland. Materials for the repair and renovation of the palace also came from many parts of the realm: tin from Cornwall, lead from the Mendip Hills, brass from the founderies around Bristol, copper from Westmorland, marble from Derbyshire and Ulster and granite from Scotland.

*The palace in the time of Charles I. The sight of it, as the royal barge moved sedately upstream from Whitehall, was indeed fit for a king – and his lesser subjects enjoyed it, too, even though they were not invited in.*

Some of the great landowners were also becoming increasingly involved with trade and industry and their growing awareness of the nation's economic potential helped to sharpen their aversion to what they were beginning to see as the undue concentration of power in the Crown.

It was against this restless background that Charles I came to Hampton Court for the first time as King, on 6 July 1625, three months after his accession. He was in so many ways unlike his father, James I – only about five feet tall, shy and reserved, and afflicted with a persistent stammer. As a child he had been

*Charles I and Queen Henrietta Maria dine as privately as seventeenth-century royals could. The scene depicted here could have been at Hampton Court, but more probably was Whitehall. In any case, this was a typical setting for dinner – then the main morning meal, usually eaten at around eleven.*

delicate and suffered from a weakness in his legs, although by sheer personal tenacity he overcame that disability in adult life and learned to ride well and to hunt and to bear himself with an impressive dignity despite his small stature.

He was well educated, although not particularly intellectual, deeply religious and a devout supporter of the Anglican church; and he disapproved of his late father's permissive attitude to sex. All the same, he had carefully studied and been much influenced by his father's treatise, *Basilicon Doron*, on the responsibilities of kingship. It told him that, under God (to whom he must ultimately be accountable), a king owed parental duties to his people – but it was not for the 'children' to question the actions of their earthly 'father', whatever they might privately think about them. In short, the treatise was an argument for the divine right of kings and was to have fatal consequences for Charles.

*Van Dyke's portrait of Henrietta Maria (1609–1669). Her marriage to Charles was 'arranged' and at first the couple bickered like spoiled children. But later they became devoted to one another.*

That first visit by the King to Hampton Court was intended to be part of his honeymoon for, just a few weeks earlier, he had married fifteen-year-old Henrietta Maria of France, sister of Louis XIII. The marriage was not one of personal choice but of political expediency – the seal on a treaty between France and England negotiated between Cardinal Richelieu and the Duke of Buckingham.

Like Charles, Henrietta was small. She had large black eyes and curly black hair but her appearance was marred by prominent teeth and her deportment spoiled by a slight spinal deformity. She was also hopelessly immature. She spoke little English, although she was to master the language in time, and when Charles went to Dover to welcome her to England she floundered half way through the formal speech she had been taught, parrot-fashion, and burst into tears.

The marriage got off to a bad start and was to remain difficult for some years. As part of the marriage contract Charles had undertaken to free English Catholics from the penal laws under which they suffered and he angered the French by failing to keep his word. Henrietta, in her turn, upset the English by refusing, as a Catholic, to be crowned with the King by the 'heretic' Archbishop of Canterbury and stayed away from the ceremony altogether.

What caused most trouble at the onset, however, was Henrietta's personal retinue of some one hundred French men and women who tried to take command of the English court and behaved in an arrogant and high-handed manner. Their conduct enraged Charles from the very moment of their arrival and his distaste particularly settled on one, Madame de Saint-Georges.

This lady had acted as a kind of governess-companion to Henrietta since the young Queen's childhood and a fussy, interfering, overweaning 'adviser' she turned out to be. Charles immediately sensed the potential danger that she presented to his domestic life and made up his mind to lose no time in putting her in her place.

As he and his bride were about to leave London for Hampton Court he refused to enter the large coach that had been made ready for himself, Henrietta, Madame de Saint-Georges and a clutch of others, and ordered up a smaller one. Into that he hustled the Queen and a couple of English ladies-in-waiting before climbing in himself. The infuriated Madame de Saint-Georges was obliged to follow in a separate coach.

Soon after the great cavalcade of attendants, servants and baggage carts had arrived at the palace, the tactless Duke of Buckingham visited the Queen in her rooms and launched an abusive tirade against her. If she did not mend her ways and put her husband before Madame de Saint-Georges she would find herself in dire trouble, he threatened. Despite her immaturity, or perhaps galvanised by the onslaught, she quietly and calmly replied that it had not been her intention to offend the King, nor would she ever wish to do so. And, she added, with unexpected quick-wittedness, she also wished to treat the Duke with all the consideration due to his rank, if only *he* would behave towards *her* as he ought.

Apart from the interference of Madame de Saint-Georges, the other problem for Charles about Henrietta was her Roman Catholicism. One other clause in the marriage contract had clearly laid down that the Queen would be free to practice her religion in officially Protestant England — but discreetly. Discretion, unfortunately, was not the outstanding trait in Henrietta's confessor, Father Bérulle, who was forever hovering bat-like over the Queen.

One night at a Court dinner in the Presence Chamber an incredible knock-about scene developed between Bérulle and the Anglican chaplain, Mr Hackett. As Hackett was about to say grace, Bérulle tried to interrupt with his version but Hackett elbowed him to one side and completed the blessing. At that, the confessor hurried around to the Queen's side of the table and prepared to pronounce a second grace. He would have succeeded but for the fact that the King swiftly intervened by signalling the carvers to begin serving the food.

At the end of the meal, Bérulle and Hackett both leapt to their feet and simultaneously began to intone the final blessing but this proved too much for the exasperated King who angrily arose from the table, grasped the Queen's hand and led her unceremoniously off to bed.

Charles's near-hysterical hatred for the French hirelings reached its peak when their ambassador, the Marquis de Blainville, arrived from plague-ridden London demanding sanctuary at the palace. The Lord Chamberlain, who was responsible for accommodation, offered the ambassador lodgings at nearby Kingston on the rather bluntly-expressed excuse that 'His Majesty never allows an ambassador to be lodged so near him.'

De Blainville obstinately refused to take this heavy-handed hint and, apparently having done his homework, pointed out that he knew of two ambassadors who had been accommodated at the palace, and so why was he being singled out for special treatment?

Patiently, it was explained to him that those two ambassadors had stayed at the palace when the King was absent. De Blainville's persistence triumphed in the end but in a way that did nothing to help relations between Charles and his wife. On Henrietta's intervention, guest rooms were provided for him and it was not long before Charles found further cause for anger in the ambassador's ever-mounting bills: bills for food for himself and his servants, who had been put into quarters in Kingston, 'and several new demands . . . for wood and coals and twenty other things'. The total cost of the visit, borne by Charles, came to £2,000.

Eventually, the King took a strong and uncompromising line, an attitude that was to serve him well in domestic matters but ill in affairs of State. One night in bed Henrietta handed him a list of French and English officials whom she proposed to appoint as managers of her finances. The French nominees, she naïvely pointed out, had been approved by her mother.

'Then I said,' Charles recounted in a letter to Buckingham, describing the bizarre honeymoon bedroom scene, 'it was neither in her mother's power, or her's, to admit any without my leave; and if she relied on that, whomsoever she recommended should not come in.' Imperiously, Charles admonished her to

1. Wolsey's Closet, the magnificent little room east of Clock Court which is all that now remains of the opulent private apartments of the palace's creator. Here the Cardinal would escape from the many cares of his powerful office.

2. The Base Court, the first of the spacious courtyards where Wolsey was greeted by the senior officers of his household when he returned from his visits to London and elsewhere.

3. The Field of the Cloth of Gold. This painting, in the Royal Collection at Hampton Court, shows the storybook setting created by the French king, Francis I, for his meeting in France with Henry VIII to secure an alliance between England and France. It failed.

4. The Tudor Kitchen. Here the master chefs, cooks and scullions created the lavish banquets which were particularly intended to impress foreign visitors by their magnificence.

5. Opposite page: The Chapel Royal. Henry VIII celebrated Mass here while his fifth wife, Catherine Howard, was heard outside screaming to be spared from execution. The King paid no heed and continued with his devotions.

*6. The Astronomical Clock, built for Henry VIII, which tells the hours, month, the day of the month, the number of days since the beginning of the year – and the time of high water at London Bridge.*

*7. Gargoyles on the roof of the Great Hall. Such carved monsters were a feature of great houses and sometimes the masons left their personal mark by modelling the faces of those of their friends or enemies.*

*8. Hampton Court from the river. No palace could have a finer frontage, for centuries the most direct and comfortable highway into London.*

'Remember to whom she spoke', whereupon Henrietta's frustration overflowed
and she poured out a stream of recriminations about how miserable she was and
how badly she was being used. Even at this long remove in time there is something
touching about the spectacle of the royal couple, she with tear-brimming eyes
and wheedling voice and he, stammering more than usual, sitting up in bed in
their embroidered nightgowns, quarrelling the small hours away.

In his report to Buckingham, Charles could not resist a certain note of smug
satisfaction about the manner in which he had succeeded in insisting on the last
word. 'I both made her hear me, and end that discourse,' he wrote. Buckingham,
whose insatiable thirst for power made him ever ready to cap any move by his
King, saw Henrietta soon afterwards and brutally and quite improperly warned
her : 'Queens of England have been beheaded before now !'

Only Charles's misguided dependence on Buckingham made it possible for him
to acquiesce in such treatment of his wife. But he no longer cared about who said
what; his one obsession was to rid himself of the malevolent retainers and, on
7 August 1626, he sent this remarkably furious order to Buckingham:

I command you to send all the French away by tomorrow out of the town. If you can, by
fair means (but stick not long in disputing), otherwise force them away like so many wild
beasts, until you have shipped them, and so the devil go with them.

When she heard the news Henrietta rushed to Charles, fell on her knees and
begged him to change his mind. At his refusal she screamed wildly, ran to the
window and plunged her fists through the glass panes. Charles carried her away,
sobbing and bleeding to her room. Her misery lingered for some time but, such
are the strange and mysterious ways of married life, what then seemed to the
Queen to be unendurable cruelty turned out to be a turning point in her life
with Charles and brought them both towards lasting devotion.

The vigorous booting out of the retainers, to whom Charles insisted on referring
contemptuously as the 'Monsers' (for *Monsieurs*), did not do much for Anglo-
French cordiality; indeed, Richelieu and others saw the incident as yet one more
example of 'perfidious Albion'. The French courtiers, however, took a revenge of
a sort by carrying off with them almost the whole of the Queen's expensive
wardrobe. They countered all demands for the return of the loot with the
allegation that the Queen had ordered them to buy the gowns for her but had
failed to reimburse the expenditure.

Despite the heated exchanges that passed between England and France,
Cardinal Richelieu was too wily a politician to allow the incident to be used as an
excuse for open hostilities and sent the experienced diplomat, Marshal de
Bassompierre to Hampton Court to try to heal the wounds.

The circumstances of the diplomat's arrival at the palace, on Sunday, 11 October
1626, were not auspicious. In the first place he and his aides turned up so late,
intentionally, it was suspected, that the elaborate meal specially prepared for
them had already been scoffed by the King and his courtiers. Secondly, and in
what certainly did appear to be a deliberate snub, de Bassompierre and his men
declined to partake of the cold collation that was hastily but hospitably set out in
place of the missed meal.

Worse still, the starchy diplomat bridled when the Duke of Buckingham told
him the King would be obliged for an outline of the purposes of his mission in
advance of the formal discussions.

In his subsequent report to his superiors, de Bassompierre detailed his reply, of which he was evidently peacock-proud: 'I said to him that the King should know what I had to say to him from my own mouth and that it was not the custom to limit an ambassador in what he had to represent to the Sovereign to whom he was sent, and that if he did not wish to see me I was ready to go back [home] again.'

Buckingham, whose own spiky temper must have been sorely tried, launched into a long, rambling explanation. It all boiled down to the fact that the business of the 'Monsers' had put Charles 'in a great passion', the Queen was still upset and 'might commit some extravagance and cry in sight of everyone', and, not to put too fine a royal point upon it, the King did not want an almighty public row.

To coin a modern phrase, Charles was undecided whether to stick or twist. Later, in the Audience Chamber and with the Queen beside him, behaving neither 'extravagantly' nor tearfully, Charles received the ambassador politely and was treated in return with equal civility. No private meeting was arranged, however, and de Bossompierre departed for London. However, four days later, he was summoned back to the palace and this time greeted by a quite different Charles who was very much consumed by that 'passion' of which Buckingham had spoked earlier.

As the two men walked and talked in one of the galleries, Charles's anger and resentment over the 'Monsers' poured out in a vituperative flood. And he astonished the equally affronted Frenchman by suddenly demanding: 'Why do you not execute your commission at once and declare war?' Stung by the insult, de Bassompierre retorted sharply: 'I am not a herald to declare war, but a Marshal of France to make it when declared!'

The raised voices attracted the attention of the ever-vigilant Buckingham who came bustling into the gallery, crying out ('impudently', as de Bassompierre rightly noted): 'I am come to keep the peace between you two!'

The outcome of this ridiculous tarradiddle was a compromise, largely effected by de Bassompierre who, for all his pomposity, was far more skilled at diplomacy than Charles: the Queen was to have a French retinue of only twenty or so hand-picked people while the members of her personal household would be mainly English and Protestant.

Not very long afterwards England did in fact find herself at war with France but the main cause was Buckingham's incompetence rather than the Hampton Court shouting match.

In a manner which was very much a reflection of his blundering interference between the King and diplomat at the palace, Buckingham took it upon himself to lead an expedition to 'aid' the Protestants of the city of La Rochelle against the French king. Quite apart from the fact that his aid had not been sought by the citizens, the venture was ill-judged and ill-prepared and ended in the rout of the British forces. It also turned out to be Buckingham's last foolish throw of the dice. As he was preparing for yet another reckless Continental campaign, the Duke was assassinated in Portsmouth by a mentally deranged naval lieutenant named John Felton.

Despite his personal sense of deprivation at the loss of Buckingham, the Duke's death freed Charles from an inept and dangerous influence but, alas for him, the damage already done to his reputation among many Parliamentarians was now irreparable. And the most important effect of the departure of the Duke, often scornfully referred to as the 'deputy king', was the re-emergence of powerful figures determined to curb the King's appetite for unbridled power.

It was understandable, however, that many guests at Hampton Court saw aspects of Charles that were very different from those portrayed by his enemies. He had, for example, most commendably transformed the Court. The carousing and loose-living of James's days had been swept away and there was now a more elegant and impressive atmosphere about the palace.

Certainly some of the new rules were uncomfortably rigid. For instance, no lady except the Queen was allowed to be seated during an audience with the King and any servant who behaved with the sloppiness which had been a feature of the previous reign was harshly dealt with. (A few ambassadors complained about their ladies having to stand but the servants seemed to prefer a better-ordered routine and held the King in great affection.)

On the other hand, the King's stiffly regal style was much compensated for by his civilised respect and love for the arts. He was a great music-lover, a small orchestra often played for him even during meals, and he surrounded himself with beautiful pictures, including works by Titian, Tintoretto and Mantegna as well, of course, as those by his great court painter, Van Dyck, and the Flemish artist, Peter Paul Rubens.

Among his greatest acquisitions were seven of the ten cartoons painted in the sixteenth century by Raphael as designs for the Vatican Palace tapestries and commissioned by Pope Leo X. Some of the three hundred or so Hampton Court pictures from Charles's time are still to be seen at the palace including Mantegna's superb nine-piece composition, *The Triumph of Julius Caesar* (for which Charles paid £10,500), and which is displayed in a special gallery in the Orangery.

Charles gave £28,000 for the magnificent collection of art works assembled over a long period by successive Dukes of Mantua and his purchasing-agents were constantly on the move around Europe in search of treasures. As a result of their untiring efforts there came to the palace a host of tapestries, furniture, carpets, bronzes, crystal, carved invories and statues.

*The Cartoon Gallery. The Raphael Cartoons, prepared as tapestry patterns for Pope Leo X, were bought by Charles I. Here they are seen as exhibited in the time of William III.*

*A panel from Mantegna's nine-piece composition, 'The Triumph of Julius Caesar', for which Charles paid £10,500. The King's purchasing agents were constantly on the prowl in Europe, searching for art treasures.*

A major addition to the palace amenities, ordered by Charles, was the cutting of a channel, known as the Longford River, more than nine miles long and twenty-one feet wide, to bring in a new supply of water from the River Colne in Middlesex. The work was begun on 8 October 1638 and completed on 16 July of the following year at a total cost of £4,102, paid for out of the Court of Wards and Liveries. This new supply of water supplemented that brought in for Wolsey and was used to feed the ponds and ornamental waters.

The project, though, was greeted with very considerable hostility by the inhabitants of Middlesex who complained bitterly of the damage to their land caused by the cutting of the channel and the occasional collapse of its banks which led to flooding.

Charles was not a king to be moved by objections from 'ordinary' people, few of whom he ever met or wanted to meet, and very soon he was considering another scheme that was to cause even greater public outrage.

This time his plan was to turn a ten-mile tract of land between Hampton Court and Richmond into a deer park, for he had inherited his father's passion for hunting. His advisers warned him that he would be infringing the rights of common land and private property to which the King replied, in effect, 'too bad', and said he had no time to waste and was already pressing ahead with the work of enclosing the new park.

*Draught of the Fishes. One of the famous Hampton Court Cartoons created as designs for Vatican tapestries by Raphael (1483–1520) whose full name, now rarely used, was Raphael Santi. He was a master of design and form and the great Rembrandt was one of the later artists inspired by his work.*

*All dressed up and somewhere to go. Charles and Henrietta Maria depicted, by the Dutch portrait painter Daniel Mytens, as they depart for the chase.*

In the end, William Laud, Archbishop of Canterbury, was brought in to reason with the King and spell out the difficulties that would be created if, in this matter, he rode roughshod over the protests of the people. Grudgingly, Charles gave in and the project was abandoned.

During his reign London was increasingly visited by the plague and Hampton Court, therefore, often became a refuge for the royal Court. When the epidemic was particularly serious – as in the summer of 1636 – the King issued proclamations forbidding anyone from the capital to come within ten miles of the palace on pain of severe punishment. Traffic on the upper reaches of the Thames (the river was then London's main commercial highway) was prohibited and the palace cooks had to draw solely on their already-purchased stocks of food since delivery normally came by boat. No servant of the neighbouring gentry of Hampton was allowed to travel back and forth to the city, and, if any disobeyed, his master's house was bolted and barred and the gentleman and his family turned out to fend as best they could until the plague abated.

In all the circumstances the drastic rules were no doubt wise. But their purpose was completely nullified by the fact that the 'isolated' Court had to be entertained and, therefore, actors were allowed in – and they came from London!

Each acting company was usually allowed £20 a week to be shared, according to status, between the managers and the individual players. Between the middle of November 1636 and the end of the following January, fourteen plays were presented and the very last in the 'season' was *Hamlet*.

Although Charles was less devoted to poetry than to music he encouraged all creative artists and was not above sparing time to help a contemporary playwright with useful and constructive criticism. When Sir Henry Herbert, the Master of the Revels, who also had responsibility for licensing plays, deleted expletives from Sir William Davenant's comedy, *The Wits*, Charles promptly ordered the restoration of the 'offending' words. They were essential to the characters, he said, and served a necessary dramatic purpose.

Shut away from the horrifying sights of the plague in London, the Court lived as well as ever at the palace. At each evening meal there were, according to a contemporary account, '86 tables well furnished . . . whereof the King's table had 28 dishes; the Queen's 24; 4 other tables, 16 dishes each, and so on; in all about 500 dishes each meal, with beer, bread, wine, and all things necessary'.

Never far from the Queen's side would be her Jester, the famous dwarf, Jeffrey Hudson. He had been 'discovered' by Henrietta in a most piquant fashion when she and Charles were being entertained to a feast by the Duke of Buckingham. A pie was set before the royal couple and when it was opened out popped Hudson – all eighteen inches of him. Henrietta was so delighted she took him into her service.

Jeffrey Hudson, born at Oakham, in Rutland, in 1619, was the son of a butcher and both his parents were of normal size. The precise facts about his dwarfishness are somewhat obscure but he claimed that he remained only eighteen inches tall from the age of seven until thirty when, for some inexplicable reason, he suddenly shot up to three feet six inches. Lack of height certainly did not affect his courage for he fought a pistol duel with a man who had insulted him, and killed his opponent with a bullet through the head, and later served on the King's side in the Civil War as a captain of horse.

At Court, and in his domestic affairs, all appeared tranquil enough for Charles.

*Henrietta Maria's Jester, the dwarf Jeffrey Hudson, painted by Mytens. From the age of seven until thirty he remained only eighteen inches tall. Then, for some inexplicable reason, he suddenly shot up to three feet six inches.*

But elsewhere, and particularly in Parliament, events were moving ominously against him and it was at Hampton Court, on 1 December 1641, that he received a document which was to mark the penultimate stage in his downfall – the so-called Grand Remonstrance.

This declaration, voted in the Commons by 159 Ayes to 148 Noes, listed the long-accumulating grievances against the King. The issues that lay behind it were many and complex, and both religious and political, but in essence they centred upon Charles's attempts to follow his father's guidance and establish absolute monarchy.

For all his education and cultivation, Charles's real trouble was that he totally lacked the ability to temporise or even to consider that there might be substance in opinions that differed from his own. He *knew* he was right and whoever thought otherwise was either stupid or a knave. (His counterparts live on in much of modern politics.) His inability to read political smoke-signals was almost pathological, as was shown by the reply he sent from Hampton Court to the authors of the Remonstrance. He promised an answer 'as soon as the weight of business permits', but meanwhile asked the Commons not to make their declaration public. To talk of 'weight of business' in the face of such a challenge and not to see that the Remonstrance was primarily intended for public consumption were the heights of royal folly.

A few weeks later Charles compounded his foolishness and sealed his doom with his reckless and irresponsible visit to the House of Commons to demand the 'surrender' of the Opposition's five leading members: Pym, Hampden, Haselrigg, Holles and Strode. In response to the King's demand to know if the 'miscreants'

*End of a royal dream. The day before his execution King Charles says an emotional farewell to two of his children, the Princess Elizabeth and the Duke of Gloucester. His other four children had escaped to the Continent.*

were present, the brilliantly-chosen words of Mr Speaker Lenthall have rung down the centuries: 'May it please Your Majesty, I have neither eye to see, nor tongue to speak here, but as the House is pleased to direct me, whose servant I am.'

In a clumsy attempt to make amends, Charles summoned seven City of London aldermen to Hampton Court and knighted every one for, after all, next to the Crown there was no greater secular power and influence than the City. But it was too late for 'generous' gestures and, in any case, the City was sheltering the five Members and shared the general outrage at the King's abuse of Parliamentary privilege. Charles went personally to the City but as soon as he realised that its great institutions were not to be bought he fled back to Hampton Court. In the streets around Whitehall, from Ludgate to Guildhall, along clustered Cheapside and from narrowly-curving Threadneedle Street across to the open spaces of Moor Fields, he had heard the infuriated cry of his subjects: 'Privilege of Parliament!'

Now from Hampton Court began the very first action by those who, in the coming conflict, would become part of the King's faction. Colonel Sir Thomas Lunsford, Keeper of the Tower, having escorted King and Queen back to the palace, rode off with two hundred men to capture the armoury at Kingston. (For his pains Lunsford was subsequently sent by the Parliamentarians back to that very Tower he had formerly commanded – only this time others held the keys.)

Hampton Court was far too vulnerable to remain a suitable refuge for long and Charles moved himself, his wife, family and Court to Windsor Castle. In the kingdom his subjects chose their allegiances – in many cases families were divided, with father against son and brother against brother – and embarked upon that worst of all abominations: Civil War.

Before he turned to the pressing business of battle, Charles sent Henrietta Maria and their young children out of the country to the Continent. With her the Queen took the crown jewels in the hope that she might either sell or pawn them to raise money towards helping her husband's cause. (She failed in the attempt.) The couple's two eldest boys, the twelve-year-old Prince of Wales (the future Charles II) and the nine-year-old James, Duke of York, remained for a time in England

Charles raised his standard at Nottingham on 22 August 1642, supported by eighty peers and one hundred and seventy-five Members of the Commons. Thirty peers and three hundred Members opted for the Parliamentary side. Those two groups were to form the nuclei of those whom, in the forthcoming struggle, Londoners were to dub 'Cavaliers', for the King and 'Roundheads' – because they wore their hair cut short – for the Parliamentarians.

The tide of war that developed out of the six-year Great Rebellion, from 1642 to 1648, swept back and forth across the country, with varying degrees of bitterness, brutality and destruction, until the defeat of Charles's forces at Naseby, near Market Harborough in Leicestershire, on 14 June 1645. A further last-gasp conflict in the spring and summer of 1648, sometimes called the Second Civil War, was quickly terminated by a Roundhead victory.

*The battle lines on the field of Naseby where King Charles's stand against Cromwell's Roundheads finally came to a disastrous end on 14 June 1645. From Naseby the road for Charles led back to Hampton Court and then to the executioner.*

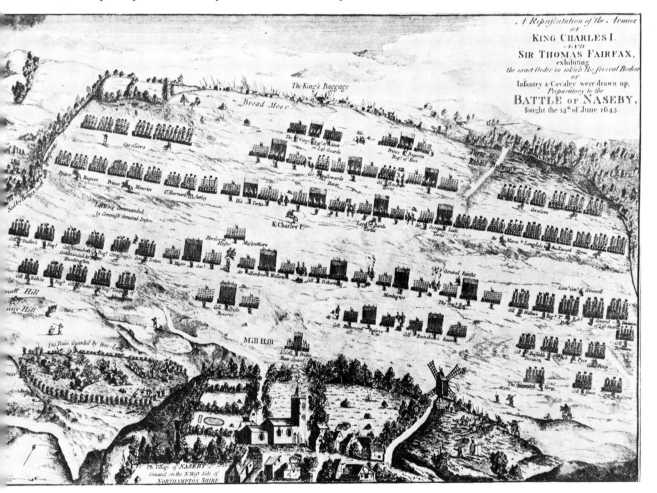

Immediately after the Battle of Naseby the Parliamentarians took possession of Hampton Court and sealed up the doors of the State apartments. And this, too, was the moment for the Puritans to take their revenge. A contemporary newspaper recorded their desecration of the Chapel Royal:

Sir Robert Harlow gave order for the putting down and demolishing of the popish and superstitious pictures at Hampton Court, where this day the altar was taken down, and the table brought into the body of the church, the rails pulled down, and the steps levelled, and the popish pictures and superstitious images that were in the glass windows were also demolished, and order given for the new glazing them with plain glass; and among the rest there was pulled down the pictures of Christ nailed to the cross, which was placed right over the altar, and the pictures of Mary Magdalen and others weeping by the foot of the cross, and some other such idolatrous pictures were pulled down and demolished.

Meanwhile, Charles had surrendered at Newark, in Nottinghamshire, to the Parliamentarians' Scottish allies in the hope, so it seemed, of trying to drive a wedge between the two countries. But the Scots were unwilling to fall for his machinations and sold him to the English Parliament for half a million pounds.

On 24 August 1647 the King returned to Hampton Court as a prisoner. He was treated with all civility and placed under what we should call today 'house arrest'. He was allowed freedom of movement within the palace, his former servants and chaplains were restored to him, and he resumed what, to all outward appearances, was his normal royal, residential life, dining with full pomp and ceremony in the Presence Chamber.

Many of the officers who had fought with him during the war were allowed in to talk to him and to kiss his hand. Occassionally and under escort, he was permitted to ride the five miles to Syon House – the name was a corruption of Zion and then usually spelt 'Sion' – where two of his children were living. Sir Thomas Herbert, a groom of the bedchamber, who was present at one of these family re-unions, later wrote:

Here the King met the young Duke of Gloucester and Princess Elizabeth, who, so soon as they saw their royal father, upon their knees they begged his blessing, who heartily gave it, and was overjoyed to see them so well in health and so honourably regarded. The Earl (of Northumberland) welcomed the King with a very noble treat, and his followers had their tables richly furnished, by his behaviour expressing extraordinary contentment to see the King and his children together, after such various chances and so long a separation. Night drawing on, his Majesty returned to Hampton Court.

One frequent palace visitor, greatly welcomed by Charles, was the tall, red-headed Mrs Jane Whorwood, whose home was in nearby Kingston. Thirty-two-year-old Mrs Whorwood, daughter of one, Ryder, a former surveyor of stables to King James I, had married Brome Whorwood, of Holton, in Oxfordshire, at the age of nineteen. She was believed by some people (without any substantial evidence) to be Charles's mistress, but the main purposes of her visits were to bring in money from the King's supporters and unfurl romantic but totally impractical plans for his escape.

She consulted the astrologer William Lilly as to what part of England Charles might safely hide in if only he could slip away from the palace. Lilly recommended Essex but, as we shall see, the King had other ideas. Later on, when Charles was a prisoner in the Isle of Wight, she showed no signs of wavering in her devotion or ingenuity. She smuggled a locksmith's file into him in the hope that he might cut his way out of his room through the barred window. And she even went to the extent of endangering her own safety and dipping deeply into her own purse by chartering a ship which for some days stood off the south coast, ready to whisk the King to a continental refuge.

Despite the futility of all her schemes, Charles spoke warmly of Mrs Whorwood in his letters where her identity was usually disguised under the ciphers 'N' or '715'.

At last the day arrived at the palace when the conqueror, Oliver Cromwell, commander of the Parliamentarian army, came face to face with the vanquished, King Charles. Cromwell was accompanied by two senior officers, Generals Fairfax and Ireton, and observers particularly noticed that, although Fairfax kissed the King's hand, Cromwell and Ireton held back while otherwise behaving courteously.

That first meeting between the two remarkable leaders is another of history's treasured moments. In appearance there were great contrasts: Charles, neat and dapper but with his unabashed regal air; Cromwell, tallish for the period, at about five feet seven inches, long-nosed, high-cheeked face splashed with the famous warts, austere but with a certain bluff, likeable countryman's style.

As is so often the case with great political opponents, there were similarities of attitude. They were both obstinate men, totally convinced of the unassailable rectitude of their causes. In Charles's case that 'rightness' derived largely from personal intuition; for Cromwell it was ordained by God. Oliver, as he never ceased to remind his supporters, did nothing but 'by the good hand of God', came to no conclusion but 'by God's will'.

The purpose of the meeting was to see if, with due reform and necessary limitations on his personal power, Charles might not be restored to his throne. It was not the kind of offer Charles was likely to accept but he contrived to show interest in the idea and, as a gesture of personal goodwill, even invited Cromwell to bring his wife to dine at the palace.

Cromwell returned for further negotiations and the two men strolled about the palace talking as intimately together as if they had been a couple of modern company chairmen discussing an amicable take-over in which both might expect to retain senior Board appointments.

Inevitably, it was chairman Charles who outsmarted himself. While he affected to be weighing up Cromwell's proposals his mind was working away hopelessly at madcap plans to outwit his rival. He was already secretly in touch with the Scots, hoping to induce them to invade England and help him to overthrow Parliament.

When news of the intrigue leaked out, as Charles might well have known that it would, the 'negotiations' came to an abrupt end and General Ireton said of the King: 'He gave us words and we repaid him in his own coin when we found he had no real intention to the people's good, but only to prevail by our factions and to regain by art what he had lost by fight.'

Charles had given his own final push to the onward roll of events and a sense of despondency settled over his supporters at Hampton Court.

In her *Memoirs*, Lady Fanshawe, wife of Sir Richard Fanshawe, lately the King's War Minister, wrote: 'The last time I saw him, when I took my leave, I could not refrain from weeping; when he saluted me I prayed God to preserve His Majesty with long life and happy years; he stroked me on the cheek and said, "Child, if God pleaseth, it shall be so; but both of you and I must submit to God's will, and you know in what hands I am."'

To Sir Richard Fanshawe the King said: 'Be sure, Dick, to tell my son (Charles) all I have said, and deliver those letters to my wife, pray God bless her! I hope I shall do well. Thou hast been an honest man, and I hope God will bless thee and make thee a happy servant of my son.'

In one of those letters to his wife, about which he spoke, Charles wrote that if misfortune befell him she was to 'continue the same active endeavours but, like thy father's daughter, vigorously assist Prince Charles to regain his own.'

At the beginning of his 'house arrest' at the palace Charles gave an undertaking to Colonel Edward Whalley, commander of the guard, that he would not try to escape. Now, two months after being confined, he suddenly announced that he could no longer abide by that pledge. He feared, he said, that some of his more hostile enemies might try either to kidnap or assassinate him and he needed to reserve the freedom to protect himself.

Whalley immediately doubled the guard but the new restraints did not entirely stop the flow of visitors and, soon afterwards, the King's daughter, Elizabeth, came to stay at the palace. She complained that the guards outside her room, off the Long Gallery on the south-west side of the Base Court, made so much noise at night that she could not sleep. Charles raised the complaint with Colonel Whalley who replied that if the King cared to renew his no-escape pledge the guards would be withdrawn. Charles vehemently retorted: 'To renew my engagement were a point of honour. You had my engagement – I will not renew it. Keep your guards!'

Subsequent events have an element of mystery that remains unresolved to this day. On 11 November 1647 Whalley showed Charles a letter he had received from Cromwell. 'Dear Cousin Whalley,' it ran. 'There are rumours abroad of some intended attempt on His Majesty's person. Therefore, I pray, have a care of your guards. If any such thing should be done, it would be accounted a most horrid act.'

Why, we may wonder, should Whalley have taken the extraordinary step of showing such a letter to his prisoner? At best it might have alarmed him and made him perhaps more of a nuisance to supervise; at worst it would have encouraged him towards a likely escape plan. There is, however, the possibility that the explanation was rather more complex: Cromwell knew that the King was determined to escape and had decided to allow him to go ahead. Then, perhaps, and we are entirely in the realm of speculation, he might be fortuitously killed while attempting his escape and that would relieve Cromwell of the need formally to commit the dreadful crime of regicide.

What we do know is that events moved swiftly. After being shown Whalley's letter Charles spent the afternoon in his bedroom – on the south side of Cloister Green Court – writing letters. At five o'clock Whalley came to the door expecting to see the King going, as was usual at that hour, to evening prayers. But the King did not appear and when Whalley questioned the servants of the royal bed-chamber they reported that Charles had said he had a considerable amount of correspondence to finish; and it was, in fact, the evening reserved for the despatch of the weekly post.

By six o'clock, according to his later account, Whalley was beginning to grow uneasy and by seven he was 'extremely restless in my thoughts, looked oft in at the key-hole to see whether I could perceive His Majesty, but could not . . .' On Whalley's instructions one of the gentlemen of the bedchamber hammered on the locked door but could raise no response.

At eight o'clock Whalley, together with the Keeper of the Privy Lodgings, went up the backstairs to the King's apartments and found his cloak lying on the floor of an empty ante-room. The keeper then opened the rear door of the royal bedroom. It, too, was deserted.

The King, aided by two of his retainers, had fled earlier that blustery and dark winter's afternoon and by then was long gone on his way to what he hoped would be refuge and freedom in the Isle of Wight.

On the bedroom table Whalley found three letters in the King's handwriting, one of them addressed to himself. It thanked him for his courtesy as royal gaoler and begged him to protect 'my household stuff and moveables of all sorts which I leave behind me in this house, that they may be neither spoiled nor embezzled. . . .' (To the very end, it seemed, poor deluded Charles must have believed that he would one day be returning to claim his crown and possessions.)

One of the other letters, addressed to Parliament, declared that 'Liberty, being that which in all time hath been, but especially now is, the common theme and desire of all men, common reason shows that kings, less than any should endure captivity . . . I thought I was bound, as well by natural as political obligations, to seek my safety by retiring myself, for some time, from the public view both of my friends and enemies.'

In his personal report to Parliament, Whalley endeavoured to explain away the escape by pointing out that Hampton Court was vast, 'hath 1,500 rooms, as I am informed, and would require a troop of horse upon perpetual duty to guard all the outgoings'. In view of Charles's open repudiation of his earlier undertaking not to escape, and the ease with which any conscientious commander could have kept the royal apartments under constant surveillance, Whalley's 'explanation' rings false.

Charles did succeed in reaching the Isle of Wight but there he found neither refuge nor freedom but further imprisonment in Carisbrooke Castle. In December 1648 he was brought back to England to stand trial for the offences he was said to have committed against the rights of his subjects and for the 'tyranny' he had exercised in the name of kingship.

On 30 January 1649, on a platform erected in front of Inigo Jones's Banqueting Hall at Whitehall, King Charles was beheaded. As the cruel axe fell, the jostling crowd, it is said, stood suddenly still and overawed, as if only then perceiving the true meaning of the momentous act perpetrated in their name. Then, significantly, their new masters, the dedicated opponents of tyranny, ordered mounted troops to ride into their ranks and disperse them. They were, after all, still only the 'common' people.

*Oliver Cromwell (1599–1658), Lord Protector, hero of the nation's temporary republic. Parliament granted him the personal use of Hampton Court and a plot to assassinate him on his way there was foiled when he decided, that day, to travel by river instead of road.*

# 7

# *The*
# *Embattled Years*

## CROMWELLIAN INTERLUDE

WHEN THE NEW PARLIAMENT finally found time to think about Hampton Court its first intention was to put the palace and its contents up for sale. The property, it said, was 'justly forfeited' by the former King, Queen and Prince of Wales because of their 'several delinquencies'.

A Parliamentary Bill authorising the sale was enacted on 4 July 1649 and, for the first time, a full-scale inventory of the palace treasures was compiled. Many of the estimated money values were ludicrously low, even allowing for the economics of the period. For example, ten pieces of Wolsey-Henry VIII tapestries, telling the story of Abraham and running to 826 yards, were valued at only £10 a yard, or £8,260. One of Titian's great works, the *Venus del Pardo*, was priced at a paltry £600 and Mantegna's immortal *Triumph of Julius Caesar* at £1,000. Altogether the palace's three hundred or so pictures were 'catalogued' at only £4,675 16s 6d. The total gross value of the palace, together with the parks and grounds of more than one thousand acres, was put at £10,765 19s 9d.

Every item down to the smallest was recorded so we know, for instance, that were was 'one paire of Bellowes' in the former Queen's bedroom, 'one small Billiard board' in the Long Gallery and 'one downe pillow' in a room formerly used by one of the senior ladies of the royal household.

*The Elephants – from the nine-piece masterly composition,* The Triumph of Caesar, *by the Italian painter, Andrea Mantegna (1431–1506). A Triumph was republican Rome's highest honour, conferred on a victorious commander and celebrated by a procession through the city to the Capitol in which animals – in this case elephants – paraded along with soldiers, priests and prisoners of war.*

The whole lot would have been sold off, irretrievably – indeed, Henry VIII's walking stick disappeared into some unknown hands for five shillings (25p) – except that Parliament had second thoughts and, fortunately for posterity, stopped the sale before it was too late. Instead it decreed that everything must be retained on behalf of the new republic which was to be known as the Commonwealth.

Those who had striven and fought for that Commonwealth owed much to the hero of the hour, Oliver Cromwell now designated Lord Protector, and, in addition to voting him a stipend of £4,000 a year, Parliament granted him the personal use of Hampton Court. For the upkeep of his household, or 'family' as it was more cosily described, he was to have £64,000 a year. In 1654, at the age of fifty-five, Cromwell formally took possession of the palace and moved in with his wife, Elizabeth, and his personal family.

As it had done for his royal predecessors, the palace captivated Oliver and, although its atmosphere was understandably far less colourful than in the time of Charles I, it soon came to resemble something of a court. Almost as if he had set himself up to be a pioneer of the modern 'British week-end', the Lord Protector made it his habit to travel down to Hampton Court on Friday evenings and return to London on Monday mornings. And, again much like a present day 'week-ending' businessman, Cromwell would often take his work with him. It was not unusual for members of the Council of State to find themselves summoned to a Saturday meeting and one observer noted that 'the great affairs of the nation are transacted with labour and care as if they were at Whitehall.'

Cromwell himself was by then being formally addressed as 'Highness' and, although none dared mock openly at his elevated status, there were others who whispered derisory comments about his plain, ordinary wife. They maliciously nicknamed her 'Old Joan' and 'the Lady Protectoress' and guffawed over her alleged bungling efforts to ape the ceremonial manner of royalty. They especially amused each other with highly embroidered tales of her stinginess. Although she came from a wealthy background she was by nature a judicious penny-watcher.

It was said that she haunted the kitchens, hovering over the cooks to make sure that no food went to waste and that no one 'fiddled' the stocks. Bitterness was naturally at the root of much of the unkind gossip but Cromwell paid it no heed. His marriage to Elizabeth was happy and she was always in his thoughts even during the most exacting of times.

Like King Charles before him, Cromwell hunted the Hampton Court deer and he particularly delighted in the company of a rather special 'inner court' consisting mainly of a group of his old wartime cronies. After the chase it was his custom to entertain these senior officers to a private supper and, once the dishes were cleared away, to give free rein to another and surprising side of his personality – a schoolboyish boisterousness. He would, it was reported, 'drink freely' and join with his friends in such outlandish pranks as 'throwing cushions and putting live coals into their pockets and boots'. At other times he would 'give order for a drum to beat, and call on his Foot Guards, like a kennel of hounds, to snatch off meat from his table and tear it to pieces . . .'

During the war the local inhabitants had taken advantage of King Charles's absence to sabotage his new water supply, the Longford River, about which they had so bitterly complained. They pulled down bridges and dammed the watercourse with stones and gravel to prevent the flooding of their land. But, to their dismay, Cromwell ordered the river to be cleared and the flow of water restored. He also diverted part of the stream to Bushy Park to fill two newly-dug ponds, then called the Harewarren ponds and now known as the Heron (a corruption of Harewarren) and the Leg-of-Mutton ponds.

He further incurred the wrath of the locals by closing off an established right-of-way through the park's Harewarren. And their reaction was summed up by questions posed in an anonymous satirical pamphlet: 'Who will have the fine houses, the brave parks, the pleasant fields and delightful gardens, that we have possessed without any right, and built at other men's cost? Who shall enjoy the delight of the new rivers and ponds at Hampton Court whose making cost vast sums of money, and who shall chase the game in the Harewarren, that my dear master hath enclosed for his own use, and for our's also that are time-servers?' No prizes were offered for identifying the person to whom the questions were addressed nor his 'time-servers'.

Another attribute that Cromwell shared with the late King was an interest in art and music and he had two additional organs installed in the Great Hall. One of the instruments was a gift from Magdalen College, Oxford, and occasionally Cromwell and his family were entertained to recitals by John Milton, the poet, who was also a very fine organist. (Milton had an official civil service post as Latin secretary to the Council of State; he translated foreign documents into Latin for which he received the equivalent of a little less than 80p a day.)

One of the major celebratory events for the Cromwells at the palace was the marriage of their daughter, Mary, in the chapel on 17 November 1657 to a widower and former royalist, Thomas Belasyse, Viscount Fauconberg. The official announcement declared: 'Yesterday His Highness (Cromwell) went to Hampton Court and this day the most illustrous lady, the Lady Mary Cromwell, third daughter of His Highness the Lord Protector, was there married to the most noble lord, the Lord Fauconberg, in the presence of Their Highnesses and many noble persons.'

Normally, service in the chapel then followed the Presbyterian form but, at the bridegroom's request, the ceremony was conducted according to the Anglican rites. Cromwell provided a dowry of £15,000 and that sum, and his agreement to the form of service, indicate the extent of his approval of the match.

Attendance at chapel was not, however, always quite so comforting for the Lord Protector. On one Sunday, it was reported, the local preacher from Hampton daringly ventured to draw a parallel in his sermon 'between David cutting off the top of Saul's garment, and the cutting off of the late King's head, and how David was troubled for what he had done, though he was ordained to succeed Paul'. The reporter committed himself to a classic understatement by observing that the sermon 'possibly' caused embarrassment.

Some other critics were also hovering, ready to give the Protector a piece of their censorious minds. One stalwart Puritan lady, a Mrs Mary Nethaway, despatched him a letter warning him of the spiritual dangers of tolerating such idolatrous statues in the gardens of Hampton Court as Venus and Adonis. But Cromwell ignored the warning.

More ominous and persistent pieces of information about the threats to his life he could not afford to brush lightly aside. Always there were whispers of possible assassination attempts and one conspirator, Miles Sindercombe, made elaborate plans to shoot the Protector as he passed through Hammersmith on his way to Hampton Court. The plot was foiled when Cromwell, who was probably forewarned by his secret agents, changed his plans and travelled to the palace by river. Sindercombe was tried and sentenced to death for high treason but committed suicide in the Tower while awaiting execution.

The State Papers of Charles II's reign record a boast by a Captain Thomas Gardiner that, in 1657, 'he intended an attempt on Cromwell, but was taken in the Gallery at Hampton Court, with two loaded pistols and a dagger, kept twelve months a prisoner and only failed to be sentenced to death on the trial.'

Cromwell travelled nowhere without protection. He wore a steel vest and whenever he journeyed to and from Hampton Court he varied the route. His coachmen and outriders, in their grey coats with silver and black trimmings, had orders to go at full gallop the whole way and stop for no one. Many of those journeys, over narrow, unmade roads and rough cart tracks, were especially agonising for the Protector after his generally declining health came to be much aggravated by a bladder stone.

The death of his favourite daughter, twenty-nine-year-old Elizabeth, at the palace on 6 August 1658, left him prostrate with grief. He took his final farewell of her as her body was carried aboard a barge and borne downstream to Westminster Abbey for he was too upset to join the mourners at the funeral. He lay in bed at the palace listening to readings from the Bible and declared that he took comfort from St Paul's words: 'I can do all things through Christ that strengtheneth me.'

Briefly he seemed to regain his composure but George Fox, founder of the Society of Friends, the Quakers, who went to Hampton Court to plead the cause of his sect, wrote: 'Before I came to him, as he rode at the head of his Life Guards, I saw and felt a waft of death go forth against him, and when I came to him he looked like a dead man.'

During the night of 17 August, only eleven days after his daughter's death, he was taken ill and on the 24th his doctors persuaded him to return to Whitehall where he could receive closer attention. At the turn of the month London was shaken by some of the worst storms the capital had experienced for centuries and on 3 September, the day after the freak weather reached its peak, Oliver Cromwell

*Richard Cromwell, son of Oliver, who 'reigned' for a short time after his father's death until popular opinion decided that a republic was not really to England's taste.*

*General Monk, First Duke of Albemarle, who initiated the moves that brought about the Restoration of the monarchy and the return from exile of the prince who became Charles II.*

died. He was nearly sixty and, in the words of the nineteenth-century historian, Lord Macaulay, was, to the last, 'honoured by his soldiers, obeyed by the whole population of the British islands, and dreaded by all foreign powers . . .' (And, one might add, also remembered for his occasional exhibitions of great cruelty, as was evidenced by some of the darker deeds of his military campaigning in Ireland.)

Cromwell was buried in Westminster Abbey amid pomp and ceremony more lavish than those bestowed on any former monarch. The cost of his funeral was put at £60,000 – an inordinate expenditure in Commonwealth values.

(His service to the state, however, did nothing to guarantee Oliver a peaceful rest. Three years later, after the House of Stuart had been restored to sovereignty, the bodies of Cromwell, General Ireton and John Bradshaw, president of the court that tried and convicted Charles I, were exhumed and hung on gallows at Tyburn (where Marble Arch now stands) and afterwards decapitated. Cromwell's trunk was buried beneath the gibbet but there were some who said that it was not really Cromwell's. The truth was supposed to be that the Protector, realising the risk of future desecration, had arranged with friends to place an unknown body in his coffin. The real corpse was then secretly buried in an unmarked plot on the battlefield of Naseby.)

Cromwell left no written document naming his successor and on the day before he died members of the Council of State had gathered anxiously around his deathbed seeking a sign. One account has it that someone whispered in Cromwell's ear the name of his son, Richard, and the Lord Protector, unable to speak, made a brief gesture of assent.

Richard Cromwell's 'reign' lasted for only five months. He was a good and honest man but his only slim claim to office was the name Cromwell. Many anti-royalists who thought mere heredity no sound basis for kingship were equally opposed to a Protector assuming power solely by virtue of being his father's son.

Rivalries, therefore, developed among some of Oliver Cromwell's former generals. One, John Lambert, made it clear that he considered he was as fitted to rule as Richard Cromwell; but most significantly, another, George Monk, decided that Lambert was unacceptable and launched the moves that were to bring Charles, Prince of Wales, back to Britain as the restored king.

Meanwhile, a nucleus of what had come to be called the Long Parliament – it served almost continuously from 1640 to 1653 and then again from 1659 to 1660 – found time amidst the general upheaval to put forward a fresh proposal for selling off Hampton Court but, happily, it failed. General Edmund Ludlow successfully intervened with a Commons resolution calling for the palace to be retained by the State as 'a place for the retirement of those in public affairs, should they be indisposed.'

In February 1660, General Monk and his army (destined to develop into the Coldstream Guards) made a triumphant entry into London and ensured the restoration of the monarchy.

As a tribute, the Commons proposed to present Hampton Court to Monk in perpetuity. But the General graciously declined the offer and, instead, accepted a gratuity of £20,000 and the honorary post of custodian and steward of the palace and its parks. (The honour was confirmed by Charles II and enjoyed by Monk for the rest of his life.)

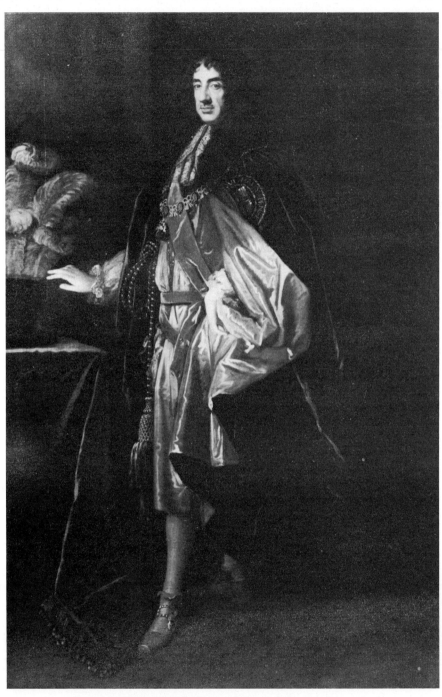

*Charles II (1630–1685), by the royal court painter, Sir Peter Lely.*
*The King enjoyed life at the palace, despite the fact*
*that his father had been a prisoner there.*

# 8

# *The Embattled Years*

## CHARLES II

CHARLES II, EXILED SINCE THE GREAT REBELLION, set foot on English soil at Dover in the dawn light of 25 May 1660. Samuel Pepys, that great diarist-reporter, was there and noted that 'the shouting and joy expressed by all is past imagination.' The 'all' was fifty thousand people and their cheers served as the proxy votes of the majority of their fellow citizens disillusioned by their experience of a republic and hoping for and expecting much from the new King.

His Majesty spent the week-end in Canterbury and entered an enthusiastically welcoming London on 29 May, his thirtieth birthday. Those near enough to have a close-up view as he rode through the streets were impressed by the sight of him. He was more than six feet tall, which was exceptional for that time. His hair was shiny black, his face long and oval, eyes brown, shoulders wide. He had charm and grace and, what the onlookers most desperately needed to see, regality. The bells rang, the capital echoed to the boom of salute by cannon, and wine and beer flowed more swiftly than the sweet Thames. With the rising sun of a new reign, Puritan England was about to sink into the shadows.

Charles came to love Hampton Court and to take a personal interest in its further development but it was not until his marriage, two years after his return to the kingdom, that he began to pay regular and protracted visits to the palace.

*Charles II's wife, Catherine of Braganza (1638–1705). She fell into a swoon at the palace when the King first introduced her to one of his many mistresses.*

*In style, Charles II enters the City of London – his narrow-street, disease-infested and crowded capital soon to be largely destroyed by fire.*

For the sake of the succession he needed a wife and, as had been the case for past monarchs, politics were more important than love. Lord Clarendon, Charles's Chancellor, was anxious for the King to take a Protestant bride. But, in the end, the choice fell upon the twenty-two-year-old Portuguese Catholic princess, Catherine of Braganza. Catherine and Charles had never met but the material prospects of a marriage were rosy indeed for a financially hard-pressed Britain – a dowry of some £360,000 plus the gift of Tangier and Bombay and free-trading rights with Brazil and the East Indies.

In terms of purely superficial feminine attractions, Catherine was no great catch. She had a small, unsmiling face, helped somewhat by large dark eyes, and crowned by lustrous chestnut hair which was unfortunately spoiled by abominable outcroppings set in tight pigtail form. Her other defect, as delicately described by Pepys' fellow diarist, John Evelyn, who met her later at Hampton Court, was 'teeth wronging her mouth by sticking a little too far out . . .'

Charles had long since concluded that the world consisted of two categories of women: wives and mistresses – and the one category by no means necessarily

Barbara Villiers, Countess of Castlemaine and Duchess of Cleveland, in the portrait by Lely. She was foremost among Charles II's mistresses.

The Restoration's greatest reporter, the diarist Samuel Pepys, who hobnobbed with leading members of the Court. He was a keen musician and just before this portrait by John Hayls was made he had composed a song, 'Beauty Retire.'

excluded the other. He accepted the political basis of the betrothal and gave the impression that if, by God's will, he should fall in love with his wife, that would be counted a most welcome bonus. Meanwhile, having acquired one principal mistress during his exile*, he lost no time at all in 'investing' in his first in England.

Almost on the first day of his arrival in London – some said it was, indeed, the very first *night* – Charles had fallen for lovely Barbara Palmer (née Villiers) wife of a young law student, Roger Palmer. Barbara was twenty, a dazzling brunette, and notoriously lascivious. Pepys, who lusted over her from a distance, declared that she had been 'a little lecherous girl when she was young', and it could well be said that, since her teens, life for her had been either bed or bored.

Before Charles her lovers had included the Earl of Chesterfield and there is no doubt that her attractions for men were powerful. (Five years after the King's return, Pepys recorded a dream 'which I think is the best that ever was dreamed – which was, that I had [Barbara Palmer] in my arms and was admitted to use all the dalliance I desired with her . . .')

The desires of King and Beauty were mutual and, just before Catherine of

* Lucy Walter, who bore him a son (1649) later to become famous as the Duke of Monmouth.

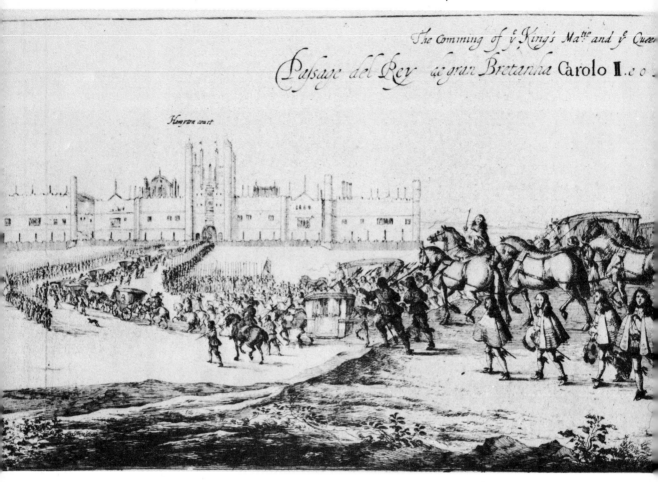

*The Comming of ye King's Matie and ye Quee*

*Passage del Rey de gran Bretanña Carolo II.e o*

*Hampton court*

*Travelling in Style. Surrounded by their retainers, Charles II and Queen Catherine arrive at the palace. The presence of Catherine's frumpish Portuguese ladies-in-attendance, whether at home or on a journey, exasperated the King.*

Braganza's arrival in England, Barbara gave birth to a daughter, Anne, which she claimed was Charles's, although it could have been Chesterfield's child. Soon she was pregnant once more, this time certainly by the King, and to ensure her 'respectability' she persuaded Charles to give her cuckolded husband an earldom. Hence she passed into history as Lady Castlemaine.

Charles met Catherine on her arrival in Portsmouth and they were publicly married in the city governor's mansion following a brief and secret Catholic ceremony. From Portsmouth the couple journeyed to Hampton Court, by way of Windsor, in a grandiose cavalcade. Their own coach was drawn by six horses and attended by a profusion of footmen, runners and men-at-arms. In their wake flowed a tide of other coaches bearing the courtiers and the ladies of Catherine's Portuguese retinue.

Although the Portuguese ladies were not to cause Charles anything like the annoyance suffered by his father at the hands of Henrietta Maria's French attendants, the English courtiers and servants viewed them askance. As the procession rolled in across the Base Court of the palace to Anne Boleyn's Gateway the onlookers found themselves being stared at by a sea of stolid, humourless, middle-aged female faces.

'Frumpish' is perhaps the most appropriate word with which to describe the

*Portsmouth to Hampton court.*

Dona Catarina *de Portsmuit ʒer a* Hamton=court

ladies who then descended from the coaches. Their farthingales had gone out of fashion in England some thirty years previously. And, as if to underline their stolidity and dowdiness, the ladies were seen to be accompanied by a flock of monks who had evidently had no recent communion with soap and water.

Like the new Queen herself, her retainers spoke little English and it is easy to imagine that they formed a starchily uncomfortable clique as they filed into the Great Hall where the royals received the greetings of the State notables – the Lord Chancellor, Lord Treasurer and members of the Privy Council. Lord Clarendon later summed up the ladies as 'old, ugly and proud, and incapable of any conversation with persons of quality and liberal education'. (He meant there to be no doubt, of course, that he was such a person.)

Other celebrities trooped to the palace, not only to pay homage to the King's new bride but to catch a glimpse of her already well-publicised 'court'. From the City of London came the Lord Mayor and the aldermen to present Catherine with a gold cup which, as an extra dividend, contained within it the cash gift of £1,000. From many cities and towns came the leading citizens.

Charles was sorely vexed by Catherine's insistence on appearing in the same unbecoming attire as her ladies. Having heard in advance of her notorious lack of dress-sense, he had presented her with a stunning English-made trousseau. She at first adamantly refused to wear it but when the King insisted she grudgingly gave way. Prompted by that minor victory, Charles nagged away at his irritation over the Portuguese ladies until, at last, they also felt obliged to put away their dismal garments and struggle, poutingly, into the latest creations. But, in the words of a future queen, they were not amused.

Apart from the desecration of the chapel, the palace had emerged intact from the nation's brief experience as a republic and the great pictures and tapestries were still there. The Queen's bedroom was now adorned by a bed which cost £8,000, had an embroidered canopy of silver on crimson velvet and was a present from the Dutch. In that room, too, stood a great mirror with a frame of beaten gold which had been given to Catherine by her mother-in-law, Henrietta Maria, widow of Charles I, who was still alive and well and living on charity. Henrietta's general personality had advanced with the years from tearful anxiety to frigid haughtiness but she approved of her daughter-in-law and the two became good friends. She had good reason for feeling a certain compassion towards any young woman to whom fell the 'privilege' of wedding an English king.

Plain as she was, Catherine did not lack spirit and she was capable of infectious vivacity. She did her best to make herself at home at Hampton Court. She enjoyed dancing and took very quickly to the English predilection for picnics of which several were organised during the honeymoon. She also won the plaudits of the English courtiers for her skill at archery.

Charles was a keen, if only moderately good, tennis player and one of his first palace projects was to improve and modernise Henry VIII's tennis court. A new floor was laid, black marble was put down to mark out the chace-lines (used in determining the fall of the ball and, therefore, the score), the roof was rebuilt and the galleries renovated.

The names of some of the workmen and their earnings have been preserved in the records. We know, for instance, that John Philips, a turner, received '6d the peece' for shaping nine wooden columns and '12d the peece' for turning four others. For seventeen days' work in squaring, working and fitting part of the stonework and cutting the black marble. John Ashlee, a mason, was paid £2 2s 6d. And Simon Winslow, the ferryman, received ten shillings for three months' service in ferrying labourers across to the palace from the Surrey side of the Thames.

When the work was completed the courtiers crowded in to watch the King play (often at six in the morning) and there is little reason to doubt that they behaved in the way Pepys had observed them at the tennis court at Whitehall: '. . . to see how the King's play was extolled without any cause at all, was a loathsome sight, though sometimes he did play very well and deserved to be commended, but such open flattery is beastly.'

Hampton Court Park also occupied much of the King's attention and he it was who was responsible for having it laid out much in the form we see today. He ordered the cutting of the great canal, the Long Water, that runs eastward across the park from the palace, and the planting of three avenues of lime-trees which he imported from Holland.

From France Charles managed to entice some of the gardeners whose creative efforts in Paris had much impressed him and there is evidence for believing that much of Hampton Court landscaping of the time was the work of André le Nôtre, the distinguished French gardener. John Rose, Charles's head gardener, had studied his craft under Le Nôtre and was responsible for the cultivation of the palace's dwarf yew trees.

In the Tilt Yard the King built a guard house for his foot soldiers and this was eventually developed into a barracks which still survives. Altogether, the cost of works in and around the palace in 1662 amounted to some £7,000.

Shortage of money continually plagued the King. He was allowed an official income of around £1 million a year but by 1662 his expenses were running at least £500,000 beyond that for he was expected to meet all administrative and personal costs. The kingdom's national debt amounted to £3 million and general economic stringency meant that Charles was far less well provided for financially than Oliver Cromwell. He even went so far as to complain that he could afford only the most frugal of meals; and he told his Parliamentary paymasters he had taken note of the fact that often when they came to visit him they hurried away as soon as hunger beckoned and 'must go somewhere else to seek your dinner'.

The King's seventeenth-century version of cash-flow trouble forced him to sell off most of the Crown lands for £1,300,000 and he was strongly criticised for concluding a £400,000 deal with Louis XIV of France which entailed handing back the port of Dunkirk captured by Cromwell. He finally gained some financial relief by persuading Parliament to grant him the Customs and Excise revenues on a wide variety of commodities – beer, cider, coffee, sherbet, tea and tobacco, among other things.

His mistresses, of course, cost him a pretty penny and many Londoners, while enjoying the re-opening of the theatres and the other social freedoms of the Restoration, grumbled about the King's preoccupation with his women and his constant absence from the Whitehall centre of government. On 30 June 1662, Pepys noted in his diary: 'This I take to be as bad a Juncture as ever I observed. The King and his new Queene minding their pleasure at Hampton Court. All people discontented . . .'

But whatever pleasure Charles 'minded' at Hampton Court it did not include domestic peace, for he was about to be embroiled in a new and extraordinary episode with Barbara Palmer, Lady Castlemaine, mother of his son whom she had named Charles.

Of all things, Barbara had recklessly decided that she wanted to be appointed as a Lady of the Queen's bedchamber. And Charles, pliable as always in the hands of his women, gave her his backing. (As one of his recent biographers, Antonia Fraser, put it: 'All his life, King Charles's method of dealing with a woman's complaints or tears was to attempt to cozen her with something to cheer her up, as a parent gives a lollipop to a child.')

Queen Catherine had known all about Barbara and her liaison with Charles even before she left Portugal. Gossip and rumour of Charles's love-life travelled far and wide across the international royal networks and consequently Catherine's mother had been able to forewarn her daughter of Barbara's existence.

By now, however, Charles had persuaded himself that his future relationship with Barbara would be no more than platonic and he seems naïvely to have believed that he could easily convince Catherine of the 'innocence' of the lady's proposed appointment. He, therefore, proceeded to draw up a list of nominations for the Queen's household with Lady Castlemaine's name at the very top.

He, alone among everyone at Court, was astonished at Catherine's outrage. 'The King's insistence,' she told Clarendon, 'can proceed from no other ground but his hatred of my person. He wishes to expose me to the contempt of the world. And the world will think me deserving of such an affront if I submit to it. Before I do that I will put myself on board any little vessel and so be transported to Lisbon.'

Spooning out the thick syrup of his diplomacy, Clarendon replied: 'I cannot believe that you are utterly ignorant as to expect the King, your husband, in the full strength and vigour of his youth, of so innocent a constitution as to be reserved for you whom he had never seen, and to have no acquaintance or familiarity with the other sex.'

Charles's reaction to Catherine's anger was both tortuous and touching. His main anxiety, it appeared, was to try to make her understand his sense of guilty obligation towards Barbara. After all, he explained, gallantly if not very accurately, he had 'ruined her reputation, which was fair and untainted till her friendship with me'. Was it not, therefore, clear that conscience and honour required him to 'repair her to the utmost of my power'? If Catherine would only accept Barbara as a lady of her bedchamber he would never ask anything more difficult of her; and, in return, Lady Castlemaine would behave towards the Queen 'with all possible duty and humility' and should she fail, even in the smallest degree, 'she shall never see my face again.'

To Clarendon, Charles wrote: 'I wish I may be unhappy in this world, and in the world to come, if I fail in the least degree of what I resolved, which is of making my Lady Castlemaine of my wife's bedchamber, and whosoever I find endeavouring to hinder this resolution of mine, except it be only myself, I will be his enemy to the last moment of my life . . .'

In the light of Charles's implacability, Catherine finally surrendered – hoping, we may imagine, that Barbara would indeed fail in her 'duty and humility'. But, despite all the high words and the wrangling, Queen Catherine had not yet actually set eyes on this much-vaunted paramour.

The great moment of encounter came in the Presence Chamber at Hampton Court on the next State occasion. The door opened upon Catherine, sitting surrounded by her stuffy Portuguese attendants, and Charles advanced across the room leading a ravishing young woman by the hand.

With wildly misplaced cunning, Charles introduced his guest as 'Lady Barbara Palmer'. Catherine appeared at first not to catch on, and offered her hand for Barbara to kiss. Then, almost certainly alerted by the buzz of excited whispering among the courtiers, her feminine intuition suddenly snapped to attention. She rose, clasping and unclasping her hands, tears welled into her eyes, her face turned ashen pale and blood ran from her nose. For a moment she stood there, stiff with shock, stifling her sobs. The next moment her eyes became glazed and she fell forward into a swoon. The King caught her in his arms and a couple of servants sprang forward and carried her away, through the ranks of the bulging-eyed courtiers, to her room.

Excitement and anticipation gripped the Court over the ensuing weeks. No one was surprised by the obvious coldness with which the King and Queen treated each other. But were the Queen's wounds so deep that they might be beyond all hope of healing?

The answer came in a totally unexpected and astonishing public demonstration by the Queen. She permitted Barbara to kiss her hand – and this time there was no swooning – she invited her to supper, she chatted to her graciously and, all in all, the two suddenly appeared to be on the most friendly terms.

The reasons for Catherine's abrupt change of mind are obscure. Had she decided that by placating Charles in the matter of what had come to be known as the 'Bedchamber Crisis' she might consolidate her marriage? Or was it, as one of her biographers, Hebe Elsner, suggests, that she had secretly been advised to obey Charles in persuance of an ultimate and more important objective – his conversion to her Roman Catholic faith?

Another consideration may also have weighed with the Queen. She was anxious to provide Charles with an heir. But, although Charles's sex life with Catherine seems subsequently to have been as active as with his women friends, all her pregnancies sadly ended in still-births.

Clarendon emerged from the Bedchamber Crisis with less honour than anyone. Having originally pressed the Queen to accede to the King's wish over Lady Castlemaine, he later castigated her for what he described as 'this sudden downfall and totally abandoning her own greatness, this low demeanour, and even application to a person she had justly abhorred and worthily condemned'.

Lord Clarendon was ever a meddlesome man who, despite public fawning and high office, fundamentally disapproved of Charles. Born Edward Hyde in 1609, he shared Charles's exile during the Cromwellian era and supervised the negotiations that led to the Restoration. His personal power was considerably strengthened by the marriage of his daughter, Anne, to Charles's young brother, James, Duke of York. When Charles became King at the age of thirty, Clarendon was fifty-one and it was this difference in years that undoubtedly accounted for much of his antagonism towards his royal master.

In July 1662 Charles and Catherine went to Greenwich to welcome the Queen Mother, Henrietta Maria, back to England. A few days later, and thirteen years after her husband's execution, Henrietta returned to Hampton Court.

There was a touch of pathos in that moment outside the Great Hall when Charles, with all due ceremony, formally received his mother whose mind must have been filled with bitter-sweet memories. Gently he led her through the Hall and into the Presence Chamber where two thrones had been set on a dais beneath the brilliant canopy of State.

Queen Catherine was there to greet her mother-in-law and, after the two Queens had exchanged felicitations, Catherine took her place on the right-hand throne and Henrietta on the left. Since Henrietta spoke no Portuguese nor her daughter-in-law any French, the King and his brother, the Duke of York, stood by the thrones and acted as interpreters. Anne, Duchess of York, was seated just below the dais to the left of Queen Catherine.

On 23 August the King and Queen made a state entry into London, travelling by river from Hampton Court. At the palace landing stage they entered the royal barge accompanied by the Duke and Duchess of York, Rupert, Duke of Cumberland, and his brother Prince Edward (both sons of Frederick V, Elector Palatine of the Rhine), and the Countess of Suffolk, the Queen's first lady of the bedchamber. Twelve scarlet-liveried bargemen rowed the barge, and the courtiers followed in a flotilla of other barges.

At Teddington, some three miles downstream, the royal party transferred to a larger, glass-windowed barge covered by a crimson awning embroidered with gold. And further down, at Putney, the royals made a final change to a huge river craft designed, as the diarist John Evelyn reported, 'like an antique-shaped open

*Frances Stewart (or Stuart), the young beauty whose favours King Charles hoped to enjoy. His importunities failed to produce the desired result and she married the Duke of Richmond. (Portrait by Lely.)*

vessel, covered with a state or canopy of cloth of gold, made in the form of a cupola, supported with high Corinthian pillars, wreathed with flowers, festoons and garlands'. Twenty-four scarlet-clad oarsmen rowed that great barge to Westminster, past river banks packed with cheering spectators and joined every few yards by escorting boats of every conceivable size and type until finally there was more than a thousand.

Overawed, like his fellow diarist, Pepys (who was watching the spectacle from a Whitehall rooftop), Evelyn wrote: 'I was spectator of the most magnificent triump that ever floated on the Thames, considering the innumerable boats and vessels, dressed and adorned with all imaginable pomp, but above all the thrones, arches, pageants, and other representations, stately barges of the Lord Mayor and companies, with various inventions, music and peals of ordnance both from the vessels and the shore, going to meet and conduct the new Queen from Hampton Court to Whitehall, at the first time of her coming to town.'

Among the floating pageants Pepys noted 'one of a King and another of a Queene, with her maydes of honour sitting at her feet very prettily'. The river was so thick with craft that Pepys could not see the water between them. But

9. The Great Hall, the superb focal point of the palace. It is almost impossible to stand in this dazzling place without feeling a sense of the triumphs and tragedies of English history.

10. *Since its foundation, gardens have been an outstanding feature and attraction of Hampton Court. Here we look across the Rose Garden towards the Great Hall.*

11. *Where this garden is now laid out there stood the Tilt Yard, the scene of the tournaments in which Henry VIII joined his knights in sporting combat — and was sometimes unhorsed.*

12. *Elizabeth I dances with Lord Robert Dudley, later the Earl of Leicester. He was one of her 'favourites' and courtiers' tongues wagged with gossip about the real, or supposed, nature of their relationship.*

13. *The justly celebrated panoramic view of the palace, by the Dutch-born painter Leonard Knyff, as seen in the reign of George I. The different styles of the original Tudor and later buildings are clearly visible.*

14. Early morning in the park, with deer. And one of the beautiful wrought-iron gates designed by the Frenchman, Jean Tijou. The craftsman who carried out the structural work is said to have died from a broken heart as the result of not receiving a penny in payment from Queen Anne.

15. The Knot Garden. Such intricate gardens were very popular in the Tudor age and this, modelled on Elizabeth I's original, was created by Ernest Law, the nineteenth-century Hampton Court historian who lived at the palace.

what most pleased this engaging reprobate-chronicler was the sight of Lady Castlemaine stepping ashore at Whitehall Palace landing steps.

'I glutted myself with looking on her,' he admitted. But he was able to leave for posterity an intriguing vignette of the breach which Barbara Castlemaine's relationship with the King had finally opened up between herself and her husband. It was strange, he wrote 'to see her Lord and her upon the same place, walking up and down without taking notice of one another; only, at first entry, he put off his hat and she made him a very civil salute – but afterwards took no notice one of another'.

Among others disembarking from the royal barge was the lovely young Frances Stewart (sometimes spelt Stuart) who was fifteen, vivacious and rather feather-brained. As Queen Catherine's maid-of-honour she became known to the Court as 'La Belle Stuart'; later countless millions saw her image since she was the original model for the Britannia who, until comparatively recently, appeared on British coins.

Charles lusted after Frances and is said to have first noticed her when she was sharing a room with Barbara Castlemaine at Hampton Court. Before long Barbara became miserable with jealousy and the King, according to Pepys, 'besotted' with Frances. Indeed, Pepys followed the example of the King (in his dreams at least) by 'demoting' Lady Castlemaine from her status as the world's most desirable woman and replacing her with Frances.

He decided that Miss Stewart 'with her hat cocked and a red plume, with her sweet eye, little Roman nose and excellent Taille [figure] is now the greatest beauty I ever saw I think in my life . . . nor do I wonder if the King changes, which I verily believe is the reason of his coldness to my Lady Castlemaine'.

The favourite pastimes of Frances at Hampton Court, as elsewhere, were blind man's buff, hunt-the-slipper and building houses out of playing cards. But they did not extend to climbing into bed with Charles, energetically as he tried to bring that about and despite the fact that he seems to have loved her in addition to wanting her. To Charles's frustration and despair she eventually married the Duke of Richmond and the King wrote a bathetic verse about his jealousy:

> While alone to myself I repeat all her charms,
> She I love may be locked in another man's arms,
> She may laugh at my cares and so false she may be,
> To say all the kind things she before said to me:
> O then, 'tis O then, that I think there's no hell
> Like loving too well.

On her death, in 1702, she was buried in Westminster Abbey where her waxen effigy may still be seen.

What with Lady Castlemaine, and Charles already ogling Frances Stewart, the triumphant river entry into London can hardly have been a matter of unalloyed rejoicing for Catherine. And something of what she had to endure was summed up in a much-told courtier's tale, inevitably scribbled down by the good reporter Pepys: watching Catherine prepare herself for the day, Barbara Castlemaine cheekily commented: 'I can't think how you can have the patience to sit so long a-dressing!' To which Catherine neatly and pointedly replied: 'Madam, I have so *much* reason to use patience, that I can well bear such a trifle.'

As the years moved on, Charles tended to spend more time at Whitehall so that his visits to Hampton Court became sporadic and were mainly occasions for hunting and hawking. On the one hand, affairs of state pressed more heavily upon him – Britain and Holland went to war over their maritime trade rivalries – and, on the other, London offered greater opportunities for the 'Merry Monarch's' pursuit of women.

Finally exasperated by Barbara Castlemaine's bossiness and attempts to interfere in political matters, Charles turned to a succession of new mistresses but concentrated his affections on Nell Gwyn – 'pretty, witty Nell', who began her career as an orange seller at Drury Lane's Theatre Royal and became one of London's most popular, bawdy actresses.

Occasions on which the whole court was obliged to move to Hampton Court were those when London's frequent visitations by the plague reached epidemic proportions. And what at first looked like no more than a routine move was made in June 1665.

The unusually hot and humid summer had followed an unusually long and cold winter. London's weekly 'Bills of Mortality' – a tally of deaths and their causes compiled by John Graunt, a Fellow of the Royal Society – clearly indicated that a severe epidemic was in progress, although no one yet suspected it would develop into history's 'Great Plague of London'.

Hardly had the King and Queen shut themselves away in the palace than the City's death toll began to mount alarmingly. From around five hundred a week in June it had risen to more than a thousand a week by the middle of July; and those 'official' figures by no means represented the actual totals. For many reasons, and not least for the fear of having their houses shut up, people often did their best to conceal their family plague deaths.

*Whenever the plague came to London the Court retreated to the safety of Hampton Court. This engraving sums up the misery of yet another epidemic. Death in the foreground, with hour-glass and fatal arrow, summons his reluctant subjects to attend upon him.*

London was, even at the best of times, a filthy, squalid, stinking cesspit where none of the most opulent residents – and rich and poor lived side by side – would dream of venturing into the streets without carefully protecting their noses. Once infection took hold it rampaged through the overcrowded City and the surrounding parishes beyond the walls. Those who pined for the recent Puritan past saw the plague as a punishment of God on the new permissive, Restoration society. More mundanely, the disease, sometimes known as the Black Death because of the fatal black swellings it raised on the victims' bodies, was endemic in Europe and borne by the fleas breeding in the fur of the vast armies of rats.

Hampton Court was by no means hermetically sealed against the outside world for, on Sunday, 23 July, Samuel Pepys paid a call at the palace, having arisen before dawn at his house in Seething Lane, next to the Tower, and arrived in a coach-and-four at nine in the morning with his friend, William Cutler.

Pepys reported that he followed King Charles into the chapel, 'and there hear a good sermon', but was rather put out at not being invited to dinner until he remembered that he was but a fleeting visitor. However, 'Cutler carried me to Mr Marriotts the housekeeper, and there we had a very good dinner and good company; among others, Lilly the painter.'

It was Sir Peter Lely (whom Pepys called 'Lilly') who painted the portraits of the ladies of the Court known as the 'Windsor Beauties' since they were first exhibited at Windsor Castle. They are still to be seen on the panelled walls of Hampton Court's Communication Gallery (which links the King's and Queen's State Apartments).

Lady Castlemaine is among them and so is Frances Stewart. There, too, is Jane Middleton, another of Charles's mistresses, although how comfortably the King and the painter were able to bear her lovely presence we can only guess since it was said of her that there was 'about her body a continued sour base smell that is very offensive, especially if she be a little hot'. In her portrait she wears a romantically dream-like expression.

Lady Falmouth, yet another of the King's conquests and noted for her readiness to blush, is also to be seen together with Elizabeth Hamilton (known to the Court as 'La Belle Hamilton') who married the Chevalier de Gramont.

All the portraits tend to look alike which is an indication either of Charles's 'pattern' in the choice of women or an endeavour by Lely not to make any one of them more strikingly attractive than the others.

A few days after his first plague-time visit, Pepys returned to Hampton Court and was received by the Duke and Duchess of York and kissed the Duchess's hand. This bit of gallantry boosted the diarist's ego greatly and to the Duchess, who was no beauty, he paid the dubious compliment of noting that she offered him 'a most fine, white and fat hand'. He was also impressed by the sight of the Duchess's 'young pretty ladies dressed like men, in velvet coats, caps with ribbands and with laced bands . . .'

There was a more important moment for Pepys on 28 January 1666 when he once more presented himself at the palace in his official capacity as clerk to the navy. The King shook his hand and, as he proudly recorded, '"Mr Pepys", says he, "I do give you thanks for your good service all this year, and I assure you I am very sensible of it."'

Pepys must have known from that encounter that his career was assured and time would show that his far-reaching reforms of naval administration had helped

*Many dogs had their day at the palace. Often when King Charles set out for a journey, as we see here, a clutch of hounds accompanied him, trotting along beside his coach.*

to lay the foundations of a modern and enduring Royal Navy – a memorable achievement for a remarkable and loveable man, born the son of an impoverished London tailor.

The arrival of winter weather had finally brought an end to the Great Plague and the Court, together with thousands of ordinary citizens who had fled their homes, was able to return to Whitehall. The total death roll for the City and its adjoining parishes was never accurately calculated. According to the Mortality Bills it reached nearly sixty-nine thousand but there seems every likelihood that it was at least double that number. Never again was London to be scourged by such a catastrophic epidemic and it has often been assumed that the reason lay in the cleansing effect of the Great Fire which followed a year later. But G. M. Trevelyan, the historian, suggests that the more probable explanation was 'an obscure revolution in the animal world; about this period the modern brown rat extirpated and replaced the medieval black rat, and the brown rat was not a carrier of the plague-flea to nearly the same extent as its predecessor'.

The Great Fire of London started at around two in the morning of Sunday, 2 September 1666, in the premises of Thomas Farynor, the King's baker, in Pudding Lane near London Bridge. It spread rapidly, aided by a north-east wind, and soon it was devouring acre upon acre of timbered buildings. Most of the City streets were narrow, with the top storeys of many houses almost touching the tops of those on the opposite side, and the timber was summer-dry.

Fires in London were commonplace but it quickly became evident that this was of a character beyond anything previously experienced. King Charles and his brother, the Duke of York, immediately went to the aid of the ill-equipped firefighters and earned the City Fathers' admiration for their personal bravery. But Charles's mother, Henrietta Maria, hastily left her home at Somerset House in the Strand and went up-river to Hampton Court; and, when it seemed possible that the blaze might reach Whitehall, the King ordered the removal of some of his furniture and other valuables to the palace. (In the event the fire stopped well short of Whitehall.)

The fire lasted for five days and virtually destroyed the whole of the City between the Tower and the Temple, taking with it eighty-seven of the ninety-seven parish churches, most of the magnificent Livery Companies' Halls and old St Paul's. More than thirteen thousand houses were reduced to ashes and nearly two hundred thousand people left homeless. The total damage was estimated at £10 million, although that figure certainly by no means represented the full cost.

From Hampton Court Henrietta Maria could plainly see the vast pall of smoke that hung over the ruined City for, as the diarist Evelyn estimated, it eventually spread out to a length of fifty miles. Fortunately the loss of life was surprisingly small – only six people, according to the official figures, and they included a housemaid trapped by the original outbreak in the Pudding Lane bakery. By some quirk of the flames Samuel Pepys's house in Seething Lane escaped unharmed.

As time passed and London was rebuilt and work began on Sir Christopher Wren's new St Paul's Cathedral – it took thirty-four years to complete – Charles became no more than a fleeting visitor to Hampton Court.

Distinguished guests were still entertained there and often regaled by one of the least civilised of the royal 'sports' – a form of deer-baiting. Four or five deer would be trapped in a large net in the park and a pack of dogs, known as 'teasers', unleashed to worry them. As the excited dogs yelped and leapt at the net the enclosed deer charged wildly about, disorientated by fear. Spectators laid wagers

*The Great Fire of London, 1666. From Hampton Court the fifty-mile-long pall of smoke was clearly visible. Charles and his brother, the Duke of York, earned the citizens' admiration by staying in town to help fight the blaze.*

on which dogs would nip the deer and how often – all of this, one visitor afterwards wrote, to everyone's 'great diversion'. When the spectators had tired of the proceedings the deer would be removed to safety, except for one or two young ones on whom the dogs would be permitted to pounce for the purpose of 'blooding'.

It was towards the end of his reign, and at Hampton Court, that Charles learned of the alleged complicity of his eldest bastard son, the Duke of Monmouth, in the so-called Rye House Plot to assassinate the King and the Duke of York. The plotters were a group of extremists angered by the defeat in the House of Lords of the Parliamentary Bill to exclude James, Duke of York, from the accession

*Charles II keeps an assignment with Nell Gwyn. The eavesdropping figure in the background is the diarist John Evelyn who, like his colleague, Samuel Pepys, was seldom short of colourful material.*

because of his Roman Catholicism. The plot took its name from the house at Hoddesdon, in Hertfordshire, close to which the murders were to have been committed.

Monmouth, who was by then a handsome, sensual man of thirty, denied any involvement and probably was innocent. He was one of Charles's twelve surviving illegitimate offspring. Lady Castlemaine was the mother of five of the other children (given the family name of Fitzroy) and Nell Gwyn of two. Altogether seven mothers bore children fathered by the King.

Charles II died at a little before noon on 6 February 1685 in the Palace of Whitehall and aged fifty-four. On his deathbed he took the crucial step for which Queen Catherine had so long prayed – he embraced the Catholic faith. His last thoughts, however, were of two of his mistresses. He asked after Louise de Keroualle, Duchess of Portsmouth, mother of his son, Charles Lennox, Duke of Richmond, and whispered: 'I have always loved her.' And he uttered those famous, final words about Nell Gwyn: 'Do not let poor Nelly starve.'

Queen Catherine, who had been unable to give her husband an heir, fled in tears and later sent a message begging his forgiveness. Charles opened his dimming eyes and replied: 'Alas, poor woman! She asks my pardon! I beg hers with all my heart.'

The fatal moments dragged slowly by and, shortly before his breathing ceased, Charles looked at those around him and apologised. 'I am sorry to be so long dying,' he said.

*Charles II's last Sunday, as imagined by the nineteenth-century painter, William Powell Frith. Soon afterwards, on his death-bed, the King consoled his wife by embracing the Catholic faith, but his final, spoken thoughts were of two of his mistresses.*

*James II (1633–1701) with his first wife, Ann Hyde. Their second daughter, Anne, was eventually to become Quee*

# 9

# *The Embattled Years*

## JAMES II

THE NEW KING, THE FORMER DUKE OF YORK whom so many people had
wanted to exclude from the throne, became James II. He was fifty-one,
arrogant, self-opinionated and an avowed Catholic. The future of the
realm hinged on the manner in which he would behave towards the
Protestants but his critics were disarmed by his first major pronouncement: 'I have been reported to be a man for arbitrary power, but that
is not the only story has been made of me, and I shall make it my
endeavour to preserve this government both in Church and State as it
is now by law established.'

An allowance of close on £2 million a year was voted to the new
King by a Parliament ready to believe him when he said he would
keep his religious opinions private. And there was no immediate
outcry when James breached his undertaking by publicly celebrating
Mass.

So far as the official records show, James did not visit Hampton
Court during his short reign. The swift passage of events afforded him
little time for leisure or relaxation.

On 11 June 1685, the handsome young Duke of Monmouth,
Charles II's illegitimate son by Lucy Walters, and James II's nephew,
landed with a small armed force at the Dorset port of Lyme Regis. He
arrived proclaiming James as a usurper and quickly rallied local
support around his standard. He marched around the west country,
building up his army to around seven thousand men, and taking the
title of 'King Monmouth'.

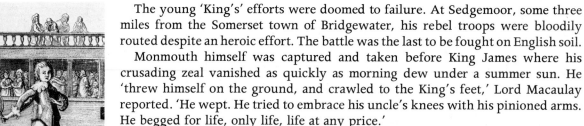

*James, Duke of York, son of King James and Mary of Modena, who later became known as the Old Pretender. He was a tennis enthusiast.*

The young 'King's' efforts were doomed to failure. At Sedgemoor, some three miles from the Somerset town of Bridgewater, his rebel troops were bloodily routed despite an heroic effort. The battle was the last to be fought on English soil.

Monmouth himself was captured and taken before King James where his crusading zeal vanished as quickly as morning dew under a summer sun. He 'threw himself on the ground, and crawled to the King's feet,' Lord Macaulay reported. 'He wept. He tried to embrace his uncle's knees with his pinioned arms. He begged for life, only life, life at any price.'

James could not afford to be merciful and Monmouth was carried off to the Tower. At the end he recovered his dignity and on the scaffold announced: 'I come here not to speak but to die. I die a Protestant of the Church of England.'

He had given the executioner six guineas as an inducement to do his work swiftly and cleanly. But the 'reward' was to no avail. The severing of the head was a grisly, botched business. The first blow of the axe made only a minor cut and the axeman struck again and again and was forced to conclude his sickening task by taking a knife to separate head from body. Spectators, outraged by the incompetent savagery, pressed forward and dipped their handkerchiefs in Monmouth's blood. In that instant, on cruel Tower Hill, they had shown James that the thirty-six-year-old Duke was their Protestant martyr.

In a malignant gesture of retribution, James sent the monstrous, drunken Judge Jeffreys to the west country to 'try' those of Monmouth's supporters who had been taken prisoner. The result was the notorious 'Bloody Assize', a fiendish mockery of justice in which three hundred and twenty people were hanged and eight hundred and forty-one were transported to the West Indies as slaves.

From his place on the Bench the unspeakable Jeffreys, swore, made coarse jokes and screamed abuse at defence witnesses. A woman, who had done no more than express admiration for Monmouth, was sentenced to be whipped through every market town in Dorset. For a similar offence a boy was ordered to be imprisoned for seven years and every year, for each of those seven years, to be flogged through those same towns.

Encouraged by the defeat of the Monmouth rebellion, James openly set about the restoration of Catholicism as the official religion of the realm. His actions were a direct challenge to Parliament and the Constitution, and the two political groups, Whigs and Tories, united against him.

In June 1688, James's wife, the Italian-born Mary of Modena, gave birth to a son, James Francis Edward Stuart. The news alarmed the King's opponents for here was a living possibility that the Catholic Stuarts could rule in perpetuity. The time for action had come. Princess Mary, King James's daughter, was married to the Dutch Protestant, Prince William of Orange, and she and her husband were invited to London.

The outcome was what is sometimes called 'the Glorious Revolution' of 1688. On 5 November Prince William landed with his Protestant army at Torbay in Devon. On that vast natural anchorage, its shorelines then dotted with a mere handful of farmworkers' and fishermens' huts, rode some four hundred ships. And from them, in the wake of the Prince, fourteen thousand armed men poured ashore – Dutchmen, Swedes, Danes, Prussians, English, Swiss and Scots.

The little groups of locals, gathered hesitantly at a distance, gaped at the great array of glittering helmets, at the Swedish cavalrymen in their black armour, the bearded Swiss infantrymen and especially at the black-faced slaves from Guiana,

*Judge Jeffreys. The dreaded Lord Chief Justice who presided over the so-called Bloody Assize from which hundreds of prisoners were sent to be hanged, drawn and quartered or exiled to the West Indies.*

attending the two hundred English gentlemen led by the Earl of Macclesfield.

In the midst of the throng, mounted on a white charger, rode the Prince himself, a pale, slender man with a high forehead and eagle-bright eyes. Beside his horse trotted forty footmen and immediately behind came riders bearing between them a banner emblazoned with the words of the cause for which William had been summoned: 'The Protestant religion and the liberties of England'.

As William and his army advanced towards London, James sent his Queen and their infant son away to the Continent and shortly afterwards followed them. His reign had collapsed in ignominy but he had not betrayed his faith and he had pursued policies which he believed were the best for his people. Cruel things were done in his name but greater cruelty has been committed in the exercise of power, not the least of it in our own times.

Initially it was proposed that William should rule as Regent, acting in place of the self-exiled James, But this would have been an unsettled and unsatisfactory regime and eventually the issue was brilliantly solved by the Marquis of Halifax. He advanced the proposal that William and his wife should govern jointly. And so it was that there began a new era – of William III and Mary II.

*William III, called William of Orange (1650–1702), landing at Torbay on 5 November 1688. He soon set about rebuilding parts of the palace with the sad result that some of the original Tudor structure was lost.*

William III as pictured by the Court painter Sir Godfrey Kneller. The King was not quite the charmer Kneller makes him appear. Behind his back women courtiers spoke of him as 'that low Dutch bear.'

Mary II (1662–1694) who shared the throne with her husband, William III. With the help of an advisory council she ruled during William's absence abroad — a testing time from which she emerged with credit.

# *10*
# *The*
# *Middle Years*

## WILLIAM III & MARY II

TEN DAYS AFTER THEIR CORONATION the new King and Queen paid their first visit to Hampton Court and, true to the form of his predecessors, William immediately fell in love with the place. The flatness of the land was a comforting reminder of Holland and, of course, the estate even had its own canal which had been dug by order of Charles II.

In any case, William had developed an immediate aversion to London. Its smog generated by the smoke of coal fires pouring from 200,000 chimneys and mingling with the river mists, inflamed his asthma and he hated the city's filthy streets. Westminster was altogether too damp for him and he found, as Wolsey had at the very beginning, that Hampton Court was remarkably dry despite its riverside site. From the outset, however, the new King looked around him with critical eyes. Pleased as he was with the palace, he could already visualise possible changes and this particular reign is of great significance in our story for, during its course, the greater part of the old Tudor state apartments was to be be pulled down and a new Hampton Court would arise.

In March 1689, a month after their initial inspection visit, William and Mary returned to the palace for a longer stay and this time Mary, too, was captivated. One of her ladies, the great Sarah Churchill, Duchess of Marlborough, recalled that the Queen ran about 'looking into every closet and conveniency, and turning up the quilts upon the beds, as people do when they come into an inn, and with no other sort of concern in her appearance but such as they express'.

As others noted, William and Mary were an odd pair. Their marriage, in London in November 1675, had been arranged for political reasons and, when told about it by her father, Mary was reported to have 'wept all that afternoon and the following day'. She was twelve years younger than he and William treated her coldly and disdainfully and soon proved unfaithful – although he was to warm to her later when he recognised the respect she had gained from their British subjects.

Mary was an attractive woman (one woman friend described her as 'beautiful as an angel') with an oval face, a full mouth, almond-shaped eyes and dark curls. She was also intelligent and despite the early, trying years of her marriage, her natural affectionate warmth remained unimpaired.

William, on the other hand, was an unattractive personality, coarse-mannered and boorish, almost totally ignorant of literature and science and particularly churlish towards women. Behind his back the ladies of the royal Court whispered of him as 'that low Dutch bear'.

He was at his happiest when fighting a battle or hunting and he seemed uncomfortable and frustrated when out of the saddle. Even his great hero-worshipper, the historian Lord Macaulay, was obliged to acknowledge William's notoriously bad temper and wrote that 'when he was really enraged the first outbreak of his passion was terrible. It was indeed scarcely safe to approach him.'

His table manners, too, were often revolting and he would dig wolfishly into his food as though desperate to nourish his frail body. Long remembered at Hampton Court was the occasion on which he dined with his daughter, Princess Anne, who was pregnant at the time with the future Duke of Gloucester. Anne's appetite was greatly whetted by a plate of the first succulent green peas of the season but, before she had a chance of being served, William snatched the dish away and slobberingly devoured the lot.

In his very earliest days at Hampton Court, William set critical tongues wagging by his petulant refusal to touch those poor suffering wretches who came to him in hope of relief from the disease known as King's Evil. From time immemorial monarchs had performed that ceremony in which they touched the ulcers and swellings caused by the scrofula and placed around each sufferer's neck a white ribbon to which a gold coin was attached. As that was being done a clergyman would pronounce the incantation, 'They shall lay their hands on the sick, and they shall recover.' (Tradition had it that those who lost or sold the gold coins broke out again in fresh ulcers. And Charles II was especially supposed to have been endowed with miraculous healing powers.)

William would have none of it. 'It is a silly superstition,' he growled. 'Give the poor creatures some money and let them go.' He was no doubt right about the basic foolishness of the business; it was his marked insensitivity to people's expectations, however misguided those might be, that was remembered of him.

He showed a similar lack of respect for others, and particularly upset church-men, by forbidding the use of music in the chapel and insisting that divine service be said and not sung. And he obstinately followed the Dutch custom of wearing his hat during the service.

The King's poor constitution may well have played some part in shaping his graceless attitudes. Apart from his other ailments, he suffered from interminable headaches and could sleep only when his head was propped up by several pillows.

William's determination to re-shape the palace also had about it an element of disdain for history and tradition. It may well seem tragic to us that much of the

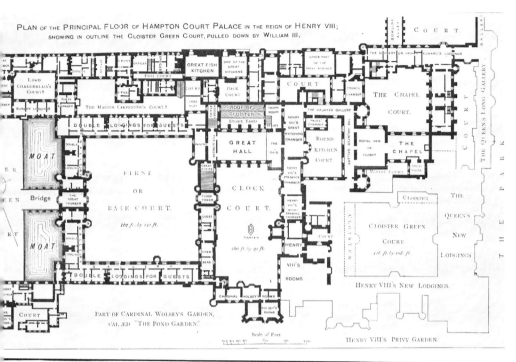

*The main floor-plan of the palace, as it was in Henry VIII's time, draws attention to William's lack of respect for tradition. For it was he who demolished Cloister Green Court shown here.*

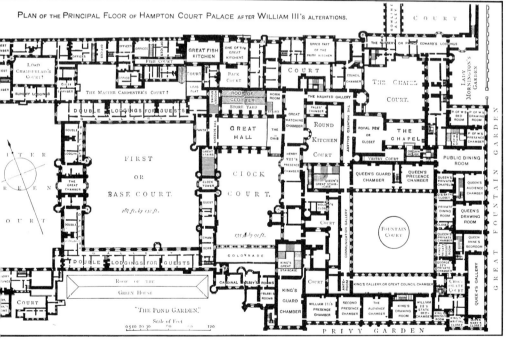

*The palace as William 're-organised' it. Ernest Law, the nineteenth-century historian who lived at Hampton Court, said the new buildings created 'an impression of pretentious meanness rather than splendour or beauty.*

original Tudor Hampton Court was to be lost. But the King wanted change and change there would have to be.

The commission for designing the new buildings was given to Sir Christopher Wren and the architect's mind at once directed itself to the prospect of creating a new Versailles. Unfortunately, that was not entirely a happy choice. Great as he

*Sir Christopher Wren, by Kneller. The great architect wanted to build a new Versailles at Hampton Court but that was not really his style. He was not helped by the King's fussy interference.*

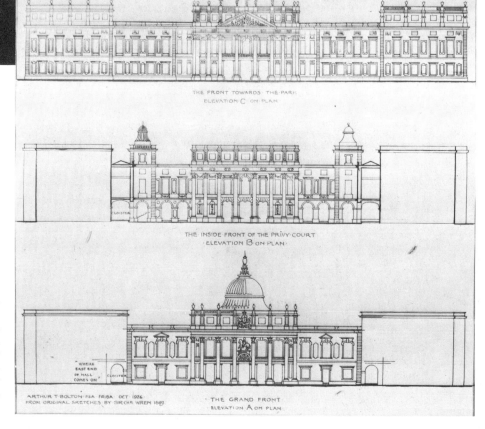

THE FIRST DESIGN FOR HAMPTON COURT PALACE · SIR CHRIS WREN · ARCHITECT · 1689
ELEVATIONS · PRINCIPAL · FRONTS · SCALE · TWENTY · FEET · TO · ONE · INCH ·

THE FRONT TOWARDS THE PARK
ELEVATION C ON PLAN

THE INSIDE FRONT OF THE PRIVY COURT
ELEVATION B ON PLAN

ARTHUR T BOLTON · PSA · FRIBA · OCT · 1926
FROM ORIGINAL SKETCHES BY SIR CHS WREN 1689

THE GRAND FRONT
ELEVATION A ON PLAN

*Wren's original design for William's 'new' palace. Wren wanted to use only Portland stone but had to include some softer material when the French blockade of the English Channel stopped stone-carrying ships sailing from Portland.*

was, Versailles was not really his style and, as things turned out, the formulation of his plans was hindered rather than helped by William's peevish, know-all interference. The King was an enthusiastic amateur architect and constantly insisted on putting Sir Christopher 'right'.

So, in the course of time, some of the lovely Tudor courts were demolished. The eventual plan called for 'the line of Long Water and the side avenues to converge on the centre point of a new East Front which was to be three hundred feet long. The new buildings were to be rectangular, the great Fountain Garden would be created and so, too, would the quadrangle to be known as Fountain Court. The buildings on the north and south sides of the Court were each to be one hundred and sixteen feet long, on the east side one hundred and ten feet and one inch, and on the west side one hundred and nine feet. As Ernest Law, the palace's nineteenth-century historian, pointed out, the reasons for the disparity in dimensions are not clear.

The development of the parks and gardens begun by Charles II was continued by William whose adviser, George London, had been a pupil of John Rose, Charles's gardener.

Work on William's buildings did not proceed without incident. In the late autumn of 1689 a newly-built wall fell down killing two workmen and injuring

*Final years of the first phase. The palace as it was before the Wren-William alterations and showing the Long Water.*

several others. The King called for an inquiry and Christopher Wren was told to send a written report to the Lords of the Treasury setting out his explanation for the accident. To his great annoyance, Wren discovered that a separate, 'rival' report had been prepared by William Talman, the Comptroller of Works who was also an architect and the builder of Chatsworth, the country seat of the Duke of Devonshire.

All the ingredients for professional jealousy were present and since Talman's stipend was 6s 10d a day, as against Wren's 4s 10d, the Comptroller may well have felt that he ought to exert his seniority.

In the middle of January 1690, Wren and Talman appeared together before the Lords of the Treasury and the encounter resulted in what now reads rather like good knock-about comedy. Their Lordships' note of the hearing records that Wren 'says the work has stood a new tryal in a hurrycane . . .' And, indeed, storm force winds had recently caused widespread damage in London and the south.

Talman, who appeared to regard that as not much of a test, declared that every stone block between the windows of the new buildings 'is crackt that one may putt his finger in'.

Enraged, Wren snapped: 'I'll putt it on this, a man cannot putt his finger in ye cracks!'

'No,' snorted Talman, 'because you've had 'em stopt!'

It is small wonder that their Lordships abandoned all hope of acquiring reliable evidence from two such brawling witnesses and decided to look for independent and impartial surveyors to rule on the safety of the work. To Wren's huge satisfaction and Talman's chagrin, the independent surveyors pronounced the work good and sound and the construction of the new buildings was allowed to proceed.

While work continued, Queen Mary was found accommodation in the palace's Water Gallery. Wren himself supervised the decorations, which included painted ceilings and panels, and that maker of masterpieces, Grinling Gibbons, produced the richly carved doorways and cornices festooned with fruit and flowers in limewood. A bathroom, then known as a 'bathing closet', was fitted with a fine white marble bath.

One of the period's outstanding cabinet-makers, Gerrard Johnson, built a number of cabinets in which Mary could display her porcelain, for she was a knowledgeable collector of chinaware and first introduced the hobby to British housewives. (She was also responsible for originating British interest in the keeping and breeding of Dutch mastiffs and goldfish and of knotting – a primitive form of crochet.)

Mary was altogether an excellent needlewoman and made coverings for chairs, couches and screens. She loved gardening and helped to supervise the laying out of the new palace gardens. From such far-off places as Virginia and the Canary Islands she imported exotic plants and planted an orangery on the south front of the site. She was particularly proud of her three garden hot-houses, each fifty-five feet long, eight feet wide at the base and five feet wide at the top.

One long abiding memorial to Mary was the long arbour of wych and Scotch elm – one hundred yards long and twelve feet wide – which formed an avenue completely enclosed and roofed in by foliage. The high terrace on the west of the Privy Garden is still known as Queen Mary's Bower.

Among the special features of Mary's Water Gallery, much admired by visitors, were the famous 'Hampton Court Beauties', a series of full-length portraits by Godfrey Kneller, the German-born painter, of the Queen's favourite ladies-in-waiting. Not everyone thought it tactful of Mary to make such a public display of just a select few of her ladies and her confidante, Lady Dorchester, asked: 'Madam, if the King were to ask for the portraits of all the wits in his court, would not the rest think that he called them fools?'

But Mary was unmoved by such criticism and Kneller was knighted for his work and presented with a gold chain and medal worth £300.

Of the original twelve portraits eight now remain and can be seen in the First Presence Chamber. There, looking extraordinarily young and innocent and leaning nonchalantly against a garden pedestal, is Lady Diana de Vere, Duchess of St Albans, whose husband, the 1st Duke, Charles Beauclerk, was the illegitimate son of Charles II and Nell Gwyn.

(Charles is supposed to have overheard Nell call to the infant boy: 'Come hither, you little bastard, and speak to your father.' When he protested, 'Nay, Nellie, do not give the child such a name,' she replied: 'Your Majesty has given me no other name by which I may call him.' Whereupon King Charles named the boy Beauclerk.)

The other 'Beauties' are: Lady Mary Bentinck, Countess of Wessex; Carey Fraser, Countess of Peterborough; Lady Isabella Bennet, Duchess of Grafton;

*Lady Isabella Bennet, Duchess of Grafton, one of the Hampton Court 'Beauties' painted by Sir Godfrey Kneller.*

Lady Mary Compton, Countess of Dorset; Lady Middleton; and Miss Pitt, afterwards Mrs Scroop. The final portrait, of Sarah, Duchess of Marlborough, was removed from the Water Gallery after Sarah's husband, the 1st Duke (and ancestor of the late Sir Winston Churchill) had temporarily quarrelled with William. In 1700 the Water Gallery was pulled down because it obstructed the view of the new buildings.

During the summer of 1690 Mary was appointed Regent for the duration of William's absence in Ireland in pursuit of James II. She was to be advised by a Council of Nine, made up of four Whigs and five Tories, to whom William declared: 'She wants experience but I hope that by choosing you to be her counsellors I have supplied that defect. I put my kingdom into your hands. Nothing foreign or domestic shall be kept secret from you. I implore you to be diligent and to be united.'

But trouble began for Mary and her Council immediately after William's departure on 4 June. A powerful French fleet of some eighty ships appeared in the Channel and sailed slowly and menacingly along the south-west coast, off Devon and Dorset. A wave of hope washed over the Jacobites, the group in England striving for the restoration of the crown to James. For England the moment was fraught with great danger and for Mary there was a special, personal test, for her uncle, Henry Hyde, 2nd Earl of Clarendon, was a leading Jacobite.

She faced the test with stern resolution. Her Council advised her that, for safety's sake, she should order the arrest of prominent Jacobites but it shied away from openly accusing Clarendon. Mary recognised the omission, accepted the responsibility that had fallen upon her and responded immediately. 'I know and everyone here knows as well as I, that there is too much against my Lord Clarendon to leave him out,' she told the Council. And so her uncle was sent to the Tower along with the rest.

The eyes of England were turned towards the sea where things went as badly as could have been feared. The French defeated the combined English and Dutch fleets off Beachy Head and so many Dutch ships were damaged that the allied commander, the English admiral Lord Torrington, ordered their destruction. The rest of the warships received the signal to flee to the sanctuary of the Thames where they threw off the pursuing enemy by hauling up the buoys marking the river's navigable channels. But the seamen's spirits were soggy with the humiliation of defeat and everywhere was heard the bitter comment that 'the Dutch had the honour, the French had the advantage, and the English the shame.'

Torrington's name was execrated. He had already earned a reputation as a fop and a womaniser, beguiled more by the pleasures of the bouncing mattress than the duties of the hazardous ocean. Even when boarding his flagship in peacetime he was usually surrounded by a bevy of courtesans and, said Lord Macaulay, 'there was scarcely an hour of the day or night when he was not under the influence of claret.' He was, in any case, so often absent from sea that his naval ratings made play with his name and mocked him as 'Lord Tarry-in-Town'.

The Beachy Head disaster brought the kingdom closer to the threat of foreign domination than at any time since the Norman Conquest. Invasion seemed imminent and suddenly there was a swift closing of ranks and a new-found unity among the people. In London ten thousand men sprang to arms and the City promised the instant raising of a further one thousand dragoons, six regiments of foot, and a regiment of horse – and all at its own expense. In the countryside farm labourers hung up their scythes and billhooks and paraded with the pikes of the militia.

Then, as quickly as the French had blown them in from the Channel, the storm clouds cleared. Word reached a cheering, bell-ringing capital that in Ireland, on 11 July, King William had gained a decisive victory at the Battle of the Boyne and King James had sped back to France.

Lord Torrington was subsequently court-martialled – appropriately aboard a warship, the frigate *Kent*, anchored in the Thames – but acquitted. Nevertheless, one of King William's first actions, when he returned home, was to sack the admiral.

Against the background of the great crisis, Hampton Court presented its own rather particular symbol of English optimism. For the new construction work had gone on despite the shortage of money caused by the military campaign in Ireland and the threat of invasion at home. And in the twelve months up to April 1691 the cost had already reached £54,484. Moreover, the presence of the French off the Dorset coast had cut off shipments of Portland stone and so, in many parts of the structure, less durable Bath stone had to be used. (It was replaced by Portland stone two hundred years later.)

By use of red brick for the surface of the walls, intermingled with Portland stone – obtained before the arrival of the French – for windows, doorways and other decorative parts, Wren did his best to retain something of the original Tudor 'flavour'. But Ernest Law complained that it produced 'an impression of pretentious meanness rather than splendour or beauty'.

The East Front, facing the Great Fountain Garden and intended by Wren and William as the main part of the new palace, was more lavishly decorated, the central area being faced with stone, highly ornamented and carved. The royal apartments were on the first floor and the whole development necessitated the destruction of two hundred yards of the Long Water at its western end.

The exterior of the South Front, overlooking the Privy Garden, was less lavishly decorated but among its points of interest are the four plain Corinthian columns supporting an entablature and bearing the Latin inscription, *GVLIELMVS ET MARIA R.R.F.* ('*Rex Regina Facerunt*') – 'William and Mary, King and Queen, built this.'

Among Wren's other notable features is the colonnade in the Clock Court which consists of seven pairs of Ionic pillars supporting an entablature and balustrade. Above the middle pair of pillars stand two large carved stone vessels and below are ornaments of foliage, masks and trophies of war.

The colonnade is eighty-nine feet four inches long and twenty-seven feet nine inches to the top of the parapet. Grinling Gibbons carved both wood and stone in the new apartments and other carving was undertaken by Caius Gabriel Cibber, the son of the King of Denmark's cabinet-maker and also the father of Colley Cibber, the celebrated actor and dramatist.

Iron gates, and magnificent screens of wrought iron which enclosed the palace gardens until the 1850s, were designed by the Frenchman, Jean Tijou, and some have survived. Each screen was ten feet six inches high, thirteen feet four inches wide, and represented some of the finest decorative ironwork ever produced in Britain. The craftsman who carried out the work, to Tijou's specifications, was Huntingdon Shaw of Nottingham.

(In 1703, nearly two years after King William's death, Tijou was still petitioning for payment of £1,889 1s 6¼d and there is a legend that Shaw died – at Hampton Court in October 1710 – of disappointment at not having been paid a single penny for his work.)

With William at home once more, life in the older part of the palace continued on its normal dreary routine while workmen scurried about their tasks on the new sections. The King himself was as restless as ever when there was no immediate military adventure to arouse his enthusiasm and even meal-times were dull affairs for he and Mary now ate only sparingly. Left-over food, and there was always plenty of it, went to members of the household.

The breakfast fare was usually new-laid eggs and bacon, washed down by drinking-chocolate imported from Holland. But the other main meals of the day did become more substantial than usual when guests were being entertained.

Dinner was still the name given to the midday meal and guests would generally have a first-course choice of capons, pullets, chicken and partridges or boiled beef, followed by turkey or goose. The second course would be pigeon or pheasant, or partridges or quail and, occasionally, 'Hen pye'. Sometimes, too, there would be sirloin of beef. Desserts often included morels (an edible fungus), truffles, jam tarts, jelly or asparagus. Supper dishes were pigeon or roast mutton or veal, followed by capons, pullets or snipe, followed by duckling or lamb. Dessert was sweetbreads, artichokes or jam tarts. On Fridays and Saturdays, and throughout Lent, fish was served and there was always a plentiful supply of claret, Rhenish wine and ale.

William's table-talk was never sparkling, except when an astute guest steered the conversation around to the subject of Holland, the country for which the King never lost his home-sickness. And at times there were events in William's life that could bring no cheer to a dinner or a supper.

One of his darkest deeds that taints the history of Hampton Court was the King's signing, in February 1692, of the order that led to the notorious Glencoe massacre.

The Highland Clans of Scotland, openly rebellious against William and Mary, had been told that they would be pardoned for their opposition if they swore oaths of allegiance to the crown by 31 December 1691. First through hesitation, and then through delays caused by bad weather, one Chief, MacIain of the MacDonalds of Glencoe, arrived for the oath-taking in the town of Inverary six days late. Yet, despite the fact that MacIain *did* give his pledge of loyalty even if it was technically a week overdue, William authorised action to be taken against him. As a result, royal troops marched to Glencoe, quartered themselves on the MacDonalds, feigning friendship, and then arose at dead of night and cold-bloodedly murdered men, women and children. Many managed to escape but among those killed was MacIain the Chief.

Lord Macaulay tried to argue away his hero's guilt on two possible grounds: either William did not intend such a crime or he was so involved in Continental politics that he had little time to attend to English affairs and even less to Scottish. But although Mary was horrified by Glencoe and wanted the offenders brought to justice, no one was punished. The King even went so far as personally to exonerate the Viscount of Stair, Secretary of State for Scotland, who had said of the MacDonalds that they were 'the only popish clan in the kingdom, and it will be popular to take a severe course with them'.

Poor Mary, whose attitude to the Glencoe tragedy shamed her husband's,

had not long to live and was destined never to occupy the new State Apartments at Hampton Court.

Death came to her, at Kensington Palace, on 28 December 1694. She had fallen ill of what was at first thought to be measles but quickly revealed itself as smallpox. The disease, always one of the great traditional killers until the discovery of vaccine, was particularly widespread in England that year. And, in a typically considerate gesture, Mary ordered that all her servants who had not had smallpox, and, therefore, enjoyed no immunity, should at once leave Kensington.

Throughout Mary's illness William slept in a room close to the Queen's bedroom on the campbed he had used in his military campaigns. And the King, who had begun married life by ignoring his 'arranged' bride, was now distraught at the prospect of her end. He told Gilbert Burnet, the Scottish-born Bishop of Salisbury whose own second wife had also died of smallpox: 'There is no hope. I was the happiest man on earth; now I am the most miserable. She had no fault –

*The body of Queen Mary II lying in state at Kensington Palace. Public mourning at the death of the Queen was lavish and moving, and both Houses of Parliament followed the hearse to Westminster Abbey.*

none. You knew her well, but you could not know, nobody but myself could know, her goodness.'

A few minutes before the Queen died, William was carried from her bedside convulsed by spasms of grief so severe that the assembled Privy Councillors thought for a time that he also was dying. Subsequent events testified to the fact that there was no counterfeit about William's heartbreaking sorrow.

Up to Mary's last moments he had retained as his mistress Elizabeth Villiers, born around 1657, cousin of that very same Barbara Villiers who had been Charles II's mistress. Macaulay said that Elizabeth, 'though destitute of personal attractions, and disfigured by a hideous squint, possessed talents which well fitted her to partake his [William's] cares'. (However, a fellow writer, Jonathan Swift, described her as the wisest woman he ever knew.)

As soon as Mary was dead William was filled with remorse about a letter once sent to him by the Queen (and which he had ignored), begging him to end his liaison with Elizabeth. He now, at last, when it was too late to bring any comfort to his departed wife, resolved to act upon that plea. He brought his affair with Elizabeth to an end and a year later helped to arrange her marriage to Lord George Hamilton, who was shortly afterwards created Earl of Orkney.

The public mourning in London for Mary's funeral was lavish and moving. Members of both Houses of Parliament, preceded by their maces, followed the hearse to Westminster Abbey – a unique Parliamentary tribute to a sovereign – and her remains were laid in the Abbey's Henry VII Chapel.

William's memorial to his dead Queen was an extension to Greenwich Palace, made in order to convert it into a hospital for seamen and something which Mary herself had wished for. Christopher Wren undertook the design work without charge.

Now that he was alone, William showed no desire to return to Hampton Court and the development work there might have been neglected altogether but for an event that occurred on 4 January 1690.

The Palace of Whitehall was destroyed by fire said to have been started by the burning of clothes hung too close to a charcoal brazier by a laundress who was herself killed in the blaze. For a time there were fears that the flames would consume Inigo Jones's great Banqueting Hall, in front of which Charles I was beheaded, but although some of its supporting columns were blackened by smoke the building was otherwise unharmed.

William was accused by some of the Jacobites of having plotted to destroy Whitehall as a means of removing further traces of the Stuarts, and certainly he shed no tears over the fire. He wrote privately that 'the loss is less to me than it would be to another person, for I cannot live there.' He also now had a good, practical reason for returning to Hampton Court and continuing his personal supervision of the reconstruction work.

On 28 April 1699 Wren presented an estimate of £6,800 for completing work on the King's rooms in the new apartments. These were all on the south, or Privy Garden, side of the palace and included the Presence Chamber – 'to be fitted for Hangings, with marble in the chimney,' said Wren – the King's Drawing Room and the Great Bed Chamber. (With the addition of two small closets, or studies, the actual cost of the work came out at £7,092 19s 0½d.) In addition there were charges by Antonio Verrio, the Italian-born decorative painter, and by Grinling Gibbons for his carvings in each of the rooms. Gibbons's leaves, flower petals, birds and musical instruments delineated in limewood remain miracles of the master craftsman's work.

The theme of Verrio's painted ceiling in the King's Bedroom, as visitors can still see, is Sleep, represented by the mythological deities including Morpheus, God of Dreams, Somnus and his attendants, and Endymion, the Shepherd, and his devoted admirer, Selene, the Moon.

But, beyond any doubt, one of the most noble features of the rooms is the King's Staircase, leading up to the first floor State apartments – forty feet high, forty-three feet long and thirty-five feet wide with ceilings and walls painted by Verrio and depicting the gods of Roman mythology at work and play. No one looking at that staircase can fail to be impressed, but down the ages critical opinion of the artistic merit of Verrio's work has been variable. The diarist John Evelyn described the paintings as masterpieces, but Horace Walpole said that Verrio had 'spoiled the work on principle'. Verrio was, indeed, a Catholic who had at first refused to accept a commission from Protestant King William.

On his return to the palace William very soon was bustling and buzzing around his architect, his master-masons and carpenters, advising there, interfering here, always knowing better than the professionals. He personally decided the size and water output of the new fountains – for which the lead pipes cost £987 14s – hovered over the creation of the famous Wilderness, converted from an orchard and laid out by his gardeners, London and Wise. And he showed especial interest and concern about the construction of the Maze on its site of just under a third of an acre.

*An early plan of the Maze. At the time it was laid out there was a European craze for such novelties which were usually called 'labyrinths' and were derived from a medieval form of religious penance.*

The Hampton Court Maze is, of course, the most widely-known feature of the palace, even to those who have never seen it. When it was created mazes were popular novelty features but their origin goes back to the Middle Ages, when they were designed as forms of penance for those who failed to keep their vows to make a pilgrimage to the Holy Land. The penitents were obliged to crawl along the

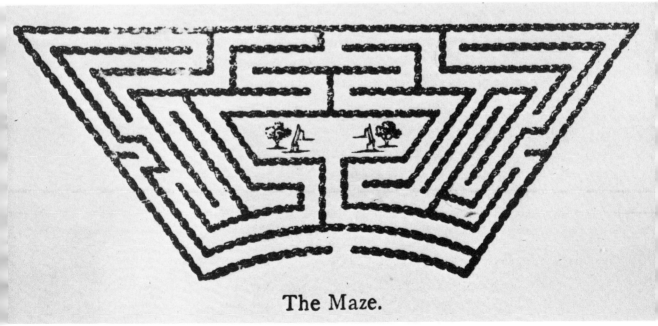

The Maze.

'puzzle' pathways on their hands and knees, reciting prayers. The difficulties they encountered by losing their way and finding no outlet were meant to symbolise the trials and tribulations faced by all who sought to follow the way of Christ. In their seventeenth-century 'novelty' form, mazes were more usually referred to as Labyrinths.

By June 1699, when William left for a visit to Holland (expressing the hope that the new palace would be completed in time for his return), construction work had reached its peak and more than four hundred men were being employed. The King arrived back in England on the morning of 4 November, landing at Margate. London was busily putting the finishing touches to the public welcome it had planned for the following day, the thirteenth anniversary of his original landing in Devon; but William was tired and neither his health nor his spirits were in fit states to endure tiring official receptions. Consequently, having spent the night of his return at Greenwich, he by-passed London and went straight to Hampton Court.

With him he carried a report on progress at the palace submitted by Talman, Wren's 'rival', who could not forbear to add a 'plug' for himself: 'The five roomes are almost finished, the great stone Stairs is done, and the Iron-work putt up, the Gallery for the Cartoons of Raphell [Raphael] is soe forward that I shall fix up the pictures in a week. The King's great Bedchamber and two closetts are in hand that his Majesty will find I have made use of my time, for it proves a greater work than I expected, and I hope it will be to his Majesty's satisfaction.'

King William found it all very much to his satisfaction. He walked around inspecting the new apartments and declared that 'for good proportions, state and convenience jointly', they were 'not paralleled by any palace in Europe'. Among many other things he was delighted with the work of a gunsmith named Harris in arranging a display of 3,141 historic weapons in the great, sixty-feet long King's Guard Chamber and granted him a royal pension for his efforts.

There still remained some work to be finished and Talman submitted estimates of £5,514 3s 1d for the completion of several rooms adjoining the King's apartments, including the Communication Gallery which formed a link with what had been the Queen's suite of rooms. Further improvement plans, some of them involving developments in Bushy Park, pushed the estimates up to £10,864, although the vigilant Board of Works cut the amount back to £8,933 11s. In a gesture respectful to his civil servants, William ordered Talman 'not in any way' to exceed that approved sum.

Pleased, as he so clearly was, with his new palace, the King was given little opportunity to enjoy it in peace and tranquility. Politically things had turned sour for the man who, as Prince of Orange, had been hailed as England's deliverer from tyranny. There were constant wrangles with Parliament and violent clashes between Whigs and Tories.

The Whigs were for maintaining the war between the kingdom and France that had rumbled on for seven years. The Tories were for disentanglement from Continental struggles and a reduction in the size of the army. Peace, of a sort, had been concluded on 10 September 1697, with the Treaty of Ryswyk, but William urged Parliament to retain an army in the interests of long-term peace. Disarmament, however, was the national mood and the army was reduced to seven thousand men. In the kingdom's politics generally, this was an era when voters switched their allegiances back and forth – akin, in many ways, to the British

INHALING VAN S.K. MAJ. aende Westeynder brug door de C.A. EIGHS.TRAET van S. GRAVENHAGE.

RECEPTION DE SA MAIESTÉ AU ...T DU WESTVND...

pattern of the twentieth century. William felt himself so burdened by political problems that at one time he even considered abdicating; and the British Museum still preserves a manuscript draft of what he had intended as his 'farewell' speech from the throne.

Other problems dogged the King. The Jacobites had been encouraged by Mary's death to come out into the open and there was constant plotting against William's life. In one plot that came to light the proposal was to ambush the King at a ferry over the Thames at Turnham Green while he was on his way to Hampton Court.

William was also beset by a 'scandal' over a grant to his former mistress, by then the Countess of Orkney. He had bestowed upon her a portion of former Irish crown property capable of producing an income of somewhere around £4,000. But his enemies exaggerated the amount to £24,000 and there was no shortage of receptive ears.

He was accused of spending too much time at Hampton Court and causing neglect and inconvenience in public affairs. There were times when he could not

*William III enters the Hague, capital city of the Netherlands. This was really always 'home' to him. He did not much care for the English – and, in time, they lost their enthusiasm for him.*

be bothered to journey to London for meetings of his Council and his ministers were obliged to go to him at the palace. They grumbled that the round trip cost them five wasted hours. Exasperated by their complaints and mindful of the effects of smog-ridden London on his health, William asked: 'Do you wish to see me dead?' Some of them had to make an effort to silence their tongues against an affirmative reply.

In the winter of 1701 William found himself waiting uncomfortably at the palace for the outcome of a general election. There was no doubt now about the poor state of his health. He was emaciated and lacked appetite. His legs were swollen and already the grey sheen of death was showing on his face. While walking in the gardens he suddenly turned to his old friend and companion, William Bentinck, Earl of Portland, and declared he felt so weak he did not expect to live another summer.

Notes of his doctor's prescriptions still exist. As a 'fumigation for His Majesty's legs', they advised: 'Take of the Roots of Florentine Orris and Tormentil, the Tops of Southernwood, Marjoram and Thyme, Olibanum and Benjamin, of each a sufficient quantity.' Pills to be taken 'early in the morning' consisted of 'a scruple' of extract of rhubarb, six grains of resin of jalap, five grains of tartar vitriolated, 'with sufficient quantity of Balsamick Syrup'.

Due, possibly, to what might now be called psychosomatic factors, William avowed that he felt 'very well' a little time after lying with his legs in a kind of portable stove designed, so the doctors said, to cause his legs to sweat and thereby drain away some of the fluids which were the cause of the swelling.

On Tuesday, 23 December, he reluctantly left Hampton Court for foggy Kensington ready for the opening of the new Parliament in which the election had given the Tories the majority. He tried to gird himself for more assiduous attention to public duties and from then on returned to Hampton Court only on Saturdays and only for the day. Never again did he sleep at the palace.

Despite an early morning attack of giddiness on Saturday, 21 February 1702, he went to Hampton Court as usual and somehow managed to place his grossly bulbous legs astride the back of his favourite horse, Sorrel, and set off for a day's stag hunting. At noon, just as William was urging him into a gallop, Sorrel stumbled on a mole-hill and the King was thrown to the ground. He was carried into the royal apartments where a doctor immediately diagnosed a fracture of the right collar-bone which he set.

William was taken back to Kensington by coach, a journey which, not surprisingly in view of the general state of the roads, succeeded in loosening the doctor's bandaging and unsetting the bone. Upon his arrival the King was given further medical attention, his broken bone was re-set and he appeared comfortable and slept soundly the whole night through.

For a time it seemed as though he might recover but on 4 March William developed a fever and the rest of his way was downhill. He was calm and courageous and remained his usual unemotional self except for a moving declaration to those who waited by his bedside. 'You know that I never feared death,' he said. 'There have been times when I would have wished it; but now that this great prospect is opening before me, I do wish to stay here a little longer.'

It was, however, too late for wishing. On the morning of Sunday, 8 March, King William reached out for the hand of his friend, William Bentinck, pressed it against his own heart, whispered a few inaudible words and died. He was fifty-two. At the laying-out of the body the attendants found, beneath the royal nightshirt, a black silk ribbon enclosing a ring and a lock of Queen Mary's hair.

William was buried privately at midnight, the cortege winding its way slowly through London's deserted streets from Kensington to Westminster Abbey, with a waxen image of the dead King lying in the funeral coach. Only when the procession reached Westminster Palace was the coffined body placed in the hearse.

The lack of public mourning for William was in marked contrast to the genuine grief people had felt at the death of Mary. The euphoria that had attended his first coming into the realm had long ago evaporated. He had not much cared for the English and they, in turn, had come to care little for him. But the happiest of all were the Jacobites who lifted their glasses in a new toast – 'to the little gentleman in black velvet'; in other words, the mole over whose hill the King's horse had fatally stumbled.

*The most elegant highway from the palace to London has always been the Thames. Here William and Mary display themselves to the fascinated crowds as they are rowed in the royal barge to Westminster.*

*Queen Anne (1665–1741) with the young Duke of Gloucester. She had an aversion to paying her bills which entailed considerable suffering for some of the palace craftsmen.*

# II
# *The*
# *Middle Years*

## QUEEN ANNE

THE ACT OF SETTLEMENT, passed in the final year of William III's reign, decreed that the sovereign of England must be a Protestant. And so it was that the crown went to Anne, daughter of King James II and his first wife, Anne Hyde, instead of to the son born to James's second wife, Mary of Modena. That son, James Francis Edward, usually known as the Old Pretender, was, like his father, a Catholic.

At the time of her accession, in March 1702, Anne was thirty-seven. In her younger days she had been reasonably attractive but now her well-rounded cheeks were red-blotched and she suffered severely from gout. She was also worn down by endless pregnancies, many of which ended in still-births, from which no child remained alive when she ascended the throne. She had put great store in the future of her son, William, Duke of Gloucester, born at Hampton Court in 1689 but he died not quite a week after his eleventh birthday.

Anne's husband – they had married in July 1683 – was Prince George of Denmark, twelve years her senior. He was handsomely blond but slow-witted and Charles II had summed him up with the dismissive comment: 'I have tried him drunk, and I have tried him sober, and there is nothing in him.' All the same Anne was attached to him.

*Anne, who prided herself on being 'entirely English' (in contrast to her Dutch predecessor), is seen here surrounded by her Knights of the Garter.*

The new Queen was crowned at Westminster Abbey on St George's Day, 23 April 1702, wearing a gown of crimson velvet and with diamonds sparkling in her hair. But because she was afflicted by a particularly severe attack of gout she had to be carried into the Abbey, for the five-hour ceremony, in an open sedan chair. Just over a month earlier she had, pointedly, used in her first address to Parliament the sentence: 'I know my heart to be entirely English.' The words 'Entirely English' were also engraved on her Coronation medal and were taken to be a jibe at the late, Dutch-born King William.

Parliament granted Anne an annual allowance of £700,000 out of which she announced she would return £100,000 to the public funds. Despite some opposition in the House of Lords, Prince George was given a life annuity of £100,000 and made Lord Warden of the Cinque Ports.

Although Anne visited Hampton Court frequently she never stayed long at any one time. She preferred Windsor and Kensington as her principal residences. However, most of her Privy Council meetings were held at the palace, certainly during the early part of her twelve-year reign.

She completed the work left unfinished at the time of King William's death including, most notably, the superb Queen's Gallery. This room, eighty-one feet long by twenty-five feet wide, has seven tall windows overlooking the Great Fountain Garden. The handsome chimney-piece is of dark grey marble surmounted by a white marble bust of Venus and with cupids on each side. During Anne's reign the walls of this room were adorned with Andrea Mantegna's nine

16. *The King's Bedroom. The allegorical paintings on the ceiling of this room are the work of Antonio Verrio, the celebrated Italian artist. Verrio, a Catholic, had at first declined to accept a commission from the Protestant King William III.*

17. The Cartoon Gallery, built by Sir Christopher Wren to house the Raphael Cartoons – designed as patterns for tapestries – purchased by Charles I. Later, at the age of eighty-six, Wren was unceremoniously sacked from his post as Surveyor-General.

18. The Queen's Gallery, on the east side of the palace, for which Grinling Gibbons carved the cornice. This is one of the most elegant apartments at Hampton Court.

19. Procession on the river. This painting of around 1640 by an unknown artist once again underlines the importance of the Thames to Hampton Court. State barges were the water-borne equivalents of royal coaches and the river banks served as grandstands for a populace anxious to catch a glimpse of the reigning sovereign.

20. In the Privy Garden, on the south side. In Henry VIII's time an arched alley of hornbeam overlooked the site of this garden and was named Queen Anne's Bower after Anne Boleyn.

21. In the reign of William and Mary, Jean Tijou was commissioned to make twelve tall, wrought-iron panels to serve as garden screens. This one depicts the Rose of England.

22. The Maze, the great 'novelty' feature of the palace that every visitor wants to see. It is said that the luckiest explorers can find their way to the middle in five minutes – but discovering the way out often takes much longer.

23. *The Queen's Drawing Room. This apartment had been planned for Mary II but she died before she could take possession and the first occupant was her sister, Queen Anne. The Antonio Verrio paintings in the room were covered up in 1741 and not unveiled again until 1899.*

pictures of *The Triumph of Julius Caesar*, which had hung in the Long Gallery in Cromwell's time.

Unhappily, the craftsmen and artists who had suffered from the tardiness of payment during the William-and-Mary rebuilding found that little was changed under Anne. The Queen had a highly cultivated aversion to paying bills.

One of the first supplicants on the list for payment was Antonio Verrio, who was still owed £1,190 for his paintings on the King's Staircase and other work. Poor Verrio was so acutely short of money that, as he pleaded, without speedy assistance he could see himself being reduced to 'great extremity'.

Anne was sufficiently moved to order an immediate payment on account to Signor Verrio of £600 – but there was a catch in her 'generosity' for, at the same time, she commissioned more work from him. The result, eighteen months later, was that he was even further in debt and without means to buy colours for the completion of the new work.

That work, which is still there for our admiration, was the decorating of the Queen's Drawing Room, the great central room on the East Front where Anne entertained. Verrio's ceiling depicts the Queen in the role of Justice and one can only hope that the irony of the chosen subject afforded the artist some quiet satisfaction. (Soon after he had finished the work Verrio's sight deteriorated and Anne was at least sympathetic enough to grant him a pension which he drew until his death at the palace in 1707.)

*Self-portrait of the Italian artist Antonio Verrio who painted the King's Staircase and King's Bedroom. He also produced other murals for the palace until his death in 1707.*

Some other creditors were given even shorter shrift than Verrio. A bill from Matthew Roberts, a plumber who had undertaken extensive pipe-laying work in the palace gardens, went straight into the royal archives marked with the single word: 'Read'.

Master bricklayer Richard Stacey's account for £6,481 0s 11½d was similarly treated, but Stacey was not a man to grin and bear bad debts, royalty notwithstanding. In any case, he was being dunned by others from whom he had ordered supplies for his work, and his anger and frustration still bubble through the archaic language of his petition to the Queen. 'Your petitioner's creditors,' the document declared, 'are generally very clamorous, but more particularly the bricklayers, Lyme-men and other persons, who furnished materials for ye said works at Hampton Court, and threaten speedily to sue yr petitioner for ye goods delivered for that service.'

Appeals of that sort made no impression upon the faceless bureaucrats of Anne's Treasury whose reply to Master Stacey is classic in its brevity and finality: 'There is no money at present for arrears.'

Jean Tijou, the designer of Hampton Court's superb ironwork, who 'prayed' for payment of £1,889 1s 6¼d, was even further along the road to perdition. 'He is indebted to several persons who threaten to imprison him,' the Treasury noted with interest – but not with sufficient concern to offer him as much as the odd farthing of his bill. The gardener, Tilleman Robart had been owed money for nine years. And Mrs Rachel Bennett, the widow of a Guard's quartermaster, was obliged to pay off the men engaged by her late husband to repair the palace barracks. She was, she said, reduced 'almost to a starving condition', but her pleas for money were in vain.

The list of debtors runs on and tediously on. It was, of course, an honour to apply one's skill for the benefit of the sovereign and, in the case of Hampton Court, for posterity. But it did not do much for personal comfort or a square meal.

Anne could not be said to be short of money. After the Battle of Blenheim, on 13 August 1704, in which the great military hero of the age, the Duke of Marlborough, defeated the French and Bavarians, she granted the Duke and his heirs the manor of Woodstock, in Oxfordshire. There the Duke built Blenheim Palace at Anne's expense. It cost her £100,000 which was a vast sum for the eighteenth century. The only condition of the gift was that every year, on the battle's anniversary, the Marlboroughs would present Anne and her successors with a standard on which three fleurs-de-lys represented the captured French colours. The traditional presentation is maintained to this day.

Until they fell out over politics, Anne (a Tory) and Marlborough's wife, Sarah (a Whig) were inseparable friends. But the letters that passed between them at Hampton Court and elsewhere, were addressed in code names. Anne was 'Mrs Morley' and Sarah 'Mrs Freeman'. Some courtiers professed relief when the close friendship ended. They thought Sarah had been too influential and nicknamed her 'Queen Sarah'.

When Anne made her very occasional long-stay visits to Hampton Court some of her advance orders could be curious indeed. For example, before arriving for a two weeks' stay in September 1710, she commanded the Keeper of the Privy Lodgings to have ready for her:

Four thousand tenter hooks of several sizes, two thousand tacks, one dozen brushes, twelve lined buckets for coal, four pound of thread of several colours, two hundred needles of several sizes, one ream of writing paper, two folio paper books, five hundred pens, a gallon of ink, five thousand wafers, and one pound of sealing wax.

That 'order' plus a few additional, minor items, cost a total of £42 and, so far as is known, the bill was paid.

During Anne's reign the old Tudor chapel at the palace was redecorated, with the reredos (the ornamental screen covering the wall behind the altar) carved by Grinling Gibbons. The floor was paved with black and white diamond-shaped marble tiles and Christopher Schrider, 'Organ-Maker to Her Majesty', built the new organ at a cost of £800. Gibbons carved its oak case.

But there was little lavish entertaining. Writing of a visit to Hampton Court, Jonathan Swift, the great satirist and pamphleteer, said: 'I dined at Her Majesty's board of green cloth [then a kind of luncheon-discussion table]. It is much the best table in England and costs the Queen £1,000 a month while she is at Windsor or Hampton Court, and is the only mark of magnificence or royal hospitality that I can see in the royal household.'

Special guests could usually expect to be offered a cup of tea – then always pronounced *tay*. This was a form of refreshment relatively new to the realm and, since it often cost as much as £1 a pound, restricted to the upper classes. The contemporary poet, Alexander Pope, included a reference to it in famous lines about Anne and Hampton Court:

> Close by those Meads for ever crown'd with Flow'rs
> Where Thames with Pride surveys his rising Tow'rs
> There stands a Structure of Majestic Frame,
> Which from neighb'ring Hampton takes its Name.
> Here Britain's Statesmen oft the Fall foredoom
> Of foreign Tyrants, and of Nymphs at home;
> Here Thou, great Anna! whom three Realms obey,
> Dost sometimes Counsel take – and sometimes Tea.

In fact, coffee was the more generally popular beverage and by the reign's end the coffee house was well established as the forerunner of the local pub, a social meeting place as well as a centre for the exchange of news and gossip. (Anne herself was fascinated by gossip which she referred to as 'twittel twattel'.)

Anne ordered a number of improvements to be made to the palace gardens, including the re-turfing of the Great Fountain Garden, after the ravages of drought, at a cost of £1,141 8s 3d. And in the two parks twenty miles of roads and avenues were repaired or rebuilt so as to ensure for Her Majesty 'passage with more ease in her chaise or coach . . .'

It was Anne's practice to follow the stag hunt in a chaise since her gout and dropsy had made horseback riding impossible. Indeed, the servants at Hampton Court noticed, with each successive visit, how the Queen's afflictions were worsening. The Page of the Back-Stairs was required to help her into her shoes and the woman of the bedchamber to pull her clothes on for her. The Page also brought the basin and ewer for the Queen to wash her hands but – because precedence must always be observed – it was the woman of the bedchamber who actually set the utensils on a table in front of Her Majesty. While Anne washed the woman knelt.

*The Rape of the Lock. This 1714 engraving illustrates the theme of Alexander Pope's poem which was based on an actual incident at the palace when Lord Petre snipped a lock of hair from Miss Arabella Fermor's head.*

In the spring of 1711 Hampton Court was the background to a notorious scandal centred upon the Toye tavern which stood outside the western entrance to the palace. (Its name was the then current spelling for 'tow' for it was sited just above the river's toyeing – or towing – place.)

There, on 27 April, a group of eighteen young men were carousing when a fight broke out between two of them, Sir Cholmley Dering, Member of Parliament for Kent, and Richard Thornhill. Dering knocked Thornhill down, breaking seven of his teeth, and stamped on him. Although Dering afterwards apologised, Thornhill refused to accept the apology and challenged his opponent to a duel which duly took place at Tothill Fields, Westminster, on 9 May.

At the duel the opponents, according to one account, 'came up like Lions with their pistols advanced, and when within four yards of each other discharged so equally together that it could not be discovered which shot first'.

However, the fact was that Dering fell fatally wounded and Thornhill was arrested for murder. At his Old Bailey trial on 18 May character witnesses testified that Dering had been a trouble-seeker and Thornhill was, therefore, convicted only of manslaughter and sentenced to be burned on the hand. Three months later he returned to the Toye tavern, and as he rode away from Hampton Court was pursued by three horsemen who caught up with him at Turnham Green where they stabbed him to death, shouting, 'Remember Sir Cholmley Dering!'

In that same year there occurred an incident at the palace that was to be immortalised in verse – of which the third canto, with its reference to tea, has already been quoted.

A group of visitors to the lodgings of one of the palace officials broke off a game of cards to drink coffee. As one of the ladies, a Miss Arabella Fermor, lowered her head to drink, Lord Petre, another visitor, noticed that a lock of her hair was falling into the china coffee cup. He at once produced a pair of scissors and, to Arabella's fury, snipped off the offending strand of hair. Despite protests, Petre refused to part with his 'trophy' and Miss Fermor left the palace deeply offended. From the event Alexander Pope fashioned his *Rape of the Lock* – written, it was said, as an attempt by the poet to heal the breach between Arabella and Lord Petre.

From Tudor times the Master of the King's Revels had acted as the censor of theatrical productions but, by a process of evolution, those duties had come to be assumed by the Master's superior, the Lord Chamberlain. In one of the last events of Anne's reign involving Hampton Court, the incumbent Lord Chamberlain, the Earl of Shrewsbury, issued from the palace, on 13 November 1712, a proclamation for the reform of the 'indecencies and disorders of the stage'. Twenty-five years later the Lord Chamberlain was formally given the power, by statute, to licence plays for public performance after he had approved the text. This form of censorship survived until 1968.

Queen Anne died on 1 August 1714 at Kensington Palace, having outlived her husband by six years. She had, of course, no children living and, under the 1701 Act of Succession, the crown was due to pass to the Protestant family of Sophia, Electress of Hanover. Anne had no enthusiasm for the Hanoverians but she realised, at the end, that her ministers had no choice except to send for the German who was to become George I.

Anne's had been a remarkable reign, not only because of Marlborough's brilliant military successes, which helped to shatter French domination in Europe, but in many other ways.

England and Scotland had been united into one kingdom, thenceforth to be known as 'Great Britain' and with a new union flag formed by the conjunction of the crosses of St George and St Andrew. (The population of the newly enlarged realm was around eight million, with some seven hundred thousand living in London and forty thousand in Bristol, the country's chief seaport.)

The reign is often spoken of as the Augustan Age of English literature. This was the beginning of Britain's foremost contribution to world culture, more marked in prose than in poetry. Among the outstanding literary creators, in addition to Pope and Swift, were Daniel Defoe (who wrote his greatest work, *Robinson Crusoe*, at the age of sixty), and Joseph Addison and Sir Richard Steele who founded the *Spectator*, one of the principal ancestors of modern newspapers and magazines.

In architecture there developed a new style of building that had its own simple but pleasing dignity and is now summed up sufficiently neatly as 'Queen Anne'.

There were, of course, other, less rewarding aspects of Anne's reign. About one out of every five people in England and Wales – a total of 1,330,000 – was a pauper and received public benefit of fourteen shillings a year. Under statute, those beggars who were male and sufficiently fit to march were drafted into the army where the infantryman's basic pay of eight pence a day was at least usually more than they could otherwise earn. Manual workers' wages averaged ten shillings (50p) a week.

In London, which was now divided into two distinct areas, the City (still the 'square mile' around St Paul's Cathedral) and Westminster (to which people of 'quality' had moved), street crime was rife. Especially at night, in the badly-lit thoroughfares, innocent passers-by were always in danger of being robbed by cutpurses (the eighteenth-century version of 'muggers'), or by bands of young 'gentlemen of fashion' armed with rapiers who roamed around looking for trouble. The gangs gave themselves colourful names and the most notorious called itself 'The Mohawks', after the North American Indian tribe.

Ordinary people drank vast quantities of beer and the better-off wallowed in port which had suddenly become highly popular because of a treaty with Portugal under which Portuguese wines were taxed at one-third less than wines imported from France. Those who had previously drunk claret now drank a similar amount of port but, since port had a much higher alcoholic content, the treaty with Portugal could be said to have contributed, unwittingly, to the widespread drunkenness for which the era was noted.

The concentration of conflict over religious issues was gradually giving way to more direct political confrontation and was centred on the two great parties, the Tories who were strongest in the rural areas and country towns, and the Whigs who drew their widest support from London and other large towns and cities. Future patterns of political struggle were already appearing in shadowy outline.

It was a good time and a bad time in which prejudice and bigotry marched shoulder to shoulder with knowledge and enlightenment. Taken as a whole, however, the reign was such that, as Sir Winston Churchill put it, the sovereign deserved 'to bear in history the title of "the Good Queen Anne"'.

*George I (1660–1727), first of the Hanoverian monarchs. He succeeded to the throne in 1714 but preferred Hanover to Britain and spent the better part of his reign there.*

# *12*

# *The Hanoverians*

## GEORGE I

THE NEW KING, GEORGE I, and his newly-acquired British subjects were at least united on one thing: each came quickly to detest the other.

George spoke no English and, at the age of fifty-four, had neither the inclination nor the energy to attempt to grapple with the language. In the eyes of a smug island race, Hanoverians were simply 'foreigners' – and that was as contemptuous a term as you could apply to anyone.

From the moment he set foot on the soil of his new realm at Greenwich, King George resolved (and was to abide by his resolution) to flit away home to Hanover whenever, and as often as, opportunity offered. In appearance he was shortish, but he had a good figure, and delicate, artists' hands with long, slender fingers. His principal characteristics, however, were a long, pointed nose and china-blue eyes. He certainly had some artistic leanings, since he loved music and the theatre. But, even so, his general personality was not pleasing and Sir Winston Churchill summed him up as 'an obstinate and humdrum German martinet with dull brains and coarse taste'.

George had been married to a cousin, Sophia Dorothea, but in 1694 he divorced her, on the grounds of infidelity, and locked her up in a German castle. Apart from the fact that she was allowed a reasonable income and a guard-of-honour, she was under house arrest and kept so for thirty-two years until her death in November 1726.

With him in his entourage of some seventy Germans George brought to England his mistress, the tall, thin Baroness von Schulenberg, and his half-sister, the corpulent Baroness Kielmansegg. The former was created Duchess of Kendal, and the latter Countess of Darlington. Horace Walpole, son of George's Prime Minister, Sir Robert Walpole, met the Countess when he was a child and later wrote this chilling description of her: 'Two fierce black eyes, large and rolling beneath two lofty arched eyebrows; two acres of cheek spread with crimson; an ocean of neck that overflowed and was not distinguished from the lower part of her body, and no part restrained by stays – no wonder that a child dreaded such an ogress!'

Gazing with wonder at the physical contrast between the two women, the King's English courtiers nicknamed the Duchess 'The Maypole', and the Countess 'The Elephant and Castle'.

Ordinary people took an immediate aversion to the ladies and whenever they passed through the streets of London or, later, on their way to Hampton Court, shouted abusive remarks at them.

On one occasion, the infuriated Duchess thrust her head out of the window of her sedan chair and attempted to admonish the insulting mob. Unfortunately, her English was not equal to the moment. 'Good pipple,' she cried, 'why do you abuse us? We come here for all your own goods.' To which a quick-witted wag unhesitatingly replied: 'Yes, damn ye – and for our chattels too!'

Hampton Court especially appealed to the King because it offered a refuge from that kind of unpleasantness; and he very soon made it his principal country home. He took with him his two chief advisers, Baron von Bernstorff, Prime Minister of Hanover, and Baron von Bothmer, a political staff of twenty three (to help him keep in touch with affairs back home in Germany), various cooks and other servants, one – just one – washerwoman, a Court dwarf, and two body-guards, named Mohammed and Mustapha, who had been captured in a campaign against Turkey.

Altogether his household totalled around nine hundred, although not all were in attendance at any one time when he stayed at Hampton Court. Working on a rota, small groups of his seventeen English gentlemen of the bedchamber helped to keep the King company at meals or strolled with him through the palace gardens. His German cooks prepared his food in the home-cooking way and sausages and ham made frequent appearances on his dining table. George liked his food, but generous eating failed to spoil his figure and neither did English beer – one of the few offerings of his adopted kingdom to which he gave praise. During most of the evening meals at the palace the King and his guests were entertained by the dwarf, Christian Ulrich Jorry, who served as an updated version of the Tudors' court jesters.

During the periods of royal residence (which were usually throughout the summer) meetings of the Cabinet were held on Thursdays, with the King presiding. Despite his lack of English, George somehow managed to follow the discussion, mainly with the aid of an interpreter, and for his benefit all official papers were translated in advance into French in which he was proficient.

(The term 'Cabinet' first came into regular use during the reign of Charles II when, for convenience sake, the King consulted with a small group of advisers rather than his large and unwieldy Privy Council. Meetings were held in the King's study known as the royal 'closet' or cabinet.)

*Sir Robert Walpole, the Whig politician who is usually regarded as Britain's first Prime Minister. Ironically, the term was originally one of contempt – suggesting that Walpole pushed himself forward in order to be first among the King's ministers.*

Political enemies of Sir Robert Walpole, whose Whig government served throughout George I's reign, accused him of behaving as if he were the King's one and only minister and referred to him, sarcastically, as 'our *prime* minister'. And so it was that the now-distinguished title of the leader of a British government came into being as a term of mockery.

(Walpole, incidentally, was also the first Prime Minister to occupy 10 Downing Street. George II offered him the house as a gift in 1732 but Walpole insisted that it should be permanently attached to the political post as an official residence.)

When George I and his retinue travelled to Hampton Court it was standard practice for all the church bells along the route to be rung. But often King and Court preferred to commute by river, travelling in a flotilla of gorgeously decorated barges and generally including a barge of musicians who serenaded the royal progress.

In 1717 the great, German-born, George Frederick Handel composed his much-loved *Water Music* especially for the King's Thames expeditions. Its first water-borne performance, by fifty musicians in July of that year, so pleased His Majesty, according to the *Daily Courant*, 'that he caused it to be played over

*George Frederic Handel, composer of the famous 'Water Music', to be played during George I's journeys on the Thames, conducts a concert of some of his works.*

three times in going and returning [between Lambeth and Chelsea]'. George I had been Handel's patron, at home in Hanover, and it may perhaps be said that any King who could admire and cultivate such a creative talent cannot have been all bad.

At Hampton Court the two German women – Maypole and Elephant – fell into the habit of promenading under the chestnuts and elms of the pathway by the Tilt Yard which consequently became known as the Frau Walk which was later corrupted by the locals to 'Frog Walk'.

A new outdoors addition to the palace, specifically installed as a gesture of welcome to the new King, comprised two large seahorses and two large tritons spouting water in Bushy Park's Diana Basin. The ornaments were cast in metal and cost £180, but Richard Osgood, the designer and craftsman had – shades of Good Queen Anne! – to wait nearly seven years for payment.

When the King walked in the palace gardens or parks six footmen went before him and six yeomen followed in his footsteps. His mistress and the Countess of Darlington occupied fourth place in the procession, borne with great care in sedan chairs by pairs of chairmen stepping so skilfully and in such exquisite rhythm that the chairs appeared to glide, as if charmed, between the beds of stocks and zinnias, geraniums and dahlias.

In 1715, James Thornhill, the decorator of royal palaces, painted the ceiling of what is now called the Queen's Bedroom. This impressive work depicts Aurora, Roman goddess of the dawn, rising from the ocean in her golden chariot. In the cornice are to be seen portraits of George I, the Prince of Wales (afterwards George II), and the Princess of Wales.

For his splendid efforts, officials of His Majesty's Works informed the Lords of the Treasury that, in their considered opinion, Thornhill deserved a fee of £457 10s. Lest their conscientious Lordships might suspect that the figure had been plucked, carelessly, from the rarefied Hampton air, HM Works explained that they had computed it on the basis of £3 11s a yard of painting 'skilfully and laboriously performed'.

This work was completed in time for the Prince and Princess of Wales to occupy Hampton Court in the summer of 1715 while the King was away in Hanover. The Prince had been appointed Regent for the duration of the King's absence and he and Caroline, his German-born Princess, deliberately set about trying to show that life at the palace need not be as stuffy and dull as his father made it.

Young Wales fancied himself as a cultivated individual although, apart from an interest in opera, he seemed to have little affection for the arts and had been known to declare, in his adenoidal fashion, that he could not abide 'boetry' or 'bainting'.

However, unlike his father, the Prince admired the English, or certainly said so, perhaps to annoy the King's Anglophobic courtiers. Occasionally he would go overboard in his commendation of the English as when he announced that he found them 'the best, handsomest, best shaped, best natured, and lovingest people in the world', and that if anyone wished to win his royal favour he had only to tell the Prince he was 'like an Englishman'.

But if the Prince, George Augustus, was neither particularly witty nor original he, and Caroline, surrounded themselves with some of the more intelligent and attractive figures of the age. Foremost among the beauties was Mrs Henrietta Howard (later Countess of Suffolk), one of the Princess's women of the bedchamber, who became mistress of George Augustus after his accession as George II.

*Henry Wise, one of the palace's supervising gardeners who, in the winter of 1710–11, widened and lengthened the Little Canal. Painting by Sir Godfrey Kneller.*

*Lancelot 'Capability' Brown, the famous landscape gardener who replaced the Privy Garden terrace steps with grassy banks on the principle that 'We ought not to go up and down stairs in the open air.'*

*William Kent, who was less well-known than 'Capability' Brown, is usually regarded as the 'true' father of landscape gardening. He and Brown were collaborators for nine years.*

She was nicknamed 'The Swiss', because of her tact and discretion, and her palace apartments were the 'Swiss Cantons', for there political and personal rivals could gather to argue their differences in the comforting knowledge that they were on 'neutral' territory. Certainly, people found it very easy to speak their minds to the receptive Henrietta. Once, nodding angrily in the direction of Duchess 'Maypole', Sophia, mother of George I, appealed to her: 'Look at that mawkin – and to think of her as my son's passion!'

Alexander Pope wrote of Mrs Howard:

> I know a thing that's most uncommon
> (Envy be silent and attend!)
> I know a reasonable woman,
> Handsome and witty, yet a friend.

At the time he and his wife took up temporary occupation of the palace it was not, however, Henrietta Howard whom the Prince was then pursuing but another celebrated charmer, Mary Bellenden. Miss Bellenden was a lively, jolly young woman, much given to singing as she tripped around the galleries of Hampton Court and she was noted for her attachment to the song *Over the hills and far away*. The poet John Gay immortalised her as 'Smiling Mary, soft and fair as down'.

The words of Mary's song may well have come to represent a hope that the Prince might disappear over the hills for she had constant trouble in warding off his importunate advances.

One of the classic Hampton Court legends has it that one day the Prince followed her, mooningly, from room to room, ostentatiously counting out a purseful of golden guineas. Every now and then he would give her a sideways glance to see how impressed she might be. Eventually her exasperation boiled over and she snapped: 'Sir, I can bear it no longer! If you count your money any more I shall go out of the room!' Oafishly, the Prince ignored the plea whereupon young Mary rose from her chair, knocked the golden coins out of his hand and swept from the room. The future king was left to grub around on hands and knees, hunting for his precious coins under tables and chairs. His pursuit of Mary Bellenden came to an abrupt end and she afterwards married Colonel Campbell, a groom of the bedchamber.

Despite his disappointment over Miss Bellenden the Prince greatly enjoyed the opportunity of playing King in his father's absence and of creating a permanent holiday atmosphere at Hampton Court.

In the mornings he and Princess Caroline delighted to board their gold and crimson-curtained barge and lie on silk cushions while the royal oarsmen rowed them slowly up and down the stream. As they glided along, the Princess's maids of honour entertained them with songs.

Later the men guests enjoyed a game of bowls and every night there were cardtable sessions which Princess Caroline, especially, doted on. In after-years one woman guest recalled that period as one of 'good sense in the morning and wit in the evening' and what she delightedly described as 'frizelation' and by which she meant flirtation.

But there were sometimes less than tranquil moments when the animosity between the German and the English courtiers bubbled to the surface. Few such moments were more memorable than that in which one large German lady inveighed against English women by declaring they made themselves pitiful by lowering their heads and looking 'always in a fright'. In contrast, the gracious lady added, 'foreigners hold up their heads and hold out their breasts, and make themselves look as great and stately as they can, and more nobly and more like quality than you English.' To the delight of her compatriots, one of the English guests, Lady Deloraine, retorted: 'We show our quality by our birth and titles, madam, and not by sticking out our bosoms.'

Relations between George I and his son had for a long time been uneasy – the Prince's popularity among His Majesty's subjects had helped to inflame matters – and when the King departed for Hanover he deliberately left his adviser, von Bothmer, at Hampton Court to spy on the activities of George Augustus.

Their knowledge that the Prince was under surveillance and officially disapproved of led some of the King's friends to adopt a haughty attitude towards the second-string royals and particularly Princess Caroline.

One of them, Lord Sunderland took the opportunity, while they walked together around the palace's Queen's Gallery, to 'lecture' Caroline and in the process lost his temper and raised his voice. When the Princess chided him for speaking so loudly that people in the garden below might hear, he growled: 'Let them hear.' What they did hear was Caroline shrieking: 'Well, if you have a mind, let 'em – but you shall walk next to the windows for, in the humour we both are, one of us must certainly jump out at the window and I'm resolved it shan't be me!'

When George I returned to Britain, at the end of January 1717, he vented his anger on his son. Word had reached him that George Augustus had carried his role of 'deputy King' too far. The Prince, so none other than Robert Walpole had admitted, 'seems to be preparing to keep up an interest of his own in Parliament independent of the King's'.

For a time the antagonism merely simmered for, in August 1717, Prince and Princess were back at Hampton Court with the King – although George was treating the Princess courteously but hardly speaking to his son.

Life at the palace resumed the uninspiring, monotonous routine which inevitably applied when the King was in residence. Alexander Pope was a guest and, after watching the ladies of the court returning from hunting, he jotted down his impressions in a letter:

To eat Westphalia ham in a morning, ride over hedges and ditches on borrowed hacks, come home in the heat of the day with a fever, and (what is worse a hundred times) with a red mark on the forehead from an uneasy hat – all this may qualify them to make excellent wives for foxhunters, and bear abundance of ruddy complexioned children. As soon as they can wipe off the sweat of the day, they must simper an hour and catch cold in the Princess's apartment; from thence . . . to dinner, with what appetite they may – and after that, till midnight walk, work, or think, which they please. I can easily believe no lone house in Wales, with a mountain and a rookery, is more contemplative than this Court . . .

In the evenings the King seldom walked or worked but preferred to sit in his room, drinking beer and watching his mistress absorbed in her favourite pastime of cutting figures and shapes out of paper. When they talked it was often about money, a subject dear to the Duchess 'Maypole's' heart. She could never have enough of the substance herself and the King lavished it upon her. After the Duke of Somerset resigned as Master of the Horse, George allowed the post to remain vacant but assigned the very lucrative stipend of £7,500 a year to the Duchess. Later she made a fortune out of the South Sea Bubble, that extraordinary and shady episode of share-floating which almost frightened the kingdom out of its financial wits in 1720. Walpole said of the Duchess: 'She would have sold the King's honour for a shilling advance to the best bidder!'

The Prince and Princess of Wales had left Hampton Court when the final break with the King occurred over a bizarre incident. On 2 November 1717 the Princess gave birth to a second son – the infant lived for only three months – and at the christening the Prince picked a quarrel with the Lord Chamberlain, the Duke of Newcastle.

'You are a rascal, but I shall find you,' screamed the Prince at the Duke. But the King, believing that at last he had recognised an English phrase, thought the final words were 'fight you', and immediately had the Prince arrested on the grounds that he was threatening a duel.

When the dust had settled and the Prince had been freed, he and the Princess were 'expelled' by the King from their home in St James's Palace. And George I even went so far as publicly to announce in the official *Gazette* that anyone visiting the Prince would be *persona non grata* at the King's Court.

Next summer, when the King moved as usual to Hampton Court, the Prince and Princess of Wales attempted, without great success, to set up a 'rival' Court at Richmond. (The Princess, it must be said, had little enthusiasm for the royal in-fighting; she was alert enough to see the harm it could do to the Hanoverians.)

Not to be outdone, the King made a special effort to put *his* Court on the map by inviting the company from Drury Lane Theatre to present a 'season' of seven plays in the Great Hall of the palace. (This unexpected instance of royal public relations appeared to work, for one of the ladies at the Prince of Wales's 'Court' wrote to a friend: 'Our world is extremely dull; though I hear there are brave doings at Hampton Court. I was much importuned to go on Tuesday to the play, but I have no notion of serving two masters.')

The Drury Lane players who went to Hampton included Colley Cibber, Robert Wilkes, Barton Booth and Anne Oldfield – all of them among the great stage names of the age. They presented *Hamlet* and Ben Jonson's *Volpone*, a few comedies and Shakespeare's *Henry VIII* with Cibber Limpeld playing Wolsey in the very setting of the great Cardinal's triumphs.

George I was hardly equipped to appreciate much of the dialogue, especially the Shakespearian verse, but he seemed to be absorbed by the action in *Henry VIII*, and generally very much pleased, for he made the company a gift of £200 – in addition to £350 to cover their expenses on the basis of £50 a performance.

The actors certainly needed to work hard because, as they discovered, the usual audience enthusiasm was missing – although this was no reflection on the cast and no offence was intended. It was all the fault of protocol. As Colley Cibber explained, when a play is staged in private before a King, 'the audience is under the restraint of a circle where laughter or applause raised higher than a whisper would be stared at.' All the same, he had to admit that such inhibitions 'had a melancholy effect upon the impatient vanity of some of our actors'.

Sir Christopher Wren was still living at Hampton Court, in a house on the Green which he had greatly improved and which he rented from the Crown authorities at £10 a year – a concessionary figure but not over-generous since the authorities owed him £341 3s 6d in arrears of salary.

But in 1718, after nearly fifty years' public service and at the age of eighty-six he was suddenly and unceremoniously sacked from his post of Surveyor-General of the Board of Works.

There was no question of senility or incompetence for Wren's mind, said Ernest Law, the Hampton Court historian, retained 'all the vigour and freshness of youth'. Some of the German courtiers, however, were jealous of the architect's success and prestige and were, therefore, anxious to see him replaced by William Benson, a man of abilities far inferior to those of Wren but who had ingratiated himself with the royal hangers-on.

Benson duly succeeded to the post but, not content with that, he added a squalid footnote to the affair by encouraging others to circulate the rumour that Wren had been guilty of malpractice. Among other things, the malicious tongues alleged, Wren had doctored his accounts, charged the King double for the workmen's wages and connived at the construction of private housing paid for by royal money.

On 21 April 1719 Wren wrote to the Lords of the Treasury refuting the charges and ending with the moving words, 'as I am dismiss'd, having worn out (by God's mercy) a long life in the royal service, and having made some figure in the world, I hope it will be allowed me to die in peace.'

A subsequent inquiry proved the allegations against Wren to be totally false and a year later Benson was dismissed. But the whole business left an indelibly black mark on the record of the royal court.

Wren spent part of his time in his London house in St James's Street. There, on 25 February 1723, he was found dead, sitting in a chair in his dining room where it was his custom to doze after dinner. He was in his ninety-first year and his St Paul's Cathedral is a finer legacy than anything bequeathed to the British heritage by George I or the rest of the asinine Hanoverians.

The inquiries into the false charges against Wren had a notable side effect: they led to other investigations which disclosed that Hampton Court was harbouring 'squatters'. Sundry people, it appeared, had simply moved in and occupied various rooms in the palace with the 'assistance' (usually encouraged by bribery) of members of the household. More surprisingly, it emerged that 'squatting', unsuspected by the royals, had been an established feature of Hampton Court since the times of Henry VIII. The King issued a sternly-worded edict, prohibiting all unofficial sub-letting. But for all that, squatting continued until the late eighteenth century.

After the silly rivalry of the two royal 'Courts', King and Prince of Wales grew cold towards Hampton Court and rarely visited the palace. They were reconciled before George I died from a stroke, on 22 June 1727, at Osnabrück, seventy miles west of the city of Hanover to which he had been returning for another of his visits. He had reigned in Britain for not quite thirteen years.

On the day the King died a large raven flew in through one of the windows of Kendal House, Isleworth, Middlesex, the home of his mistress. Some time before George had 'promised' that if he pre-deceased her he would endeavour to return to her world in some form. She treated the bird with reverence and devotion until it finally took off again. She herself lived on for another sixteen years, dying at Kendal House in 1743, aged nearly eighty-five and enormously rich.

*George II (1683–1760) with his wife, Caroline of Anspach, and their family, painted by William Hogarth.*

# 13

# *The Hanoverians*

## GEORGE II

A YEAR AFTER HIS FATHER'S DEATH the new King, George II, and his Queen, Caroline, began the first of their regular visits to Hampton Court.

Mrs Henrietta Howard was still in residence in her dual capacity as the Queen's lady of the bedchamber and the King's mistress. Queen Caroline was fully aware of the liaison and accepted it as best she might while subjecting Mrs Howard to petty humiliations as often as she could. For example, when Mrs Howard appeared each night with the royal bedtime hot chocolate the Queen obliged her to kneel while proffering the cup.

Henrietta at least attempted some resistance to the degrading ritual, as the Queen herself reported in a letter to Lord Hervey, the Vice-Chamberlain: 'She said that positively she would not do it; to which I made her no answer then in anger but, calmly, as I would have said to a naughty child, "Yes, my dear Howard, I am sure you will; indeed you will. Go, go, fie for shame! Go, my good Howard; we will talk of this another time."'

Whether they did talk of it another time we don't know. But certainly Mrs Howard surrendered and did as she was commanded.

Caroline had ordered that the room adjoining her dressing room should be set up as a private chapel and it was her habit, as she dressed in the morning, to leave the communicating door slightly ajar so that she could listen to her chaplain, Dr Isaac Maddox (later Bishop of Worcester), intoning prayers.

The prayers, however, were not allowed to interrupt the Queen's gossip with her ladies and in his memoirs Lord Hervey satirised the routine morning scene as part of a playlet:

*1st Parson (behind the scenes):* From pride, vainglory, and hypocrisy, from envy, hatred and malice, and all uncharitableness . . .
*2nd Parson:* . . . Good Lord, deliver us!
*Queen:* I pray, my good Lady Sundon, shut a little that door; these creatures pray so loud one cannot hear oneself speak. *(Lady Sundon goes to shut the door.)* So, so, not quite so much; leave it enough open for those parsons to think we may hear, and enough shut that we may not hear quite so much.

In real life, as distinct from Hervey's 'dramatised' version, Caroline once did insist that the door should be completely closed and bellowed to Dr Maddox, shut off on the other side, to know why he had stopped praying. Portentously, the reverend doctor shouted back that it was not in the nature of his holy office to 'whistle the word of God through the keyhole'.

Despite the elaborate efforts made by the King, during his days as Prince of Wales, to outshine his father's Court, life at the palace soon became as dreary and uninspiring as it had been under George I.

Stag hunting in the parks, every Wednesday and Saturday morning for five hours at a stretch, was the principal form of diversion. Henrietta Howard peevishly noted: 'We hunt with great noise and violence and have every day every tolerable chance to have a neck broke.'

Queen Caroline, who did not share her husband's passion for climbing into the saddle to chase terrified stags, followed the hunt from a distance in a chaise – hoping, perhaps, to see Henrietta break her neck.

George II, incidentally, drew the line at hunting foxes. He told the fox-hunting Duke of Grafton he thought it undignified for any man of 'quality' to be 'spending

*Stag hunting for five hours at a stretch in the palace parks, every Wednesday and Saturday morning, was a favourite diversion for George II and his friends. The artist John Wootten depicts a 'kill.'*

all his time in tormenting a poor fox that was generally a better beast than any of those that pursued him; for the fox hurts no other animal but for his subsistence, while those brutes who hurt him did it only for the pleasure they took in hurting'. The Duke, who was a very large man, explained that he hunted only for exercise. At which the King snappily suggested he try walking since 'with your corpse of twenty stone no horse, I am sure, can carry you within hearing, much less than within sight, of hounds!'

In the evenings the King exchanged the bouncing saddle for a different form of recreation in Henrietta's bed. His nocturnal visits were timed to begin precisely at nine and Sir Robert Walpole was amused to learn that George could often be seen pacing the gallery outside his mistress's rooms, impatiently consulting his watch and waiting for the hands to reach the appointed hour.

After her husband had succeeded to his brother's title as Earl of Suffolk, life and status improved somewhat for Henrietta at Hampton Court. But she grew wearied of George's public treatment of her which was often bad-tempered and churlish. According to one piece of gossip the final break-up of the relationship was hastened by an incident one morning in the Queen's dressing room (with the parsons praying away behind the half-closed door). The King unexpectedly walked in and snatched away a piece of linen with which, for modesty's sake, Henrietta was about to cover the Queen's naked breasts. 'Is it because you have an ugly neck yourself that you love to hide the Queen's?' he shouted.

Eventually, Henrietta resigned from her post in the Queen's service and left the palace and the Court. The King's enemies, as reported on by Hervey, commiserated with her and said she had 'undergone twenty years' slavery to (George's) disagreeable temper and capricious will' and sacrificed her time, reputation and health 'to his service and pleasure'.

By the time she left the Court, Henrietta was in her early forties – middle-aged by early eighteenth-century standards – and no longer very attractive. She was not without financial resources. The King had allowed her £2,000 a year while he was still Prince of Wales and £3,200 after he ascended the throne. He also bought for her a villa – Marble Hill, near Twickenham, in Middlesex – for which he paid around £12,000. But he could well afford that purely material return for her past devotion. His state allowance, the Civil List, was about £900,000 a year, a huge amount for the time and far greater, in actual value, than any 'salary' ever bestowed on a British sovereign. In addition, Queen Caroline was allowed £100,000 plus the gifts of Somerset House, in London, and Richmond Lodge.

Neither money nor the departure of a rival was of great benefit to Caroline's domestic life for she complained that George continued to vent his bad temper upon her. 'I can say nothing but it is contradicted,' she sighed. But the King's anger and injudicious outbursts may well, literally, have had a deep seated cause for he was a lifelong martyr to piles from which no medication brought him relief.

He was particularly irritated by Caroline's frequent fussy decisions to move pictures from Kensington Palace to Hampton Court and fumed over her habit of constantly dropping into aristocratic homes in order to spy out the possessions.

'You don't see me running into every puppy's house to see his new chairs and stools,' he told her. 'Nor is it for *you* to be running your nose everywhere and trotting about the town to every fellow that will give you bread and butter, like an old girl that loves to go abroad, no matter where, or whether it be proper or no.'

The persistence of George's irritability finally drove the Queen to consult Walpole who made the remarkably outspoken proposal that the King should perhaps be provided with a replacement for his former love, Henrietta. Still more remarkable, the idea won the support of the royal daughter, Princess Caroline, who said: 'I wish with all my heart he would take somebody else, that mama might be a little relieved from the *ennui* of seeing him forever in her room.'

Walpole thought it would be a very good idea if the Queen herself were to choose the King's new playmate – a classic royal example of keeping family matters within the family. High on Walpole's list of nominees was Camilla Colville, wife of Charles, the second Earl of Tankerville. She, Walpole suggested, was 'a very safe fool, and would give the King some amusement without giving Her Majesty any trouble'.

Mention was also made of handsome promiscuous Lady Deloraine, the thirty-five-year-old governess of the youngest royal princesses. But she, Walpole objected, was 'a very dangerous one – a weak head, a pretty face, a lying tongue, and a false heart...' With such attributes she must have seemed readily acceptable to George and she it was who, in due course, became his new mistress.

Lady Deloraine may have had a false heart but she had a secure purse. For she later confided to Walpole that 'old men and kings ought always to be made to pay well'. The good lady had a husband and a child and a heavy thirst for alcohol. Having quenched the thirst at one gathering she was asked about her 'pretty' baby boy and replied that he was fathered by her husband but added, giggling, 'But I will not promise whose the next shall be!'

Personal events in the lives of George and Caroline had a curious way of turning into carbon copies of the life of George I. George, when Prince of Wales, had been at the receiving end of his father's hostility and now the succeeding King and Queen had developed a bitter aversion to their son, Frederick, the current Prince of Wales.

The dislike even had, at its roots, a cause similar to that which had alienated George I from his son – the royal couple were almost pathologically jealous of the way Prince Frederick courted popularity. Queen Caroline snorted: 'Popularity makes me sick, but Fritz's popularity makes me vomit!'

The King totally ignored his son and, even when they were in the same room together, treated him as though he were invisible. The Queen, referring to her son and his wife, Augusta, spoke of his 'silly gaiety' and 'rude railleries', and of her 'flat stupidity'.

Hardly a day passed at Hampton Court, it was said, without King and Queen publicly expressing the warm parental wish that the Prince 'might drop dead of apoplexy'.

The spirits of the royal couple were much uplifted in the summer of 1737 when both Houses of Parliament rejected the Prince's request for an increase in the £50,000 a year granted to him by his father. But it was at Hampton Court, shortly afterwards, that the family quarrel reached a bizarre climax.

Tittle-tattling Court gossips had spread the rumour that Princess Augusta was pregnant but, when Queen Caroline put the question directly to her, Augusta replied simply, 'I don't know'. Caroline, never a woman to take 'don't know' for an answer, re-phrased the question as though Augusta might be only slightly pregnant: 'Is it, then, the beginning of your being with child?'

Obstinately, Augusta repeated that she didn't know and Caroline immediately sensed the sour aroma of conspiracy. Someone was deliberately trying to keep the senior royals in the dark, for some devious reason. And who might that be? The name 'Fritz' popped up on the scoreboard of the Queen's mind – yet another addition to the tally against him.

The King, backed by Walpole, was determined that, if there were to be a birth, it would take place at Hampton Court where he could personally ensure the child was genuinely a royal product and not a 'substitute' infant. A message conveying that command was to have been sent to the Prince and Princess of Wales at their home, St James's Palace, but it was delayed on the assumption that the Princess was unlikely to be confined before October.

Queen Caroline refused to believe that the Princess was pregnant and, when some of her courtiers insisted that the early signs were evident, replied: 'For my part, I do not see she is big; you all say you see it, and therefore I suppose it is so, and that I am blind.'

She was also convinced that her son would find some way of disobeying the Hampton Court command. She warned Walpole: 'Sir Robert, we shall be catched; he will remove her before he receives any orders for her lying in here . . .'

On the evening of 31 July 1737 the Princess dined with the King and Queen at the palace and afterwards went to bed in the room, still known as the Prince of Wales Bedroom, on the northern end of the building's East Front. She had only just climbed in between the sheets when it became clear that she was in the first stage of labour.

For Prince Frederick it was a testing moment. Within an hour or two the expected child would arrive there, in the palace, and that would be a 'victory' for his father. He acted swiftly. With the aid of the Princess's dancing master and one of his equerries he hauled Augusta from the bed and half carried, half dragged her down the nearby staircase.

Two attendant courtiers tried to intervene and the Princess cried out for mercy and moaned that the pain of being moved was like the agony of the rack. But the only response from the huffing and puffing Prince, gripping his wife all the more firmly, was to hiss 'Courage! Courage!' And, 'with the encouragement of a tooth-drawer or the consolatory tenderness of an executioner', as Lord Hervey reported, he told her 'it would be over in a minute'.

On the way down, the trio of Princess-bearers encountered several frightened servants, but the panting Prince warned them to keep their mouths shut. At last, without arousing any general alarm in the palace, the men bore poor writhing Augusta across to the cloisters of Fountain Court, past the Chapel Royal and then, by back ways, to a side door in the West Front.

Outside the door the half-comatose Princess was heaved and hoisted into a coach. The Prince and the helpers hastily climbed in and the coachman was ordered to make for London and St James's Palace at full gallop. Mercifully, the Princess was probably too far gone towards temporary oblivion to be aware of what her body suffered during the leaping, wracking coach ride.

They reached St James's Palace at ten o'clock where the idiot Prince was obliged to scurry around making urgent preparations for the lying-in. Servants had to be sent from door to door in the neighbourhood to beg such necessities as a warming-pan and napkins. Frederick at least managed to rustle up a midwife but for some extraordinary reason – possibly because they had been stored away – he could not lay his hands on bed-sheets. Consequently the first Princess of the kingdom went into final stages of labour between two tablecloths.

At 10.45 she was delivered, as Lord Hervey unfeelingly and inaccurately put it, of 'a little rat of a girl, about the bigness of a large toothpick'. (She grew up to be a fine, handsome woman, later became Duchess of Brunswick and lived to the age of seventy-six despite her unpropitious entry into the world.)

While all these incredible capers were taking place, the King and Queen, in blissful ignorance, were absorbed in the challenges of the card-table.

At half-past one in the morning the Queen was awakened by Mrs Charlotte Tichburne, her woman of the bedchamber, who said the Prince had sent a message to say his wife was in labour.

Queen Caroline, assuming the birth was imminent in the palace, shrieked: 'My God, my nightgown! I'll go to her this moment.' Smugly, Mrs Tichburne replied: 'Your nightgown, madam, and your coaches, too! The Princess is at St James's.'

'Are you mad, or are you asleep, my good Tichburne?' the Queen shouted and quietened down only when the truth finally sank in. By that time the hubbub had aroused the King and he responded to the extraordinary news by upbraiding his wife. He cursed her in German, telling her: 'This is all your fault! There is a false child will be put upon you, and how will you answer it to all your children?'

While the torrent of words rained down upon her the Queen hastily pulled on her clothes and at half-past two boarded her coach, leaving the King still muttering and seething. She reached St James's at four and was met by the Prince, dressed in nightgown and nightcap, who spilled out the story of the 'escape' from Hampton Court – not omitting the fact that he had strained his back in supporting his wife in the coach.

Prudently, in view of the hostility between them, Caroline thought it best not to ask the Prince for an explanation of his escapade. She went at once to the Princess, treated her with great kindness and expressed sympathy over her 'horrible suffering'. She kissed the baby, whispered that she was a poor little creature and added, 'you have arrived in a disagreeable world.'

The Prince continued to yammer on about the coach journey. The Queen listened stony-faced and, at the end, turned and directed a tirade of criticism at Lady Archibald Hamilton, one of the Princess's ladies, who had gone with Augusta to St James's.

Barely pausing for breath she snarled: 'At the indiscretion of young fools, who know nothing of the dangers to which this poor child and its mother were exposed, I am less surprised; but for you, my Lady Archibald, who have had ten children, that with your experience, and at your age, you should suffer these people to act such a madness, I am astonished, and wonder how you could, for your own sake as well as their's, venture to be concerned in such an expedition.'

The luckless Lady Archibald Hamilton who, in the bedroom at Hampton Court, *had* protested to Frederick about his folly, turned to the Prince and cried in exasperation: 'You *see* – sir!'

As Queen Caroline was about to leave, the Prince told her he would report to the King later that day at the palace. But she warned him: 'I fancy you had better not come today; to be sure the King is not well pleased with all this bustle you have made; and should you attempt coming today nobody can answer what your reception may be.'

The Queen was comforted by one thought: the child could not, as she put it, be 'spurious'. If the Prince had concocted a conspiracy in order to provide himself

*Frederick, Prince of Wales, who engaged in a ludicrous and public quarrel with his father, George II, poses with the Knights of the Round Table, a re-creation of the King Arthur legend.*

with an heir – he then had no son – he would surely have selected a boy as a 'substitute' child and not a girl.

Queen Caroline returned to Hampton Court to find that during her absence the King had worked himself up into a frothing rage. When he heard her account of events he summoned one of his aides, Lord Essex, and ordered him to deliver the following message to the Prince of Wales:

The King has commanded me to acquaint your Royal Highness: That his Majesty most heartily rejoices at the safe delivery of the Princess, but that your carrying away her Royal Highness from Hampton Court, the then residence of the King, the Queen, and the Royal family, under the pains and certain indication of immediate labour, to the imminent danger and hazard both of the Princess and her child, and after sufficient warnings for a week before to have made the necessary preparations for that happy event, without acquainting his Majesty or the Queen with the circumstances the Princess was in, or giving them the least notice of your departure, is looked upon by the King to be such a deliberate indignity offered to himself and to the Queen, that he has commanded me to acquaint your Royal Highness that he resents it to the highest degree, *and will not see you*. [Underlined in the original].

If Frederick had used his head and not been surrounded by fulsome flatterers, who kept their wiser thoughts to themselves, he could have saved the situation with a graceful apology. Instead, he tried to bluff it out and sent a series of letters to Hampton Court attempting to justify himself. He even denied that the Princess had answered 'I don't know' when the Queen asked about her pregnancy.

The correspondence, back and forth, soon turned into an almost daily charade, each side trying to outdo the other in recriminations. In his letters the Prince ceased referring to his mother as 'your Majesty' which infuriated Queen Caroline, not solely for the lack of respect but because it reminded her of Frederick's past fatuous insistence that he, as Prince of Wales, was superior in rank to her. He had conceived the notion that, in the royal pecking order, he stood *between* King and Queen. But, as Lord Hervey commented: 'How he made it out, God knows!'

When the Prince had first aired his preposterous notion, Queen Caroline joked: 'My dear Fritz, let your quality be ever so great, the King, if I was to die, would never marry *you*!'

In their turn, the King's letters continually raked through the cold ashes of the Hampton Court 'escape'. Again and again they went over the whole incident, stage by stage. Like energetic potmen in a tavern polishing up the tankards to impress the tetchy landlord, Lord Hervey and Sir Robert Walpole scrubbed and rubbed at the King's words, ever bringing back for approval new and maliciously gleaming versions.

Letters from Hampton were succeeded by memoranda, once more reviewing the fateful night and loaded with quick-firing demands to the Prince to repent and submit to duty. The most decisive was addressed: 'From the King at Hampton Court to the Prince at St James's, September 10, 1737.' It expelled Prince Frederick and his family from St James's Palace, 'When it can be done without prejudice or inconvenience to the Princess.'

At her Hampton Court breakfast table the following morning the Queen, according to that industrious fact-gatherer Hervey, 'every now and then repeated, "I hope in God I shall never see him again."' And the King muttered: 'Thank God, tomorrow night the puppy will be out of my house.' The Prince, he complained, was surrounded by 'boobies and fools and madmen'.

George II followed up his memorandum to the Prince by notifying all peers, peeresses and privy councillors that 'whoever went to the Prince's Court should not be admitted into the King's presence'.

Prince Frederick was warned not to remove any furniture or other fittings at St James's that properly belonged to the King. But when Lord Hervey diffidently suggested that ornamental chests might be exempt from the order, since the Prince and Princess could not carry their clothes 'like dirty linen in a basket', the King snapped: 'Why not? A basket is good enough for them.'

On Monday, 12 September, the Prince and Princess of Wales moved out of St James's to Kew. The King's reaction on hearing that some members of their Court had gone with them was one of unconcern. 'He [the Prince] is such a fool he will talk more fiddle-faddle nonsense to them in a day than any old woman talks in a week,' he said.

Princess Augusta made a tentative move towards a reconciliation by writing to the King to say she would have come to see him at Hampton Court but decided not to only for 'fear of offending'. George replied that he was sorry she had been a victim 'of your husband's unpardonable conduct' – but he offered no invitation for a visit.

By this time the Hampton Court 'royal birth scandal' had become public knowledge. In London delighted citizens snapped up printed copies of lampooning verses in which the Prince was usually described as *Griff*, the nickname given him by his father many years before and in happier times. These pamphlets and broadsheets reflected the Prince's popularity for most of them mocked the King.

In the light of that popularity Prince Frederick then made a new and even sillier move. He had some of his own letters to the King printed and published with some parts of the originals altered and amended to strengthen his public case.

The King responded rather cleverly. All the Prince's letters had been written in French, but rather bad French. George, therefore, employed Hervey to make precise, literal translations into English. These were then printed on sheets and divided into two columns, with the originals on the left and translations on the right. George II himself paid for the nationwide distribution.

Much of this whole extraordinary affair had, of course, closely paralleled events between George II, when *he* was Prince of Wales, and his own father. He and Caroline had been expelled from St James's Palace and George I had publicly warned that their courtiers would not be received at his Court. The mirrored image of the latest events appears not to have impressed George II, however.

Frederick was advised that it might be to his advantage to dig out some of the letters his father had written to George I during the family quarrel of the previous reign. But they were not to be had. All except three had been burned by the late King's mistress, 'Maypole' Duchess of Kendal, on George II's orders.

During that summer of 1737, in the midst of the royal birth 'scandal', Queen Caroline was twice taken ill at Hampton Court. On both occasions the symptoms were the same – bouts of violent vomiting and nausea which lasted for three or four hours and then suddenly ceasing, leaving the Queen feeling reasonably well again.

When the Court returned to London in November the Queen was again taken ill, but this time more seriously. The medication prescribed by her doctor which, naturally, included bleeding and dosages of snake-root and brandy only made her worse.

Prince Frederick sent a note of sympathy and asked if he might visit the Queen, but the King vehemently refused to allow it. 'He wants to come and insult his poor, dying mother, but she shall not see him,' he cried. 'No, no! He shall not come and act any of his silly plays here – false, lying, cowardly, nauseous puppy!'

As she lay exhausted, Queen Caroline took heart from the knowledge that the Prince would not be seen at her deathbed. She whispered: 'At least I shall have one comfort in having my eyes eternally closed – I shall never see that monster again.'

Eventually the doctors discovered the cause of the sickness: an umbilical rupture, the legacy of past child-births and clearly indicated by a large swelling in the abdomen. Surgeons lanced the swelling, releasing a great deal of pus but did nothing to repair the basic damage.

Several more lancings followed but the whole clumsy procedure increased the septicaemia and it was evident that the Queen was beyond rescue. She patiently endured great agony until she died at just after ten on the evening of 20 November. Just before the end, according to Hervey, she said, 'I have now got asthma – open the window,' followed by the one word, 'Pray.'

Some unknown wag summed up the feeling of many of George II's subjects in a couplet displayed in London at the Royal Exchange:

> Oh, death, where is thy sting?
> To take the Queen, and leave the King!

George II showed great grief at the death of his wife but the generally poor opinion of him was not improved when it became known that he was being consoled in his mourning by his mistress, the Hanoverian Amelia Sophia de Walmoden. Soon afterwards the King created her Countess of Yarmouth.

From time to time George took the Countess to Hampton Court but the royal visits were usually only for a day or a few days at the most. During his visits he dropped into the habit of resting on his bed for an hour or two in the afternoon and he would sometimes conduct discussions with his ministers while lying flat on his back. William Pitt, his Secretary of State, gained much royal regard for the respectful manner in which he always knelt at the bedside – on a cushion.

With other ministers George often exhibited some of the more outlandish forms of his bad temper. When especially angered he would snatch off his wig and kick it around the room. In time, the onset of deafness and near-blindness made him even more irascible.

George II died at Kensington Palace, on 25 October 1760, of a massive heart attack. He was seventy-seven and had reigned for thirty-three years. Not all post-mortem judgments on him were harsh. William Pitt declared that 'the late good old King had something of humanity and, among other and royal virtues, he possessed justice, truth and sincerity in an eminent degree.' Perhaps Pitt really believed what he said, but as a summing up of the former monarch his tribute leaned much further towards colourful sentiment than to strict accuracy.

Despite an abortive attempt, the feud between the King and the Prince of Wales was never patched up and lasted until the Prince's death, nine years before his father's.

Frederick's popularity had also waned as the years passed and his departure was marked by a number of cuttingly satirical verses, the most notable of which was:

> Here lies Fred,
> Who was alive and is dead.
> There's no more to be said.

During George II's reign two rooms at Hampton Court, both overlooking Fountain Court on its northern side – the Queen's Presence Chamber and the Queen's Guard Chamber – were remodelled by having the ceilings raised. As part of the ornamentation of the fifty foot long Guard Chamber, a great white marble chimney-piece was installed with sides representing Yeomen of the Guard.

The East side of Clock Court was largely rebuilt and the George II Gateway was added, with the carved date, 1732, marking the completion of the additional State rooms made for the King. The Queen's Great Staircase, which leads up to the Haunted Gallery to the north and the Communication Gallery to the south, was completed and decorated by William Kent. Its wrought iron balustrade is by Tijou.

When dining formally with guests, George II used the Public Dining Room, on the palace's East Front, which had been converted from a music room. It was originally eighty feet long but is now reduced to nearly sixty, and is thirty-one feet wide.

In 1750 an Act of Parliament authorised the building of a bridge from East Molesey on the Surrey side of the Thames across to Hampton Court. On 13 December 1753 the bridge, comprising seven wooden arches, was opened to traffic but it proved to be altogether too frail and, twenty-five years later, was replaced by another wooden, but sounder structure.

Lord Halifax, Keeper and Ranger of Bushy Park, closed the public right-of-way across the Park to the outrage of the locals. His lordship, however, had not

*An engraving, dedicated by the artist John Vardy to George II, showing a 'Perspective View of the Magnificent Gothic Hall at Hampton Court.'*

*Part of the palace and gardens as they were in the time of George II. During the reign the east side of Clock Court was largely rebuilt and George II's Gateway added.*

bargained on the active opposition of a local Hampton Wick shoemaker named Timothy Bennett. Mr Bennett, in no way overawed by such powerful gentry, took his lordship to law and, as a result, public access to the Park has been preserved.

Queen Caroline enjoyed the gardens at Hampton Court, although she does not seem to have been actively concerned in their development. Elsewhere she left her mark – in the linking together of ponds in London's Hyde Park to form the Serpentine. And the royal birth affair certainly ranks as an important footnote in the annals of gardening, for Augusta, Princess of Wales, may be taken, as Mollie Sands, historian of Hampton Court gardens said, 'to have been the real founder of Kew'.

*George III (1738–1820). His autocratic policies contributed to Britain's loss of her American colonies and thereby to the emergence of the independent United States of America.*

# 14

# *The Hanoverians*

## GEORGE III

GEORGE III, SON OF THE LATE PRINCE OF WALES, and born one year after his sister's 'royal birth scandal', is remembered in the history of Hampton Court not for staying *at* the palace but for staying *away* from it.

His reasons for writing the place off as a royal residence are uncertain. But the most generally accepted story, told in later years by his son, the Duke of Sussex, is that his decision could be traced back to a strange incident involving his grandfather, George II.

Young Prince George and the King (so the story goes) were strolling through the palace's State Apartments when suddenly, and for no apparent reason, the old man turned nasty and boxed the boy's ears. This so impressed itself on the Prince's memory that when he finally became King himself he decided he could not bear to live at the scene of the insult.

George had not had an altogether propitious start in life. He was brought up against the background of the feud between his father and George II, coddled and over-protected by his widowed mother, and not given much opportunity for social or intellectual stimulation. From his teens, too, he was subjected to frequent attacks of sickness which mainly took the form of nausea and vomiting.

*Queen Charlotte (1744–1818), wife of George III to whom she bore nine sons and six daughters. Many of Hampton Court's pictures and much of its furniture were moved to Buckingham House in London which the King bought for Charlotte and which was later rebuilt as Buckingham Palace.*

George III is remembered now as the King who 'lost' Britain her American colonies and was 'mad'. On both counts he has been harshly judged; and modern medical detection has shown beyond much doubt that George was not insane, in the generally accepted sense, but suffered from the condition known as porphyria. This is a rare disorder due to a defect in body chemistry which causes widespread damage to the nervous system. It is always accompanied by other clinical symptoms and those that appeared in George, in his youth, were the forerunners.

In 1761 George entered into an arranged marriage with seventeen-year-old Princess Charlotte Sophia of the miniature duchy of Mecklenburg-Strelitz on the Baltic coast of Germany. She was an amiable young woman but, many thought, plain to the point of being ugly. (As she grew older her looks actually improved and Horace Walpole delivered himself of the cutting remark: 'I do think the *bloom* of her ugliness is going off!')

George had been in love with the equally young Lady Sarah Lennox but, as time passed, he became devoted to Charlotte and for £21,000 he bought Buckingham House, later rebuilt as Buckingham Palace, to serve as a private family residence. That also became another reason why George deserted Hampton Court.

The State Apartments at Hampton were now no longer the scene of great state occasions and many of the pictures and much of the furniture was moved either to Buckingham House, which soon became known as Queen's House, or Windsor. But the palace was by no means empty of people.

George III instituted the system, still operating today, of alloting suites of Hampton Court apartments to families of those who had, in some way or other, given notable service to the Crown – the so-called grace-and-favour accommodation. During his reign around forty such apartments were allocated.

By opening up the palace in a properly controlled way, the King hoped to keep out squatters who, as we have seen, had been helping themselves to rooms since Henry VIII's time. He gave orders to the staff that no one was to be allowed to occupy apartments without first obtaining a warrant specifying the precise rooms to be allocated.

A surviving warrant, addressed to Mrs Mary Anderson, under-housekeeper, and signed by Lord Hertford, the Lord Chamberlain, gives an example (with original punctuation and style) of the specified details:

These are to require you to deliver to Sir Robert Hamilton, Bart, the Keys and Possession of the Apartments in the Outer Lodging of Hampton Court Palace which, when the Court was there, were used by Their Royal Highnesses The Princesses Amelia and Caroline, Also to deliver to the said Sir Robert Hamilton the Keys and Possession of the Garretts immediately over, and of Three Rooms under the said Apartments, the whole to be held by him till further Order. And for so doing this shall be your warrent. Given under my Hand this 26th Day of April, 1775. In the Fifteenth Year of His Majesty's Reign. (Signed) Hertford.

Even four years before the date of that warrant, Hannah More, the author and evangelist, was writing to Horace Walpole: 'The private apartments are almost all full; they are all occupied by people of fashion, mostly of quality; and it is astonishing to me that people of large fortune will solicit for them.'

One applicant who did not succeed in acquiring an apartment was the great lexicographer and essayist, Dr Samuel Johnson. The good doctor had been graciously received by the King at Queen's House and allowed to browse in the magnificent library there. Ever afterwards Johnson heartily defended the King and his much-abused government and said: 'Sir, they may talk of the King as they will, but he is the finest gentleman I have ever seen.'

In his formal application to the Lord Chamberlain, written from his house in

Bolt Court, Fleet Street, London, on 11 April 1776, Johnson said:

My Lord: Being wholly unknown to your lordship, I have only this apology to make for presuming to trouble you with a request – that a stranger's petition if it cannot easily be granted, can be easily refused. Some of the apartments at Hampton Court are now vacant, in which I am encouraged to hope that, by application to your lordship, I may obtain a residence. Such a grant would be considered by me as a great favour; and I hope, to a man who has had the honour of vindicating his Majesty's government, a retreat in one of his houses may not be improperly or unworthily allowed. I therefore request that your lordship will be pleased to grant such rooms in Hampton Court as shall seem proper to,
My Lord,
Your lordship's most obedient
and humble servant,
Sam Johnson.

Despite its elegantly flowing style, the application failed to move Lord Hertford who replied with a single, snooty sentence: 'The Lord Chamberlain presents his compliments to Mr Johnson and is sorry he cannot obey his commands, having already on his hands many engagements unsatisfied.'

Johnson wrote his letter a few hours before he dined with his worshipping biographer, James Boswell. But nowhere in his famous *Life* does Boswell mention Johnson's effort to secure a Hampton Court apartment. It seems possible that the great man half expected to be turned down and, when he was, saw no good reason to make the failure public.

Inevitably, a minority of palace occupants exploited the royal favour. Without permission some of them even set about making structural alterations and others sub-let their apartments. The Lord Chamberlain issued warnings but when these

*'A Kick-Up At A Hazard Table.' Thomas Rowlandson, the caricaturist, was one of the most pungent visual commentators on the seamier side of eighteenth-century life. In this cartoon the card-table gamblers fall out among themselves.*

*24. Fountain Court. The Tudor Cloister Green Court was demolished to make way for this courtyard by Sir Christopher Wren. The magnificent many-windowed buildings are of brick faced with Portland stone.*

*25. The East Front of the palace, also designed by Wren with some 'assistance' – which usually meant interference – from William III. The royal apartments were on the first floor of the building which looks out across the Great Fountain Garden.*

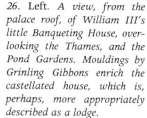

26. Left. *A view, from the palace roof, of William III's little Banqueting House, overlooking the Thames, and the Pond Gardens. Mouldings by Grinling Gibbons enrich the castellated house, which is, perhaps, more appropriately described as a lodge.*

27. Below left. *The Privy Garden seen from the palace roof. On a summer's day Queen Mary – who ruled jointly with her husband, William of Orange – would sit in a bower on the edge of this garden, sewing and pausing occasionally to admire the flowers that she, as a keen gardener, loved.*

28. Right. *The Long Water at daybreak. It was Charles II who ordered this great canal to be dug and William III particularly loved it since it was a reminder to him of his native Holland.*

29. Below. *Long Water and the Fountain Garden. William III had planned to adorn this garden with thirteen fountains, but one suffices. And with the Long Water at one end and the East Front of the palace at the other what more is needed?*

30. Right. *Privy Garden and South Front. This part of the palace exterior is less lavishly decorated than the East Front. But one of its notable features is the Latin inscription which, in translation, reads: 'William and Mary, King and Queen, built this.'*

31. Queen Anne's Orangery, on the south side of the palace. The building, similarly to the Banqueting House, is of warm red brick and it is made additionally elegant by the white sash-windows. House-martins find here many attractive corners for their nests.

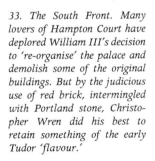

32. The Great Vine of Hampton Court – the world's most famous vine that has been growing and flourishing here since 1768. The annual crop of Black Hamburg grapes sometimes amounts to as many as six hundred bunches, each bunch averaging around twelve ounces.

33. The South Front. Many lovers of Hampton Court have deplored William III's decision to 're-organise' the palace and demolish some of the original buildings. But by the judicious use of red brick, intermingled with Portland stone, Christopher Wren did his best to retain something of the early Tudor 'flavour.'

LE TRIOMPHE DE L'AMOUR.

proved ineffective the King added his personal weight to the pressure. He instructed Lord Hertford to spell out to Mrs Anderson his strong objection to sub-letting. Part of Hertford's letter to the under-housekeeper, dated 20 July 1780 reads:

I am to signify to you His Majesty's pleasure in order that it may be communicated to the several persons who possess apartments in Hampton Court Palace that such practice will not be permitted in future. Those who have lodgings in it, of which neither they nor their families make use, are expected to give them up and return the keys into your hands . . . This mode of transfer prevents His Majesty from favouring such persons as he may think most proper to indulge with lodgings. His Majesty, so far from being consulted or his own pleasures being necessary to give lodgings to any person who may apply for them, will not even know, except by accident, the persons residing in his palaces . . .

The only effect of this royal instruction, however, was to encourage the offenders to take greater care in concealing their private deals and the practice of sub-letting continued for almost another sixty years.

The apartments had their share of unusual and, occasionally, tragic lodgers. One of the most notable, in that second category, was the author, Richard Tickell, a brother-in-law of the playwright Richard Brinsley Sheridan.

*'The Bridal Night.' A satirical view of the Prince of Wales, later George IV, and his bride on their way to the nuptial bed. A servant bears a sack of money representing the Prince's frequent dips into the public purse.*

On 4 November 1793, Tickell died in a fall from his bedroom window, on the South Front of the palace. His head, so it was recorded, made a hole 'a foot deep in the gravel walk' sixty feet below.

The playwright's sister, Mrs Alicia Le Fanu, gave this account of Tickell's death:

It had frequently been his delight to sit and read on a parapet wall, or kind of platform before his window, in one of the upper apartments of the palace; he much delighted in the situation, which was constantly filled with flower-pots.

About twelve at noon, while his carriage was waiting to convey himself and his family to town for the winter, Mrs Tickell left the room for a moment and on her return, not finding him there, she ran into an adjoining chamber, which commanded a view of the garden beneath, where she beheld her husband lying on the ground; but before she reached the fatal spot he had expired.

At the inquest into the tragedy the jury returned a verdict of accidental death. But it is more likely that Tickell committed suicide. What the jury did not know was that, six months before, he had written to Warren Hastings – first British governor-general of India, later tried, and acquitted, for cruelty and corruption – saying he was in trouble and needed a loan of £500. The loan was granted. Another notable occupant, whose life certainly ended in suicide, was Thomas Bradshaw, private secretary to the Duke of Grafton, who was, for a time, George III's Prime Minister.

Grafton had been a reluctant Prime Minister who preferred his private life and pleasures to politics although he had remained in office out of a sense of duty. He was a Fitzroy, and a descendant of that illegitimate son sired by Charles II on Nell Gwyn, and Horace Walpole summed him up as a man who thought 'the world should be postponed to a whore and a race horse'.

(All the same, he opposed retaining the tax on tea in Britain's American colonies – the fuse that lit the political dynamite under George III's throne and led to the creation of the United States. Unfortunately, or perhaps, in retrospect, American citizens might say 'happily', the Duke was outvoted by his own Cabinet.)

Grafton became involved with one Nancy Parsons, daughter of a tailor in London's Bond Street, who was usually known as Mrs Horton, from the name of the West Indian merchant with whom she had lived.

The Duke was besotted with Nancy and she does seem to have been an hypnotically attractive woman. For her, he left his wife, who was also one of the era's great beauties, and flaunted her around the town. At the opera they were seen by, or at least reported to the famous and pungently satirical 'mystery' commentator, *Junius*, who employed his talents to bring down Grafton's administration. (The attacks somewhat backfired since Grafton was succeeded by the bungling Lord North during whose term of office the American colonies were finally lost.)

*Junius* suggested that Thomas Bradshaw had been awarded his Hampton Court apartments through the influence of Grafton and as an expression of the Duke's gratitude for Bradshaw's efforts as a go-between with Nancy. He certainly benefited handsomely – he was allocated a suite of around no fewer than sixty rooms, just off the Haunted Gallery and known as the Haunted Gallery Lodgings.

Bradshaw was, even more incredibly, later made a Lord of the Admiralty.

But he squandered his money and shot himself in 1774. Two years after that suicide, Nancy married Charles, 2nd Viscount Maynard.

Lord North, who was Prime Minister from 1770 to 1782, and a close friend of the King, also found himself installed at Hampton Court, by a rather curious turn of events.

In 1771, George III offered to appoint North as Keeper and Ranger of Bushy Park with which went the Keeper's Lodgings at the palace, above the King's Guard Chamber and Presence Chamber, overlooking the Privy Garden. North was keen to have this sinecure post but, since it was an office under the Crown, he could not accept it and still retain his House of Commons seat. Obligingly, the King arranged to confer the honour on North's wife, Anne, and the couple were able therefore to take up residence in the palace.

The names of North and George III are usually coupled in the story of the disastrous war against the American colonists. North privately opposed the war but he was under the strong influence of the King who, in effect, controlled Parliament through a small group known as the 'King's Friends'. And he was, literally, in the King's debt to the extent of a royal gift of £20,000, made available when the weight of money troubles nearly broke the Prime Minister.

After his retirement from public life, North could often be seen shuffling around Hampton Court, an awkward, clumsy man with a wide, thick-lipped mouth and prominent, hopelessly myopic eyes. He died in 1792 but his widow continued to live at the palace until her death five years later.

In 1764 the palace gardens came under the supervision of Lancelot Brown, better known to history as Capability Brown, from his habit of saying, after inspecting a piece of land, that it 'had the capability' of being turned into an

*The Great Fountain Garden at the palace as it was some sixty-five years before the famous supervising gardener 'Capability' Brown was appointed.*

*Earlier days of the Great Vine, planted from a cutting taken for 'Capability' Brown from a Black Hamburg vine then growing at Valentines, near Wanstead, in Essex.*

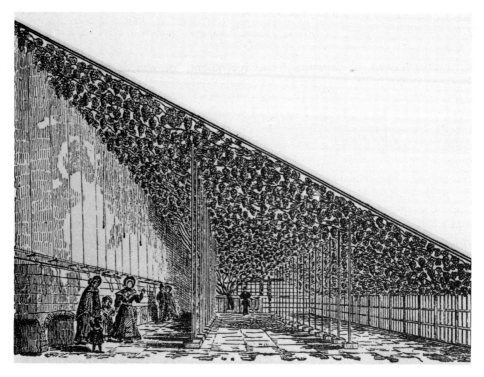

impressive garden. The architect, William Kent, although less well-known than Brown, is usually regarded as the true 'father' of landscape gardening and he and Brown were collaborators for nine years.

Brown, born in 1715 in Northumberland and first employed as a kitchen gardener by Lord Cobham, was a favourite with the nobility and other owners of great country houses. He laid out the grounds of Blenheim and Kew and, in the year of his appointment at Hampton Court, planned the lake at Blenheim. For his services at the palace he received the then enormous sum of £2,000 a year and he was provided with Wilderness House, west of the Lion Gate, as a residence.

He replaced the terrace steps in the Privy Garden with grass banks under the dictum that 'we ought not to go up and down stairs in the open air.' But his most memorable achievement was the planting of the great vine – the most famous in the world – now seventy-eight inches round at its base and with a main 'branch' of one hundred and fourteen feet. Its origin was a cutting taken for Brown from the Black Hamburg vine then growing at Valentines, near Wanstead, in Essex.

In his record of the palace, Ernest Law, writing in 1891, said of the vine:

Various conjectures have been advanced to account for the great size to which it so quickly grew. Some have surmised that its roots have made their way into the vast drains of the palace, or into a neighbouring cesspool, and that it has, in fact, been nourished on sewage. This, however, is not the case . . . If its luxuriance is to be ascribed to any special cause it is more likely due to the roots having penetrated to the bed of the river, which is not more than sixty feet from the end of the vine-house.

Brown's principal approach to landscape gardening was to emphasise the undulating lines of the natural terrain. Unfortunately, this developed into a mannerism which usually took little or no account of differing situations or historical background. But, so far as the grounds of Hampton Court are concerned, Brown, happily, left well alone. The palace gardens historian, Mollie Sands, wondered, indeed, if 'Capability' had real talent, 'or was he merely a clever charlatan, who knew just enough to exploit the fashion of the times?' But, whether Brown was really talented or merely acquired gullible clients, he amassed a fortune and became High Sheriff of Huntingdonshire.

The gardens and grounds meant little to George III since he seldom saw them. But there is one anecdote attaching to one of his rare visits to Hampton Court.

It was said that one day George, and a group of courtiers out hunting, attempted to follow the hounds over the bridge from the Surrey side of the river. Despite an imperious cry of 'The King!' Mr Feltham, the keeper, closed the toll gate and announced: 'I'll tell you what, hang me if I open my gate again until I see your money! I pay £400 a year for this bridge and I laid out £1,000 upon it. I've let King George through, God bless him! I know of no other king in England. If you have brought the king of France, hang me if I let him through without the blunt [ready cash]!'

The King then appeared and poor, embarrassed Feltham bowed low and hastily opened the gate. George was sufficiently amused by the incident to order a special and substantial payment for the toll-keeper – far more than the usual guinea paid for the passage of a royal party. As he crossed the bridge on a later occasion, the King put his head out of his carriage window and shouted to Feltham, with a grin: 'No fear of the king of France coming today!'

There was, indeed, no fear of anyone of royal note spending time at the palace which, apart from the 'official' residents, the unofficial sub-tenants and a handful of squatters, began to wear an air of neglect and desertion.

One visitor noted that 'the princely halls have nothing to echo back but the hurried footsteps of a single domestic, who passes through them daily to wipe away the dust of their untrodden floors, only that it may collect there again.'

There were just the occasional colourful incidents to breathe some life into the near-dead palace. One young woman, who seems to have been ignorant of the palace's open-house facilities, if not of other more worldly matters, complained that the difficulty of finding a private room obliged her admiring colonel to make love to her 'on a stone staircase'.

George III died at Windsor, on 29 January 1820, a pathetic figure, alone in the fantasy world of his dementia where, only a little time before, he was said to have saluted a tree in the muddled belief that it was the king of Prussia.

His had been a tumultuous reign, not only because of American Independence, but because of riots that were both political and economic in origin. At the same time it was a reign that saw the emergence of growing public involvement in politics and the birth of an era in which ordinary people would increasingly begin to seek the accountability of those placed to rule over them – the genesis of modern parliamentary democracy.

*George IV (1762–1830). A prolific spender and gambler, he maintained a royal stud at the palace where he bred race-horses. In the Goodwood Cup, run on 11 August 1830, his horses took the first three places.*

# 15

# *The Hanoverians*

## GEORGE IV & WILLIAM IV

NINE YEARS BEFORE THE DEATH OF GEORGE III, and in consequence of the King's disability, Parliament was obliged to create his son, George Augustus Frederick, as Prince Regent. And it was the forty-nine-year-old Prince who now became George IV.

The new King was handsome and gifted but he was also a profligate spender and a gambler and had chosen debauchery as one of his other enthusiastically-pursued hobbies. He collected mistresses, on whom he lavished expensive gifts, and at the age of twenty-one he secretly and, without his father's legally required consent, married the lovely widow, Maria Fitzherbert. He subsequently contracted an official, arranged marriage with the German princess, Caroline of Brunswick, but though, in line of duty, the couple produced a child, they detested each other and eventually separated.

George IV was a ludicrous monarch but he had artistic abilities which expressed themselves through such projects as the building of the Pavilion at Brighton, the reconstruction of Buckingham Palace and the creation of that stately London thoroughfare, Regent Street. The trouble was, he did these things at the expense of his ordinary impoverished subjects and, until the day he died, Parliament groaned over his ever-accumulating debts. (At one time he was spending £10,000 a year on clothes. His coronation robes cost £24,000 and his crown £54,000.)

*George IV's dissolute style of life and his self-indulgent grossness shocked and angered many of his subjects. Here he is depicted as 'A Voluptuary.'*

*High life under the Hanoverians. A peep into the Green Room of a group of idle upper class citizens preparing themselves for their amateur theatricals.*

But he did visit the palace occasionally mainly to inspect the royal stud where he bred his own racehorses. His yearlings, sold on the Monday of each Epsom race week, fetched around £200 each – some return, at least, to set against the £30,000 a year the King spent on the stud. As far as winners were concerned he had one notably successful day, in the Goodwood Cup, run on 11 August 1830, when his horses took the first three places: 1, *Fleur-de-lys*; 2, *Zingaree*; and 3, *The Colonel*,

If the King was seldom seen at Hampton Court there was, nevertheless, a royal presence there in the person of George's brother, the Duke of Clarence (subsequently William IV), who succeeded Lord North's window as Ranger of Bushy Park and took up residence in Bushy House, a substantial mansion.

The Duke formed a wining and dining society, the Toy Club, named after the local hostelry. Most of its members were drawn from the neighbouring gentry and it met monthly for whist drives interspersed with the singing of songs (usually bawdy) and the serving of the Duke's favourite dish, marrow pudding.

A stanza of one of the more 'respectable' club songs, unearthed by Ernest Law, ran:

> With some *Toy* or other all mortals are pleased,
> Their fancies delighted, their troubles appeased;
> The globe through all quarters they search for their sport,
> But no prettier they'll find than at sweet Hampton Court.

During George IV's reign the palace began to be visited by sightseers – the first trickle of what was to become a flood and turn Hampton Court into a major tourist attraction. There were some notables among the visitors. William Wordsworth, the poet, was there and so was the Duke of Wellington, 'The Iron Duke', and the novelist, Mary Russell Mitford, author of that memorable and delightful book, *Our Village*.

Miss Mitford wrote ecstatically: 'What a beautiful place! What a real palace!' And, in an oblique reference to the King's devotion to Brighton, she asked: 'How can anybody leave Hampton Court and live in the Pavilion?'

The Duke of Wellington was responsible for adding a new name to part of the palace. He was much taken with the discovery that, on warm summer days, elderly lady residents gathered in one of the window recesses outside the East Front and there gossiped the hours away. From a distance the wagging tongues reminded the Duke of the sound of cats and he therefore designated the place as 'Purr Corner'.

During George IV's ten-year reign, maintenance costs of the palace, including wages, averaged £5,000 a year with a further £2,880 for the gardens.

Compared with the total cost to the nation of the King himself, those were moderate sums. His debts were formidable and endless and when he died, on 26 June 1830, an unusually bitter editorial in the London *Times* asked: 'What eye has wept for him? What heart has heaved one throb of unmercenary sorrow?' All that the people could do after his departure, said the editorial writer, was to pay 'for his profusion' and ensure that similar profligacy was not allowed in the future.

The new King, William IV, hated his late brother's rebuilt Buckingham Palace and it was with great reluctance that he left Bushy House. For some time, when he was still Duke of Clarence, he had lived there, in what one observer called a state of 'perfect domestic character', with his mistress, the remarkable Mrs Dorothy Jordan.

Mrs Jordan, born Dorothy Bland in 1761, was the illegitimate daughter of a Welsh mother and Irish father. She grew up to become one of the most popular actresses of the age. The essayist William Hazlitt depicted her as the essence of femininity in features, voice, manners, laugh and what he called 'fine animal spirits'. She was, in short, 'all gaiety, openness and good nature'.

Clarence was immediately smitten by her and they lived openly and happily as unofficial husband and wife. When she appeared at London's Drury Lane Theatre the Duke was usually to be found hovering in the wings, admiring her performance. Her many theatre-going 'fans' had no difficulty in picking out her

*Dorothy Jordan, actress and mistress of the Duke of Clarence (later to be William IV) by whom she had ten illegitimate children. In this picture, by John Hoppner, she portrays the Comic Muse.*

coach, whether in London or in and around Hampton and Bushey as its crest included an anchor as a tribute to her lover's service in the Royal Navy.

Althogether, in thirteen of the twenty years of their association, Dorothy Jordan bore the Duke no fewer than ten illegitimate children. The public interest in the frequency of her pregnancies naturally gave rise to ribald comments. One magazine writer quipped: 'Mrs Jordan is shortly expecting to produce *something*, whether a young Admiral or a Pickle Duchess it is impossible yet to tell.'

Duke, mistress and children made Bushy House a lively and well populated retreat. Clarence was an affectionate father but the costs of the household added to his burdens for, like his predecessor, he was soon running into debt. He gave Dorothy £1,000 a year and much of what she earned from the theatre went towards supporting children from previous love affairs and contributed to the lavish entertaining in which she and her lover delighted.

There were some who chose to believe, unjustifiably, that the Duke was 'sponging' on his mistress and a typical example of doggerel ran:

> As Jordan's high and mighty squire
> Her playhouse profits deigns to skim,
> Some folks audaciously inquire
> If *he* keeps her, or *she* keeps him?

Clarence's father, George III, was less concerned about his son having a mistress than about what he was allowing her. 'A thousand, a thousand!' he is supposed to have barked. 'Too much, too much! Five hundred quite enough – quite enough!'

When he was not occupied with his large 'unofficial' family, the Duke busied himself at Bushy and Hampton commanding the local yeomanry, sitting as a magistrate and pursuing the hobby he had inherited from his father: farming.

On one occasion, it is said, a doctor who had been pronouncing on the fitness of local recruits to undertake military service, remarked upon the excellent handwriting with which the Duke signed the necessary papers.

'Why,' the Duke replied, 'the fact is, that when I served as a midshipman (and you must know I served my regular time), I was obliged to keep a log-book, and my captain had a particular aversion to bad writing. I thus acquired a habit of writing legibly, and I also acquired a habit which has been of the greatest use to me through life, and that is of recording the occurrences of the day. Every night of my life I make it a rule to set down (as I used when a midshipman with the log-book) the occurrences of the day and, by so doing, submit my actions to the scrutiny of a self-examination. The habit is a good one. I have tried, and proved it.'

Important actions which the Duke eventually decided to submit to the scrutiny of a self-examination centred, inevitably, on money. He came to the conclusion that he needed money more than he needed Mrs Jordan, and the large brood of children he and his mistress had produced, and to which he gave the family name Fitzclarence, were proving a constant drain on his resources. Dorothy Jordan suspected there was something amiss for she said: 'I believe when I am out of the gate at Bushey Park I am very soon *forgot.*'

The arrival on the scene of a Miss Catherine Tylney-Long, an attractive young woman with a fortune thought to be around £500,000, raised the Duke's hopes. But his attempts to woo her failed ignominiously and, immediately after that, he was equally unsuccessful in seeking to win the hands of other wealthy women. He was no great catch – pudgy and coarse-mannered and looking more like a man in his mid-fifties than mid-forties. In any case he had no reason to expect that he would accede to the throne; ahead of him, in line, were George IV's daughter, Charlotte, and his own elder brother, Frederick, Duke of York.

In October 1811 a letter from the Duke, ending their twenty-year affair, reached Mrs Jordan in Cheltenham where she was appearing in the aptly-named comedy *Devil to Pay.* According to her earliest biographer, James Boaden, writing in 1830, she turned up at the theatre that same evening, 'dreadfully weakened by a succession of fainting fits'.

Copy-book true to stage tradition, however, she was determined not to disappoint her eagerly expectant audience. She went on in her roll of Nell, a character supposed, at one point in the play, to be made laughing drunk by a conjuror. When poor Dorothy Jordan reached the scene she tried to laugh but burst into tears. With supreme presence of mind, the actor with whom she was playing adjusted his lines, to cover her distress, so the audience heard him say: 'Why, Nell, the conjuror has not only made thee drunk, but has made thee *crying* drunk!'

The Duke at least arranged to provide generously for Mrs Jordan and made her a settlement of £4,400 a year to cover the needs of herself and her daughters, including two from her previous love affairs. Despite her earlier anguish she spoke well of the Duke and his 'liberal provision'. But there were many former neighbours of the couple at Bushey and Hampton who regretted the break up

*William IV (1765–1837). He was known as the 'Sailor King' because of the early years he spent in the Royal Navy. The crest on the side of his mistress's coach included an anchor – a tribute to her sea-dog lover.*

of the 'happy domestic scene' on their doorstep.

Unhappily, Dorothy Jordan lost most of her money as a result of fraud perpetrated by Frederick March, one of her sons-in-law, and she died in poverty in France, and neglected by her children, on 5 July 1816.

It was the deaths of his niece, Charlotte, and his brother, Frederick, that brought the Duke to the throne as William IV. And by then he had married Princess Amelia Adelaide of Saxe-Meiningen, mainly on the grounds that marital status entitled him to a larger state allowance.

Adelaide was twenty-six at the time of their marriage and, although no beauty, she was an affectionate and kindly natured young woman who was, in time, to influence William considerably for the better. His manners improved, he dropped his habit of telling crude, dirty jokes in mixed company and his courtiers were impressed by his sudden and unexpected politeness.

His admiration for Adelaide was genuine and he made that clearly known in some of his public speeches. Recalling one such speech, Dr John Watkins wrote in his 1831 biography of William: 'Her Majesty also was observed to be much moved by the affectionate manner in which the King had spoken of his connubial happiness, and that in her presence.'

Although the King and Queen made Windsor their residence, William appointed Adelaide as Ranger of Bushy Park and gave the locals the right to visit Bushy House without any admission charge. Dr Watkins reported: 'In grateful respect for this benevolence, the people of Hampton entered into a subscription to celebrate His Majesty's birthday yearly, by appropriate festivities, and an entertainment to the poor.'

William favoured the idea of turning Hampton Court into a museum and he ordered a large collection of pictures, most of them second-rate, to be moved to the palace from other royal residences including Buckingham Palace and Windsor.

For a cost of £400 he restored the great King's Staircase, which had not been repaired or redecorated for fifty years. But he foolishly removed Henry VIII's astronomical clock – the works had long ceased to operate accurately – and replaced it with a clock from St James's Palace. (In 1879 the original clock, with a new mechanism, was brought back.)

William also planned to demolish the then dilapidated riverside Banqueting Hall built for William III. But the Hall was saved by a happy accident. The King happened to mention his plan to a friend, Sir James Reynett, as the two were walking around the palace on an inspection visit. Sir James immediately protested: 'Don't do that, sir, I pray you. If you will allow me to occupy the Hall I will undertake to put it in repair and take care of it.' William agreed and Reynett restored the building and used it as a summer residence until his death in 1864.

The flow of sightseers to the palace which had begun, as we have seen, in the previous reign, increased summer by summer. Admission was one shilling and the first, but not very enthusiastic, Hampton Court conducted-tour guides appeared.

A guide was sometimes the deputy-housekeeper but more often one of the housemaids. And visitors, says Ernest Law, were shown, or rather 'driven', through the State Apartments by one or other of these ladies 'who pointed out the pictures with a long stick, calling out in a loud voice at the same time, the names of the subjects and their painters to the awe-stricken company – a procedure that allowed of little opportunity for studying or enjoying them'.

One colourful story of the period centres on the Chapel Royal. In the summer of

1831 a young woman visitor fainted and was carried out into the open air by Sir Horace Seymour, a handsome widower who had fought with the Duke of Wellington at Waterloo. On each of the two succeeding Sundays other young women also fainted and on every occasion Sir Horace readily offered his Samaritan service.

All that swooning much irritated Sir Horace's aunt, Lady George Seymour, who complained that, unless something were done, the affliction would 'degenerate into an epidemic'. Having, therefore, obtained the chaplain's permission, she posted the following notice on the chapel door:

Whereas a tendency to faint is becoming a prevalent infirmity among young ladies frequenting this chapel, notice is hereby given that, for the future, ladies so affected will no longer be carried out by Sir Horace Seymour, but by Branscombe the dustman.

Branscombe, the dustman, was denied his moment of glory for, from the Sunday on which Lady Seymour's notice appeared, the 'infirmity' vanished as suddenly as it had developed.

King William's own infirmities, culminating in a bout of asthma, brought his life to a close on 20 June 1837 at Windsor. He was two months short of his seventy-second birthday.

At Kensington Palace his eighteen-year-old niece wrote in her diary: 'Poor man, he was always very kind to me and he *meant* it well I know . . . He was odd, very odd and singular, but his intentions were often ill-interpreted.' The niece was Victoria, daughter of Edward, the late Duke of Kent and Victoria of Saxe-Coburg, who was now Queen.

Politically, the reign of William IV, 'Sailor William', had been one of great significance. Against a background of rioting, especially in the Midlands and Bristol, Parliamentary reform had laid the foundation for modern democracy. Local government had been reconstructed and freedom granted at last to the slaves of the West Indies.

But respect for the monarchy was at its lowest ebb. People had grown sickened of the Georges, and William, the last reigning son of George III, had added his quota to the general disdain. There were many who would have been delighted to witness the emergence of a new republic. Young Victoria changed their minds, however, and the British royal line owes its survival to her.

*Like so many of their predecessors, King William and Queen Adelaide processed by way of the river on some of their major state occasions.*

*The Excursion-Van, one form of Victorian transport for a day's outing. In this type of contraption, among others, the first sightseers descended on the publicly-opened palace.*

# 16

# *The*

# *Later Years*

## QUEEN VICTORIA

LADY EMILY MONTAGUE, WHO SERVED AS Hampton Court's Lady House-keeper until the first year of Queen Victoria's reign, has a rather strange claim to fame in the history of the palace. For by departing this life she unwittingly opened the doors of the state apartments to the kingdom and the world.

While she filled her honourable office, small fees had continued to be charged to visitors mainly to supplement her salary. But on her death, in April 1838, the immediate need for that particular source of revenue ceased. And so it was that the young Queen took what, to the surprise of herself and many other people, turned out to be a momentous decision: the palace was to be opened to the public *free of charge*.

The new free-admission system came into operation in November 1838 and the plan was that the gates should be opened on five days a week – excluding Friday (which was to be kept as a cleaning day) and, of course, Sunday.

However, the ladies of the housekeeping staff, who were to act as guides and custodians of the conducted-tour parties, very astutely spotted a distinct lack of entreprencurial enterprise in the arrangement. Among themselves they reasoned thus: large crowds of ordinary people would surely want to take advantage of their first opportunity to see inside a palace; and large crowds of people would certainly mean a very useful flow of gratuities for the ladies; but large numbers would be unlikely to visit the palace on any day except Sunday, for that was the one work-free day of the week. Conclusion: extra, privately-pocketable income must depend on Sunday opening.

*Harris, one of the trio in Jerome K. Jerome's classic 'Three Men in a Boat', declared that the way through the Maze was 'absurdly simple.' A crowd, equally simple, follows him in.*

The obvious problem would be with the authorities. Any suggestion of Sunday opening would undoubtedly meet with their horrified opposition. The ladies, therefore, adopted a cunning ploy. When the crowds turned up on the first Sunday after the official free-admission system came into force (hoping, if perhaps not expecting, to find the door open) the ladies let them in. The following Sunday even bigger crowds arrived and they, too, were admitted. And so it went on until when, at last, the authorities caught on to what was happening they reacted as the clever ladies of Hampton Court had suspected they would: rather than risk a public outcry against what was rapidly developing into a mass invasion, they turned a blind eye to the sharp practice by their staff and Sunday opening stayed.

Others were less tolerant. The idea of any free admission at all had set off puritanical protests from the well-heeled who were astonished and wounded by the decision of their nineteen-year-old, inexperienced Queen to open a royal palace to those whom they charmingly referred to as the 'lower orders'. They predicted that the invaders would undoubtedly wreck the place, carry off the moveables and generally behave like a rabble.

But *Sunday* opening held out even more dire prospects. It would, said the critics, send Britain hurtling down the slippery, sinful slope towards the 'Continental Sunday' (with which no other horror on earth could be compared). A tidal wave of licentiousness and drunkenness would sweep down the Thames. 'Hampton Court on a Sunday,' thundered one divine, 'will be hell on earth.'

Certainly the invasion of the 'lower orders' was of a far greater strength than anyone could have forecast. As winter turned to spring they poured out of the fetid stews of London in droves and made their way to the palace on foot, in dog-carts and pony-traps and in horse-drawn charabancs. Before long, the annual total of visitors had topped the 80,000 mark.

And to the disappointment of all those who had voiced their hysterical forebodings, the vast hordes of working class families behaved impeccably – indeed, as one observer commented, their behaviour was a good deal more civilised than that of many of their 'betters' who had inhabited the palace in the past.

It was not only the palace and its treasures that gripped the visitors' imagination. They wandered in awe around the gardens and parks. The mere fact of being free to walk in such places was an experience in itself for those normally confined to dismal, smog-ridden Victorian London.

Others eventually caught on to the financial rewards to be gained from the freely-opened palace, among them the directors of the London and South Western Railway who, in 1849, opened a branch line to Hampton Court. (Average journey time from Waterloo, with stops at intervening stations: 45 minutes.) And, over Victoria's reign as a whole, the average annual total of visitors ran at 220,000.

(Forty years later the original edition of Jerome K. Jerome's great comic classic, *Three Men in a Boat*, gave the palace added publicity. According to the book, one of the three men, the delightful know-all Harris, had once attracted a vast following at Hampton Court Maze by declaring, airily, that the solution to the puzzle was absurdly simple – 'You keep on taking the first turning to the right.' Inevitably, of course, Harris got lost along with his infuriated followers. But thousands of readers of the book, so it was said, descended on the Maze on the equally erroneous assumption that *they* would solve the problem by adopting the opposite course to Harris – by taking every turn to the left.)

Whatever they may have felt about the Sunday visitors' invasion, the grace-and-favour residents continued to live the rest of the week in quiet and secluded comfort. Their greatest excitement came in 1842 when they battled in the High Court against a proposal by the Hampton parochial authorities to end their immunity against paying a poor-law rate. Their test case was brought in the name of Lady Emily Ponsonby 'and others'. (Lady Ponsonby, widow of Major-General Sir Frederic Cavendish Ponsonby, lived in the south-west wing of the West Front.)

In their argument before the Queen's Bench, the residents' lawyers pleaded that, technically, their clients were neither tenants nor occupants since, in law, the actual 'occupier' was Her Majesty who could at any time resume possession of the entire palace. But the court ruled that occupation was a benefit and, therefore, rateable. As a result the local authority decided on a total annual payment for all the palace residences of not less than £500 which meant, in effect, that the individual occupants paid between £7 and £15 year depending on the size of their apartments.

The court case was instrumental in giving outsiders a glimpse of those grace-and-favour apartments. Some, it was said, consisted of 'spacious drawing rooms, dining rooms, bedrooms, servants' rooms, kitchens and other domestic offices, suitable for the residence and accommodation of persons with considerable household establishments; and are now, and always have been, occupied by persons of rank and distinction; and others are occupied by persons of respectable station'.

In the middle and late eighteen-hundreds the summer crowds who flocked to Hampton Court delighted in strolling through the gardens or just sitting in the shade of the trees.

Residents provided their own furniture and fittings and any repairs necessary before a new occupant moved in were carried out at the Crown's expense. If occupants wanted more extensive decorations than those provided by the authorities they shared those costs with the Crown. But payment for any additional, major alterations was the responsibility of the occupant and, in some cases, the court heard, these had amounted to £1,000 or more. All redecoration or alterations had to be approved by HM Office of Woods and Forests and every two years Crown officers inspected each apartment. If any repairs were necessary occupants were ordered to carry them out at their own expense.

Even although they had been saddled with rates, the grace-and-favour residents did at least still enjoy the advantage of being immune from civil process, so long as they remained within their apartments. That was especially helpful to any debtors who otherwise were likely to end up in a debtors' prison, as did the father of one of the Queen's most illustrious subjects, the novelist Charles Dickens.

Hampton Court did, in fact, have the distinction of producing its own debtor – a Colonel Rose who shared an apartment with his mother-in-law, Mrs Margaret Vesey, on the south side of Clock Court.

Rose, according to Ernest Law, who was himself a palace resident,

. . . could not venture outside the palace without exposing himself to the risk of arrest. For a long time he used to take his exercise on the top of the palace, pacing up and down the vast lead flats of the roof, from which secure and lofty position he looked down on his baffled pursuers.

Once, however, having imprudently come down into the Barrack Yard, the bailiffs, who were on the watch, pounced on him in an instant, and proceeded straightway to march him off triumphantly to the debtor's prison.

But the insolvent colonel, though captured, was not yet at the end of his resources, for, managing to divert their attention for a moment, he suddenly escaped from their grasp, vaulted over the railings on to the Towing Path, rushed to the riverside, plunged in and swam – in the midst of a shower of stones from the exasperated bailiffs thus balked of their prey – across to the Surrey side of the Thames where, in a different county, his person was inviolable from the writs issued in Middlesex.

The bailiffs may have been easily identifiable within the precincts but the multifarious authorities who had a hand in the day-to-day palace functions were rather more shadowy. For Victorian bureaucracy – Charles Dickens's Circumlocution Office – was firmly installed, to the constant irritation and frustration of the residents.

It was, for example, ordained that the cleaning of the outside of all the windows was the sole responsibility of the Office of Woods and Forests while none but the minions of the Lord Steward's department was allowed to clean the insides. But very rarely indeed could the two departments manage to co-ordinate their activities, so most windows stayed dirty on one side. (Precisely the same problem applied at Buckingham Palace, incidentally.)

One lady resident discovered that she could obtain more convenient access to the gardens if a permanently locked door at the foot of the staircase next to her apartment could be opened. She was advised to apply to the Lord Chamberlain's office which retained all door-locking powers. She did so and the door was duly unlocked but, she was told, she could not then actually *open* the door; only the Lord Steward's department could do that. She thereupon put in her application

*A Victorian concert held in the Great Hall in aid of the Lancashire Distress Fund. Lancashire's textile industry was badly hit when the American Civil War cut off supplies of cotton from the southern states.*

to the Lord Steward and, in due course, the door was opened. But, asked one of the Lord Steward's officials, did she, as it were, in a manner of speaking, propose to *pass through* the door? She did. Ah, then that really did complicate matters somewhat since only the Board of Works was permitted to grant access.

Patiently, the lady resident put in her request to the Board of Works and, after a suitable time for consideration, it was granted. But, it was put to her, if she *passed through* the door did she then contemplate going so far as to venture into the garden? Yes, indeed she did – since that was the whole point in asking to have the door unlocked in the first place. Well, in that case, there was just a tiny bit of a problem. Only the First Commissioner and the Board of Office of Woods and Forests could endow her with the right to step *into* the garden. Finally, the lady received that permission, too, and as far as history records she succeeded in completing her plan to go straight from her apartment into the open air. Whether or not she collapsed there from exhaustion we don't know.

In June 1838 Hampton Court hit the newspaper headlines – not an easy task since headlines then were barely visible – as the setting for murder. Private John Rickey, aged thirty-two, of the 12th Lancers, left his duties as stable sentry and shot and killed Sergeant James Hamilton.

There was something of an enigma surrounding the fatal incident since Rickey and Hamilton were said to be on good terms; and Rickey is supposed afterwards to have declared that he really intended to kill Troop Sergeant-Major Joseph Murphy.

According to the evidence at the Old Bailey trial Rickey was spotted by Hamilton lurking near Sir Horace Seymour's apartment carrying a cavalry pistol in each hand. When the sergeant advised him not to be an idiot and return to duty Rickey replied: 'Hamilton, if you do not go back I'll shoot you.' The sergeant stood his ground and Rickey fired both pistols.

At the trial one of the witnesses who spoke up for Rickey was Murphy, the supposed intended victim. He had known the prisoner, he said, for nine years and 'during that time I always considered him a quiet, harmless, inoffensive man and, in consequence of my approval of his conduct, I selected him to clean my horse and appointments which was of some pecuniary benefit to him. I saw him in custody after the misfortune had happened. His eyes were staring and rather wild, and his counternance was flushed. I believe he had been drinking.'

Counsel for the defence accepted that the prisoner had fired the fatal shots but argued, in mitigation, that Rickey was drunk at the time and not responsible for his actions – an argument much disapproved of by the judge in his summing up. The jury returned a verdict of guilty but added a recommendation to mercy which the judge, clearly again much put out, reluctantly undertook to convey to Her Majesty. Rickey was sentenced to death but later reprieved and sent to life imprisonment.

The trial proceedings carry a vague hint that perhaps all was not really sweetness and light between the private and the sergeant-major, despite Rickey's 'pecuniary benefit'. But privates in Victoria's armed forces did not rate much consideration or interest. It is perhaps significant that, although Rickey had served in the regiment for eleven years, no one seemed certain as to whether he was married or not, although one witness 'thought' he was.

Of more pressing concern to the residents was a fire – one of the first recorded in the palace's history – which broke out at around seven-thirty on the morning of 14 December 1882 in private apartments in the Gold Staff Gallery on the upper floor of the south front. It was started by the overflowing of spirit from a small spirit lamp used by a servant for making tea.

The blaze was quickly put out by the palace fire-brigade using a typical steam fire-engine of the period which could pump seven hundred gallons of water a minute. Three of the palace's one thousand rooms were badly burned and half a dozen others slightly damaged. The resulting repair bill totalled £4,000. There was one fatality. The tea-making servant, whose spirit lamp caused the fire, ran back into the blazing rooms to rescue her few possessions and died from suffocation.

An inquiry into the mishap led to the building of fire-proof walls and steel doors and, another ultra modern touch, the installation of electric fire-alarms. In the State apartments, hot-water central heating replaced the old coke-burning stoves.

Despite those precautions a much more serious blaze occurred four years later, on 19 December 1886. It began with the overturning of a lighted candle, on the first floor of the north-east corner of the old Tudor buildings, overlooking the Chapel Court, and spread rapidly. This time the fire was much more than the palace firemen could deal with and help was summoned from a dozen neighbouring brigades. For more than three hours they fought the flames and when those were finally extinguished it was seen that nearly forty rooms in the Tudor wing had been destroyed or damaged. Restoration, in the original style, cost £8,000.

As a result of the two fires the residents were required to contribute towards fire insurance for the palace and to share in an annual £50 water rate payable to the Grand Junction Water Works Company for an extra water supply to be maintained at a constantly high pressure. A new nine-inch main was laid at a cost of £2,100.

Extra sightseeing crowds from London's East End poured in immediately after the fire to inspect the blackened ruins. Many came from public houses used as picking-up points – the Coach and Horses (of which there were no fewer than fifty-five so-named in London), the King's Head (ninety such), White Hart (seventy) and from Rising Suns, Crowns, Black Horses, the Prospect of Whitby and a few particularly oddly named pubs such as Naked Boy and Woolpack, Pickled Egg, Running Footman and World Turned Upside Down.

They stared in silence, almost as if in mourning. For they had adopted Hampton Court Palace – it 'belonged' to them and ever since it has been regarded as being part of the public domain, history's great showplace.

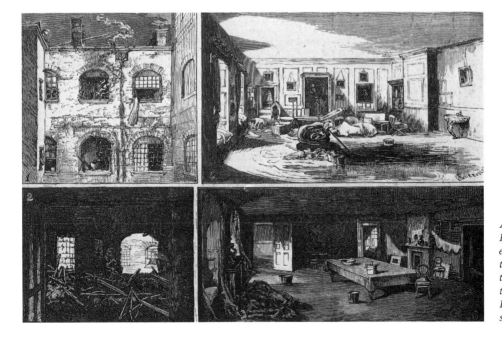

*Aftermath of the first Hampton Court fire in December 1882. It broke out in the private apartments in the Gold Staff Gallery on the upper floor of the South Front. One person – a palace servant – was killed.*

*There are few better places for studying history-on-the-spot than Hampton Court, and by this early poster London Transport saw the tourist value of appealing to, among others, the nation's schoolteachers!*

A harassed school teacher from Hayes
Took her children to Hampton Court Maze,
They got thoroughly lost
At a moderate cost
And then had a wonderful time admiring
the Great Vine and imagining Henry VIII
serving double faults on the Tennis Court.
It was easy to get there, too — Green Line
Coaches 716, 716A, 718 and 725 run to the gates

# 17

# Legends and ghosts

NOT SURPRISINGLY, IN VIEW OF its long history, Hampton Court has its legends – and, of course, its allegedly resident ghosts.

Sometimes late at night, it is said, the ghost of Jane Seymour, Henry VIII's third wife who died in childbirth, can be seen emerging from a door on the eastern side of Clock Court. The spectre is supposedly dressed in white, carries a lighted phantom taper and wanders forelornly up and down stairs and in and out of rooms, passing through closed doors in authentic spirit fashion.

The so-called Haunted Gallery, between the Round Kitchen Court and the chapel, takes its name from reported visitations by the apparition of Catherine Howard, Henry's fifth wife, who was beheaded on his orders on Tower Green in February 1542.

The story is that Catherine escaped from the palace room in which she was being held prisoner, pending her removal to the Tower. She ran along the gallery to plead with Henry, who was celebrating Mass in the chapel, but was chased and held by the guards and carried back to her room. As she was dragged away she gave vent to a piercing scream which was heard all over the surrounding area and could certainly not have been missed by the King. But he paid no attention and continued with his devotions.

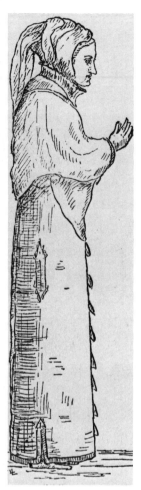

*An impression of the ghost of Mistress Sibell Penn, Edward VI's nurse, who was said to have been seen and heard working at her phantom spinning wheel.*

Occasionally over the succeeding years (so the story continues) the shadowy form of a woman in a billowing white gown has been seen to approach the door leading to the royal pew, which adjoins the chapel proper, but to flee away suddenly, uttering a blood-chilling scream, and vanish. Unearthly shrieks in the night were reported to have been heard as late as the middle of the nineteenth century.

There have been no recent reports of such incidents although in May 1945 Miss Lilian D. Irwin wrote to the *Sunday Times* newspaper to say that her father, a former resident, had told of seeing a

. . . female form in curious old-world dress walking in the grounds of Hampton Court. He remarked to his companion about her odd appearance and was amazed that his friend saw no one and could not understand what my father was talking about. This occurred at noon and, during lunch, my father asked the waiter who replied that it would be Catherine Howard he had seen as she had been "Walking a great deal lately".

A man at an adjacent table overheard the talk and related that he was an artist working in one of the galleries, and on several occasions a hand had come between him and his work. On this hand was a remarkable ring of which he had made a drawing and identified it with a ring known to have been worn by Catherine.'

In 1829 grace-and-favour residents living in the south wing insisted that they could hear mysterious mutterings in a woman's voice and a subdued whirling noise – all sounding from behind one of the walls. At about the same time others reported having seen a strange female figure which walked in a 'long, grey robe, with a hood over her head and her lanky hands stretched out before her'.

At first the authorities dismissed all this as mere superstitious gossip, but eventually they decided to still the chattering tongues (or so they hoped) by direct investigation. Workmen cut a hole in the wall and, to the embarrassment of the watching officials, stepped through into a long-forgotten, sealed-off room. There, in the half-light of the musty chamber, they saw a sixteenth-century spinning wheel.

At that time, Hampton Church was being demolished and the work had disturbed the grave of Mistress Sibell Penn, Edward VI's nurse who had plied her skill at spinning in the palace up to the time of her death in 1562. The theory, therefore, of the mutterings, whirlings and apparition was that Mistress Penn, no longer allowed to rest in peace, had returned to continue her tasks interrupted 267 years before.

According to Henry Ripley, the nineteenth-century historian of Hampton village, the Hampton curate, the Reverend Merewether, a churchwarden, the foreman of the church demolition work and a workman, had an alarming experience when they visited Mistress Penn's uprooted grave at night.

As they approached the graveside 'they were staggered to hear low moaning sobs proceeding from its vicinity. They gaped, their knees trembled, the lantern dropped from the hands of the foreman and was extinguished and then, to their horror, they saw that a strange unearthly glow was diffused over the monument, and that the previously recumbent effigy of Mistress Pen had left the position it had retained for two hundred and sixty-eight years (sic), and was sitting up, with hands over its eyes, sobbing piteously.'

Stories about Sibell Penn's 'haunting' of the palace abound. She is, for example, said to have been seen by Princess Frederica of Hanover who lived for a time at

Hampton Court, in the late 1800s, with her husband, Baron von Powel Rammingen.

On 7 March 1881, Frederica gave birth to a daughter, Victoria, and soon afterwards was astonished to awake to find a strange old woman bending over the cradle. The stranger suddenly vanished but the incident gave rise to the legend that Mistress Penn had returned not only to her spinning but to her nursemaiding. If there was such a visitation it was no omen of good fortune for the baby Victoria, for she died within three weeks of her birth.

(The tragedy of the infant's death, incidentally, led to Princess Frederica opening a post-natal convalescent home for 'poor and delicate married women' near the palace. As part of the fund raising campaign Hampton Court's Great Hall was opened for an evening's public entertainment for the first time since 1731. There was a concert, two one-act plays, and interlude music was played in the minstrel's gallery by the band of the Kneller Hall Military School of Music.)

A ghost is also alleged to have been encountered, on a June afternoon in 1929, in the house near the palace once occupied by Sir Christopher Wren. A boy of about eight, dressed in the costume of a page of Charles II's time, suddenly appeared among the guests at a garden party, made his way upstairs to the top floor and disappeared. The boy-ghost – since that was what, afterwards, those present assumed him to have been – paid no attention to anyone but appeared so real and purposeful that guests instinctively stood aside to let him pass.

The servants at the house were later questioned and emphatically declared that no child had been admitted. Children were not, in any case, invited, and a child appearing at the front door in 'fancy dress' would hardly have escaped scrutiny by the hostess. But what seemed to have clinched matters for the perfectly 'respectable' guests, who most vehemently insisted that the haunting *had* occurred, was the fact that the upper part of the house to which the boy hurried had no door or other outlet. Had he been a flesh and blood boy, and not a wraith, he could not have left the house, they said, except by returning down the stairs.

*There was a time when visitors from London could go to the Palace by tram and this charming poster was part of London Transport's efforts to publicise the service.*

# 18
# The
# Palace Today

HAMPTON COURT'S POPULARITY WITH VISITORS shows no sign of waning. In the early 1980s the number of people annually viewing the State Apartments runs consistently close to half a million. But palace officials estimate that another million-and-a-half visitors go just to see the gardens and the parks. The peak visiting months are April, July and August.

All royal Household interests – the royal collection, the use of the State rooms and the Chapel Royal – are the responsibility of the Lord Chamberlain who is personally represented at the palace by the Chief Steward (at the time of writing, General Sir Rodney Moore). But day to day administration and maintenance is vested in the Department of the Environment which operates through its Directorate of Ancient Monuments and Historic Buildings and its resident superintendent (currently Mr Ian Gray).

Henry VIII's wine cellar was cleared of intrusive partitions in 1923 and restored to its original state and the beer cellar was opened to the public after similar clearance and restoration in 1928. The Great Kitchens were restored as late as 1978.

In 1924 Ernest Law, the historian who lived at the palace, planted the Knot Garden based on the sixteenth and seventeenth centuries' concept of intertwined dwarf box borders enclosing herb and flower beds. He wrote: 'The patterns of interlacing bands of ribbons are taken entirely from those designed and published by the old masters of the time of Elizabeth and James I. The interspaces are planted with such old English flowers as tulips, hyacinths and daffodils.'

Also in 1924 lawns and a rose garden were laid out in the Tilt Yard and the sole surviving Tudor tower of five that at one time overlooked the Yard was turned into a teahouse.

*Restoration of historic tapestries. Part of the work of the Textile Conservation Trust, housed at Hampton Court.*

Historical research is continually being undertaken at the palace and almost every year minor archaeological discoveries are made. One of the latest and most important was the discovery of the Tudor east window of the Chapel, disclosed during preparatory work for the installation of a new lift.

The main changes at the palace in recent years have been those affecting the grace-and-favour system. As we have seen, in Queen Victoria's time nearly a thousand rooms were converted into forty-five separate apartments granted by the sovereign's grace and favour to the widows and children of distinguished servants of the Crown.

However, the practice of allocating grace-and-favour apartments for private residential use was discontinued in 1972. People who were in residence at the time continued to occupy their apartments (some are still there today) and other accommodation is now reserved for staff whose duties require them to live-in at the palace. But these large and expensive-to-run apartments are no longer popular and in latter years there has been a growing move towards their occupation by craft organisations, connected with historic buildings and their interiors, such as the Embroiderer's Guild and the Textile Conservation Centre.

The latter is a non-profit making teaching and working establishment under the direction of Mrs Karen Finch OBE who originated the project. It offers conservation of textiles of all kinds and training to graduate students and museum employees in textile conservation. Its work involves, among much else, the restoration of palace tapestries and it fulfils a most important role in helping to pass on highly valuable and very specialised skills.

The palace also houses the headquarters of the Building Conservation Trust (director, John Griffiths RIBA) in what was formerly a grace-and-favour residence and home to Field-Marshal Viscount Wolseley, an eminent figure of the Victorian period. The Trust was set up to promote the proper conservation, alteration and maintenance of both old and new buildings.

*Today the palace is also home to the Building Conservation Trust, set up to promote the proper care, alteration and maintenance of all types of buildings, both old and new.*

One very important recent event at the palace – which adds to its status as a 'living' institution – has been the construction of air-conditioned galleries in which to display some of the earliest paintings, including those on wood panels which, for their continued survival, require a carefully controlled environment.

Many of the major works at the palace are from the Queen's Collection, some of them from Windsor and Buckingham Palace, and there is also a reserve collection of other important paintings open at present only to scholars. Altogether the value of art works at Hampton Court at this date – 1983 – is probably somewhere in the region of £300 million.

November 1982 was an historic month for the palace, recalling the link with William and Mary, when Queen Beatrix of the Netherlands, in the course of a state visit, held a banquet at Hampton Court at which Queen Elizabeth II and other members of the British royal family were the principal guests. This was the first occasion in modern times that one reigning sovereign had entertained another at the palace.

In that same month in the palace in which the command for the preparation of the original authorised version of the Bible had been given, the fifth authorised version was presented and marked by a service of dedication in the Chapel Royal.

As time progresses, the fascination of Hampton Court Palace continues to grow. For, indeed, every stone of it is part of a memorial to an extraordinary, part-glorious, part-malodorous past which has helped to shape the twentieth-century's United Kingdom.

# Selected Bibliography

BURTON, Elizabeth. *The Elizabethans at Home*, Secker and Warburg, 1958.

CAVENDISH, George, *Life of Cardinal Wolsey*, London, 1827.

CHAMBERLIN, Frederick. *The Private Character of Queen Elizabeth*, John Lane, The Bodley Head, 1921.

CHAPMAN, Hester W. *The Last Tudor King: A Study of Edward VI*, Jonathan Cape, 1958.

CHETTLE, G. H. (additions by John Charlton). *Hampton Court Palace*, Department of Environment guidebook, HMSO, 1978.

CHURCHILL, Winston. *History of the English-Speaking Peoples*, 4 vols, Cassell, 1956.

CIBBER, Colley. *Apology for His Life*, London, 1740.

COLE, Henry. *Handbook for Hampton Court*, London, 1843.

CURTIS, Gila. *The Life and Times of Queen Anne*, Weidenfeld and Nicolson, 1973.

DEFOE, Daniel. *Tour Through Great Britain*, London, 1742.

DODD, George. *Food of London*, London, 1856.

ELSNA, Hebe. *Catherine of Braganza, Charles II's Queen*, Robert Hale, 1967.

FAIRHOLT, F. W. *Costume in England*, London, 1846.

FERGUSON, Charles. *Naked to Mine Enemies: Life of Cardinal Wolsey*, Longmans Green, 1958.

FRASER, Antonia. *Cromwell: Our Chief of Men*, Weidenfeld and Nicolson, 1973.

FRASER, Antonia. *King Charles II*, Weidenfeld and Nicolson, 1979.

GREEN, David. *The Gardens and Parks at Hampton Court and Bushy*, Department of Environment guidebook, HMSO, 1974.

GREGG, Edward. *Queen Anne*, Routledge and Kegan Paul, 1980

HATTON, Ragnhild. *George I: Elector and King*, Thames and Hudson, 1978.

HEATH, James. *Flagellum, or the Life and Death, Birth and Burial of Oliver Cromwell, the Late Usurper*, 1663.

HUTTON, William Holden. *Hampton Court*, London, 1897.

JORDAN, W. K. ed: *The Chronicle and Political Papers of King Edward VI*, George Allen and Unwin, 1966.

LAW, Ernest. *The History of Hampton Court*, 3 vols, London, 1885–91.

LEASOR, James. *The Plague and the Fire*, George Allen and Unwin, 1962.

LINDSAY, Philip. *Hampton Court: a history*, Meridan Books, 1948.

LINGARD, John. *The History of England*, 8 vols, London, 1819–1830.

MACAULAY, Thomas Babington, 1st Baron. *The History of England*, 4 vols, Dent (Everyman edition), 1966.

MASTER, Brian. *The Mistresses of Charles II*, Blond and Briggs, 1979.

MELVILLE, Lewis. *The First George in Hanover and England*, 2 vols, London, 1908.

MINNEY, R. J. *Hampton Court*, Cassell, 1972.

MORRIS, Edward E. *The Age of Anne*, London, 1877.

PEPYS, Samuel. *Diary*. G. Bell and Sons, 1970–76.

PREBBLE, John. *Glencoe*, Martin Secker and Warburg, 1966.

SANDS, Mollie. *The Gardens of Hampton Court*, Evans Brothers, 1950.

SMITH, Lacey Baldwin. *Henry VIII: The Mask of Royalty*, Jonathan Cape, 1971.

TREVELYAN, G. M. *Illustrated English Social History*, 4 vols, Penguin, 1964.

VAN DE ZEE, Henri and Barbara. *William and Mary*, Macmillan, 1973.

WALPOLE, Horace. *Anecdotes of Painting*, London, 1762.

WATSON, D. R. *Life and Times of Charles I*, Weidenfeld and Nicolson, 1972.

WOOD, Margaret. *The English Mediaeval House*, Ferndale Editions, 1981.

# *Index*

Numbers in italics refer to black-and-white illustrations;
*plate* numbers refer to colour photographs.

Addison, Joseph 149
d'Albon, Jacques 41
Amelia Adelaide of Saxe-Meiningen, Princess
   (Queen of William IV) 188, *189*
American Independence, War of (1775–83),
   background to 178, 179
Anderson, Mary 175, 177
Ann of Denmark, Princess (Queen of James 1)
   65, 66, 67, 74
Anne, Queen (r. 1702–14) 120, *142, 144*
   appearance 143; ill-health 143, 144, 147;
   coronation 144; state allowance 144; at
   Hampton Court 146–7; relations with
   Duke and Duchess of Marlborough 146;
   death 148; reign of, reviewed 148–9
Anne, Princess (1950–   ) 205
Anne, Duchess of York 111, 115
Anne Boleyn *see* Boleyn, Anne
Anne of Cleves (1515–57) 29
d'Annebaut, Claude 31
Armada, Spanish (1588) 61
Augusta, Princess of Wales 164–6, 168, 171
Augustan Age 149

Bancroft, Richard 69
Banqueting Hall 75, 93, 136
*Basilicon Doron* (James I) 79
Bassompierre, *Marshal* de 81
Beachy Head, defeat of English and Dutch
   fleets at (1690) 132
Beatrix of the Netherlands, Queen (r.
   1980–   ) 205
Beauclerk, Charles 131
Belasyse, Thomas, Viscount Fauconberg 98
Bellenden, Mary 156
Bennet, *Lady* Isabella, Duchess of Grafton *131*
Bennett, Timothy 171
Benson, William 159
Bentinck, William, Earl of Portland 140
Bernstorff, Baron von 152
Bérulle, *Father* 80
Bible, The: James I Authorised Version
   (1611) 69, *71*; fifth authorised version 205
Black Death *see* plague
Blainville, Marquis de 80
Blenheim, Battle of (1704) 146
Blenheim Palace 146, 180
Boleyn, Anne (1507–36) *20, 21, 24*, 25–6
Book of Common Prayer, issue of, reaction
   to 38–40
Boswell, James 176
Bothmer, Baron von 152, 157
Bothwell, Earl of 59
Boyne, battle of the (1690) 133
Bradshaw, Thomas 178–9

Brighton Pavilion 183
Brown, Lancelot 'Capability' *155*, 179–81
Brunswick, Duchess of 166
Buckingham, Duke of 75, 79, 81, 82
Buckingham House 175; *see also 174*
Buckingham Palace 183, 185, 194; *see also*
   *174*
Building Conservation Trust *204*
Burton, Elizabeth 29
Bushy House 184–8 *passim*
Byrd, William (1543–1623) 57

Cabinet (term), derivation of 152
'Capability Brown' *see* Brown, Lancelot
Caroline of Anspach (Queen of George II) *160*
   as Princess of Wales 154, *155*–8 *passim*;
   relations with King 161, 163–4; morning
   routine 161–2; state allowance 163;
   relations with Frederick, Prince of Wales
   (son) 164–9; ill-health and death 169;
   achievements 171
Caroline, Princess (daughter of George II) 164
Caroline of Brunswick, Princess 183
Castlemaine, *Lady* Barbara *see* Palmer,
   Barbara
Catherine of Aragon (1485–1536) *20*, 25
Catherine of Braganza (Queen of Charles II)
   *104, 106, 107*; appearance and
   temperament 104, 107–8; marriage 106;
   retinue of 106–7; relations with Queen
   Mother 108; and Barbara Palmer 109–11;
   state entry into London 111–13; and
   death of King 119
Catherine Howard *see* Howard, Catherine
Catherine Parr *see* Parr, Catherine
Cavendish, George, *quoted* 15, 17, 18, 20
Cecil, Robert (Lord Salisbury) 63, 65
Cecil, William (*later* Lord Burghley) 52, 59
Charles I (r. 1625–49) 70, *76, 78, 85, 88*; as
   Prince of Wales *71*, 74, 75; socioeconomic
   conditions at time of accession 77–8;
   appearance and temperament 78–9, 87,
   91; marriage and problems associated
   with 79–82; and divine right of kings 79,
   87; reform of Court etiquette 83; love of
   the arts 83, 86; life and imprisonment at
   Hampton Court 86, 90–3; political
   problems 87–8; and Civil War 88–90, 91;
   meetings with Cromwell 91; execution 93
Charles II (r. 1660–85) 101, *102, 104, 106,
   107, 116, 118, 119*, 126; returns to
   England 103, *104*; appearance and
   character 103; and Hampton Court 103,
   108–9, 114; marriage 104, 106–8;
   mistresses 104, 105–6, 109–10, 113, 114,

115, 119; pastimes 108, 117–18; state allowance and financial difficulties 109; 'Bedchamber Crisis' 109–11; state entry into London 111–13; political problems 114; and Fire of London 116; Rye House Plot 118–19; illegitimate children 105n, 106, 109, 119; death 119; *quoted* 143

Charles, Archduke of Austria 54

Charlotte, Princess (daughter of George IV) 187, 188

Charlotte Sophia of Mecklenburg-Strelitz, Princess (Queen of George III) *174*, 175

Cheke, *Sir* John 34–5, 36

Church of England 41

Churchill, Sarah, Duchess of Marlborough 132; *quoted* 125

Churchill, *Sir* Winston, *quoted* 149, 150

Cibber, Caius Gabriel 133

civil unrest (1549) 38–9

Civil War (1642–52) 88–93

Clarendon, *Lord* (formerly Edward Hyde) 104, 109, 110, 111

coffee and coffee houses 147

Coke, *Sir* Edward 73, 74

Coke, Frances 73–4

Colville, Camilla 164

Counter-Reformation 55, 59

Cox, *Dr* Richard 34–5

Cranmer, Thomas, Archbishop of Canterbury (1533–53) 30, 35, 41

Cratzer, Nicholas 30

Cromwell, *Lady* Mary 98

Cromwell, Oliver, Lord Protector of England (1653–8) 91, 93, *94*; appearance and temperament 91, 97; state allowance 96; life at Hampton Court 96–8; love of art and music 98; marriage of daughter (Mary) 98–9; life of, threatened 99; death of daughter (Elizabeth) 99; ill-health and death 99, 101; funeral 101; exhumation and desecration of corpse 101

Cromwell, Richard *100*, 101

Cromwell, Thomas, Earl of Essex 27, 29

Culpepper, Thomas 30

Daniel, Samuel 67

Darnley, Earl of 59, 65

Defoe, Daniel 149

Deloraine, *Lady* 164

Department of the Environment 203

Dering, *Sir* Cholmley 148

Dorchester, *Lady* 131

Drury Lane players 158

Dudley, Arthur 54

Dudley, Guildford 44

Dudley, *Lord* Robert (*later* Earl of Leicester) *53*, 54, 55, 56; *plate 12*

Dudley, John, Earl of Warwick (*later* Duke of Northumberland) 39, 40, 41, 43, 44

Edward VI (r. 1547–53) *21*, 30, 31, *32*, *34*; birth 27, 33; baptism 27–8; appearance and temperament 33, 36, 41; early years 33–5; health of 34, 36, 40, 41; education 34–5, 36; coronation 35; marriage,

attempts to arrange 36, 44; personal and political problems 36, 38–40; forms alliance with France 40–1; death 41; successor to, struggle over 43

Elizabeth I (r. 1558–1603) 48, 50, 53, *plate 12*; birth 25; and Act of Succession 26; as Princess 27, 30, 43, 45–7; appearance and character 51, 56, 57–8, 63; marriage suitors 47, 51–4, 56; education 52; relations with Dudley 54; sex-life, rumours concerning 54–5; life of, threatened 54, 55, 61; persecution of Catholics 55; ill-health 50, 55, 58; economic problems 55; and Mary Queen of Scots 56–7, 58–9, 61, 63; love of music (and other pastimes) 57; life at Hampton Court 57, 61–3; death 63

Elizabeth II (r. 1952–    ) 205

Embroiderer's Guild 204

enclosures 38

Essex, Earl of 55

Evelyn, John 118, 137; *quoted* 104, 111–12, 117

Falmouth, *Lady* 115

Fanshawe, *Lady*, *quoted* 91–2

Fanshawe, *Sir* Richard 92, 93

Field of the Cloth of Gold (1520) *plate 3*

Fire of London (1666) 116–17

Fitzherbert, Maria 183

Fitzpatrick, Barnaby 35

Forty-Two Articles (1553) 41

Fotheringay Castle, execution of Mary Queen of Scots at (1587) *60*, 61

Fox, George, *quoted* 99

Fraser, *Lady* Antonia, *quoted* 109

Frederica of Hanover, Princess 200–1

Frederick, Prince of Wales 164–9, 170

Frederick, Duke of York 187, 188

Gardiner, *Captain* Thomas 99

George I (r. 1714–27) *150*; his unpopularity 151, 152; absence from England 151, 155–7; appearance and character 151; wife 151; and mistress 152, 154, 157–8, 159, 169; life at Hampton Court 152, 153, 154, 157–8, 159; additions to Hampton Court 154–5; relations with Prince of Wales (son) 157, 158, 159; death 159

George II (r. 1727–60) *160*; as Prince of Wales 154, 155–7, 158, 159; mistresses 155–6, 161, 163, 164, 169–70; life at Hampton Court 161, 162–3, 170; state allowance 163; temperament 163, 170, 173; ill-health 163; relations with: Queen 163–4; Prince of Wales (son) 164–9, 170; death 170; additions and changes to Hampton Court 170–1

George III (r. 1760–1820) *172*, 186–7; and Hampton Court 173, 175, 179, 181; early years 173; ill-health 173–5, 181; marriage 175; death 181; reign of, reviewed 181

George IV (r. 1820–30) *182*; as Prince of Wales *177*; expenses and debts 183–4, 185; marriages 183; projects 183; and

Hampton Court 184; death 185
George, Prince of Denmark (husband of
　Queen Anne) 143, 144
Gibbons, Grinling 130, 133, 136–7, 147; *see
　also plates* 18, 26
Glencoe, massacre of (1692) 134
Glorious Revolution (1688) 122–3
Goddard, William, *quoted* 58
Grafton, Duke of 162–3, 178
Grand Remonstrance (1641) 87
Gray, Ian 203
Great Fire *see* Fire of London
Greenwich Palace, extension to 136
Grey, *Lady* Jane (Queen: 10–19 July 1553)
　*42*, 43–4, *48*
Guadra, da (Spanish ambassador) 52, 54
Guildford, *Sir* Henry 19
Gwyn, Nell (*c.* 1650–87) 114, *118*, 119

Hackett, *Mr* 80
Halifax, *Lord* 170–1
Halifax, Marquis of 123
Hamilton, *Lady* Archibald 166
Hamilton, Elizabeth 115
Hamilton, *Lord* George 136
Hamilton, James, Earl of Arran 51–3
Hamilton, *Sergeant* James 196
*Hamlet* (Shakespeare) 86, 158
Hampton Court *10, 11, 24, 31, 78, 127, 129,
　137, 171, plates* 8, 13
　administration and maintenance (1980s)
　　203
　archaeological discoveries 204
　architectural features 10, *11*, 12, 13;
　　*plate 7*
　artists and craftsmen 13, 129–30, 133,
　　136–7, 138, 144–5, 147, 154–5, 170,
　　180
　payments and wages of 23, 108, 130,
　　133–4, 136–7, 145–6, 155, 180
　art works 83, *84, 85, 97*, 115, 131–2, 137,
　　144–5, 154, *156*, 188, 205
　astronomical clock 30, 188; *plate* 6
　Banqueting Hall 188; *plate* 26
　Base Court *plate* 2
　beer cellar 203
　building materials 12, 128, 133; *see also
　　plates* 27, 33
　Cartoon Gallery 83, *plate* 17
　Chapel Royal *plate* 5
　climatic conditions 12, 125
　Clock Court 12, 133, 170
　Cloister Green Court *127*
　Communication Gallery 115
　East Front 133; *plate* 25
　events/incidents 74, 148, 165–9, 177–8,
　　188–9, 196
　festivities and entertainments *17*, 18–19,
　　57, 61, 67–8, 97, 158, *184, 195*, 201
　Fountain Court 129; *plate* 24
　George II Gateway 170
　ghosts and legends 199–201
　Great Hall 12, 23–4, 98, *171, 195*, 201,
　　*205; plate* 9
　Great Kitchens 21, 203; *plate* 4

great vine 180; *plate* 32
Haunted Gallery 199
history: original design 12, 13, *127*;
　conveyed to Henry VIII 20; additions
　and changes by: (Henry VIII) 21, 23,
　26, 28–9, 30; (Charles I) 84, 86;
　(Charles II) 108–9; (William III) 125,
　126–32, 133, 136–7, 138; (Queen
　Anne) 144–6, 147; (George I) 154–5;
　(George II) 170; (George III) 179–81;
　(William IV) 188; becomes neglected
　47, 181; put up for sale 95–6, 101;
　Wren's work on *127, 128, 129, 133*,
　136; *plates* 24, 25, 33; squatters in
　159, 175, 181; grace-and-favour
　system/residents 175–7, 178, 179,
　193–6, 197, 200, 204; as a tourist
　attraction 185, 188–9, *190*, 191–3,
　197, *198*, 202, 203; fires 196–7
hunting *71*, 72–3, 97, 117–18, 147, 157,
　162, 181
King's bedroom 136, 137; *plate* 16
King's Staircase 137, 188
legends and ghosts 199–201
location 10
maintenance costs 185
Maze 137–8, 192–3; *plate* 22
Orangery, *plate* 31
parks and gardens 12, 28–9, 84, 97, 108,
　129, 130, 138, 147, 154, 170–1,
　179–81; *plates* 10, 11, 14, 15, 20, 27,
　28, 29, 30
Presence Chamber *17*
Public Dining Room 170
Queen's bedroom 108, 154, *156*
Queen's Drawing Room 145; *plate* 23
Queen's Gallery 144; *plate* 18
Queen's Great Staircase 170
Queen's Guard Chamber 170
Queen's Presence Chamber 170
as a refuge from plague 20, 86
South Front 133; *plates* 29, 33
state occasions 16–18, 31, 40–1, 98–9,
　111–12, 205
tapestries 13–14, 24, 95, *204*
tennis court 21, 108
Tilt Yard 26, 109, 154; *plate* 11
Tudor chapel 15, 23, 147
Water Gallery 130–1, *132*
water and sewage system 12–13, 84, 97
wine cellar 23, 203
Wolsey's apartments 13–14, 15, *17*;
　*plate* 1
*Hampton Court Beauties* (portraits) 131
Hampton Court conference 68–9
Handel, George Frederick (1685–1759)
　153–4
Hastings, Warren 178
Hatton, *Lady* 73
Hay, James 66
Hazlitt, William, *quoted* 185
Henrietta Maria of France (Queen of Charles
　I) *78, 79, 85*, 92; appearance and
　temperament 79, 108; relations with King
　79–81; into exile 89; as Queen Mother

108, 111, 116, 117
Henry II, King of France (r. 1547–59) 39
Henry VIII (r. 1509–47) *21, 26, 34; plate* 3;
    life at Hampton Court 18–20, 22–3, 26–8;
    Hampton Court conveyed to 20; additions
    and changes to Hampton Court 21, 23, 26,
    28–9, 30; pastimes 21, 26–7; appearance
    and character 21, 26, 29; relations with:
    Catherine of Aragon 20, 25; Anne
    Boleyn 20, 21, 25, 26; Jane Seymour 25,
    26, 28; Anne of Cleves 29; Catherine
    Howard 29–30, 34; Catherine Parr 30–1;
    Edward VI (son) 33; Wolsey 20–1; break
    with Rome 25; ill-health and death 30, 31
*Henry VIII* (Shakespeare) 158
Henry, Prince of Wales (son of James I)
    69–70, *71*
Herbert, *Sir* Henry 86
Herbert, Thomas, *quoted* 90
Hertford, *Lord* 175, 176, 177
Hervey, *Lord* 161, 169; *quoted* 162, 163, 165,
    166, 168
Howard, Catherine (*c.* 1521–42) 29–30, 199,
    200
Howard, Henrietta (*later* Countess of Suffolk)
    155–6, 161, 163
Howard, *Sir* Robert 73, 74
Hudson, Jeffrey 86, 87
Hunsdon, *Lord* 63
Hyde, Anne (1st wife of James II) 111, *120*,
    143
Hyde, Henry, 2nd Earl of Clarendon 132


Jacobites 132, 133, 136, 139, 141
James I (r. 1603–25) *64, 72*; appearance and
    character 65, 66, 68, 69, 70, 72; honours-
    for-money scheme 65–6; and Hampton
    Court Conference 68–9; life at Hampton
    Court 67–8, 70, 72–3, 75; and death of
    Queen 74; financial and political problems
    68–9, 74–5; death 75
James II (r. 1685–8) *120*; as Duke of York
    111, 116, 118–9; appearance and
    character 121; state allowance 121; and
    Hampton Court 121; and Monmouth
    Rebellion 122; restoration of Catholicism
    122; flees country 123
Jeffreys, *Judge* George, Lord Chief Justice
    122
Jerome, Jerome K. 192
Johnson, Gerrard 130
Johnson, *Dr* Samuel 175–6
Jones, Inigo (1573–1651) 68, 75
Jordan, Dorothy (*née* Bland) 185–6, 187–8
*Junius* (satirical commentator) 178


Kent, William *155*, 180
Keroualle, Louise de, Duchess of Portsmouth
    119
Kett's Rebellion (1549) 38–9
Kew Gardens 171, 180
Kielmansegg, Baroness (*later* Countess of
    Darlington) 152, 154, 156, 157
Kneller, Godfrey 131

Lambert, John 101
Lark, Thomas 12
Laud, William, Archbishop of Canterbury
    (1633–45) 86
Law, Ernest 129; *quoted* 133, 159, 180, 185,
    188, 194; *see also plate* 15
Le Fanu, Alicia, *quoted* 178
Leicester, Earl of *see* Dudley, Lord Robert
Lely, *Sir* Peter 115; *see also 102, 105, 112*
Lennox, Charles, Duke of Richmond 119
Lennox, *Lady* Sarah 175
le Nôtre, André 108–9
Lilly, William 90
Lingard, John 54
London, George 129
Lord Chamberlain's licence for public
    performances, origin of 148
Ludlow, *General* Edmund 101
Lunsford, *Colonel Sir* Thomas 88


Macaulay, *Lord* 134; *quoted* 101, 122, 126,
    132, 136
Macclesfield, Earl of 123
MacIain, Chief of the MacDonalds 134
Maddox, *Dr* Isaac (*later* Bishop of
    Worcester) 161, 162
Mar, Earl and Countess of 65
Marble Hill House 163
March, Frederick 188
Margaret of Navarre 52
Marlborough, Duke of 146, 148–9
Mary I (Mary Tudor) (r. 1553–8) *46*; and Act
    of Succession 26; as Princess 27, 28, 30,
    43; accession of 44; marriage 44; false
    pregnancies 45, 47–8; ill-health 45;
    relations with Princess Elizabeth 46–7;
    and Hampton Court 45, 47; persecution
    of Protestants 48; death 48
Mary II (r. 1689–94) *124, 141*; as Princess
    122; relations with King 126, 135–6;
    appearance and character 126; interests
    and pastimes 130; appointed Regent 132;
    meals at Hampton Court 134; and
    Glencoe massacre 134; death and funeral
    135–6
Mary Stuart, Queen of Scots (r. 1542–67) 53,
    55, 60; relations with Elizabeth I 58–9,
    61; execution 61
Mary of Modena (Queen of James II) 122,
    123, 143
*Measure for Measure* (Shakespeare) 70
Melville, *Sir* James 56–7
Middleton, Jane 115
Milton, John (1608–74) 98
*Mirror of the Sinful Soul, The* (Margaret of
    Navarre) 52
Mitford, Mary Russel 185
Monk, *General* George 100, 101
Monmouth, Duke of 105n, 118, 119, 121–2
Monmouth Rebellion (1685) 121–2
Montague, *Lady* Emily 191
Moore, *General Sir* Rodney 203
Moray, Earl of 59, 65
More, Hannah, *quoted* 175
More, Sir Thomas (1478–1535) *quoted* 25

Murphy, *Troop Sergeant-Major* Joseph 196
Musselborough, battle of (c. 1547) 36

Naseby, battle of (1645) *89*, 90
Nethaway, Mary 99
Neville, *Sir* Edward 19
Noailles, de (French ambassador) 53
Norfolk, Duke of 59
North, *Lord* 178, 179

*Othello* (Shakespeare) 45
*Our Village* (Mary Russel Mitford) 185
Oursian, Nicholas 30
Oxford, *Lord* 57

Palace of Whitehall 12, 119, 136
Palmer, Barbara (*née* Villiers, *later* Lady
     Castlemaine) 105–6, 109–11, 113, 114,
     115, 119, 136
Parliamentary voting, 'division' system,
     origin of 25
Parr, Catherine (1512–48) 30–1, 34
Parsons, Nancy (Mrs Horton) 178, 179
Penn, *Mistress* Sibell 200–1
Pepys, Samuel (1633–1703) *105*, 115–16, 117;
     *quoted* 103, 105, 108, 109, 112–13
Philip II, King of Spain (r. 1556–98) *46*;
     marriage (to Mary Tudor, 1554) 44; and
     Elizabeth I 47, 52, 53–4
Pitt, William ('the Elder', *later* Earl of
     Chatham) (1708–78) 170
plague 20, 68, 86; (1665) 114–15, 116
Platt, *Sir* Hugh 62
Ponsonby, Lady Emily 'and others', case of
     193
Pope, Alexander (1688–1744) 148, 149;
     *quoted* 147, 156, 157
Puritans 68–9

Raleigh, *Sir* Walter 55, 69
Rammingen, Baron von Powel 201
*Rape of the Lock* (Alexander Pope) 148
Raphael cartoons 83, *85*, 138; *see also plate* 17
Redman, Henry 12
Reformation 25
Regent Street (London) 183
Reynett, *Sir* James 188
Reynolds, *Dr* John 69
Richelieu, *Cardinal* (1585–1642) 79, 81
Rickey, *Private* John 196
*Robinson Crusoe* (Daniel Defoe) 149
Rohan, Francois de 41
Rose, *Colonel* 194
Rose, John 129
Royal College of Surgeons, The *205*
Rye House Plot (1683) 118–19
Ryswyk, Treaty of (1697) 138

Saint-Georges, *Madame* de 79–80
St James's Palace 48
St Paul's Cathedral 159
Sands, *Lord* 19
Sands, Mollie, *quoted* 171, 181
Sarah, Duchess of Marlborough 146
Schrider, Christopher 147

Schulenberg, Baroness von ('Maypole',
     *later* Duchess of Kendal) 152, 154, 157–8,
     159, 169
Settlement, Act of (1701) 143, 148
Seymour, Edward, Duke of Somerset, Lord
     Protector (1547–51) 35–6, 38–40
Seymour, *Lady* George 189
Seymour, *Sir* Horace 189
Seymour, Jane (c. 1509–37) 21, 25–8 *passim*,
     199
Seymour, *Admiral* Thomas 36–8, 43
Seymour, William 70
Shakespeare, William (1564–1616) 68, 70,
     158; *quoted* 21n, 45
Shrewsbury, Earl of 148
Sidney, *Lady* 54
Sidney, *Sir* Henry 41
Sindercombe, Miles 99
Somerset, Edward Seymour, Duke of *see*
     Seymour, Edward, Duke of Somerset
Somerset House 36, 163
Sophia Dorothea (divorced wife of George I)
     150
Sotheron, Robert 54
South Sea Bubble (1720) 158
*Spectator* 149
Stair, Viscount of, Secretary of State for
     Scotland (c. 1691) 134
Steele, *Sir* Richard 149
Stewart (Stuart), Frances *112*, 113, 115
Stuart, *Lady* Arabella 70
Stuart, James Francis Edward ('Old
     Pretender') 122, 143
Succession, Act of (1534) 26
Sunderland, *Lord* 157
Swift, Jonathan (1667–1745) 136, 149;
     *quoted* 147
Syon House 90

Tallis, Thomas (c. 1515–85) 57
Talman, William 130, 138
tea 147
Textile Conservation Centre 204
Thames river, importance of to Hampton
     Court 12, *94*, 111–13, *141*, 153, *154*, *189*;
     *plate* 19
Thirty Years War (1618–48) 75
Thornhill, *Sir* James 154–5; *see also* 156
Thornhill, Richard 148
*Three Men in a Boat* (Jerome K. Jerome)
     192–3
Throckmorton, *Sir* Nicholas 36, 37
Tichburne, Charlotte 166
Tickell, Richard 177–8
Tijou, Jean 133–4, 146, 170; *see also plates*
     14, 21
Torrington, *Lord* 132, 133
Tory Party 122, 138, 149
Toy Club 185
Toye tavern scandal 148
*Triumph of Julius Caesar, The* (Mantegna)
     83, *84*, 95, *96*, 144–5
Tylney-Long, Catherine 187

Union, Act of (1707) 149

Verrio, Antonio 136–7, 145; *see also plate* 23
Victoria, Queen (r. 1837–1901) 189
Villiers, Barbara *see* Palmer, Barbara
Villiers, Elizabeth (*later* Countess of Orkney) 136, 139
Villiers, George (*later* Duke of Buckingham) 73
Villiers, *Sir* John 73, 74
*Vision of the Twelve Goddesses* (Samuel Daniel) 67
*Volpone* (Ben Johnson) 158

Walmoden, Amerlia Sophia de (*later* Countess of Yarmouth) 169–70
Walpole, Horace (1717–97) 137; *quoted* 152, 175, 178
Walpole, *Sir* Robert (1676–1745) 152, 153, 163, 164, 165, 168; *quoted* 157
Walshingham, *Sir* Francis 61
Walter, Lucy 105n
*Water Music* (Handel) 153–4
Watkins, *Dr* John, *quoted* 188
Wellington, Duke of ('The Iron Duke') 185, 189
Whalley, *Colonel* Edward 92–3
Whig party 122, 138, 149, 153
Whitgift, John, Archbishop of Canterbury (1530–1604) 68
Whorwood, Jane 90–1
William III (William of Orange), King of England (r. 1689–1702) *124, 139, 141*; 'invades' England 122–3; appearance and character 123, 126, 129; health 125, 126, 140; relations with Mary II (wife) 126,

135–6, 141; alterations to Hampton Court 126–30, 133, 136–8; in Ireland 132, 133; life at Hampton Court 134; and death of Mary II 135–6; and Palace of Whitehall fire 136; political problems 134, 138–40; assassination plots against 139; criticism of 139–40; death and funeral 140–1
William IV (r. 1830–7) *188, 189*; as Duke of Clarence 184–8; marriage 188; and Hampton Court 188; death 189; reign of, reviewed 189
William, Duke of Gloucester 143
'Windsor Beauties' (portraits) 115
Wise, Henry *155*
witchcraft, laws against, repealed 38
*Wits, The* (*Sir* William Davenant) 86
Wolseley, *Field Marshall Viscount* Garnet Joseph (1833–1913) 204
Wolsey, *Cardinal* Thomas (1473–1530) *8, 9, plate* 1; appearance and character 10, 16; household 10, 14–15; ill-health 12, 20; peak year 12; income 12; mistress 12; designs and furnishes Hampton Court 12–14, *plate* 1; life at Hampton Court 15–16; as a host 16–19; relations with Henry VIII 18–20; death 20
Wordsworth, William (1770–1850) 185
Wren, *Sir* Christopher (1632–1723) 117, 127, *128*, 129, 130, 133, 136, 158–9; *see also plate* 17
Wyatt, *Sir* Thomas 45

York Place 12